THE INHERITORS

STAN LEE

SOLDIER
ZERO

DAN ABNETT
ANDY LANNING
JAVIER PINA
RAMON BACHS

VOLUME THREE

ROSS RICHIE Chief Executive Officer • **MATT GAGNON** Editor-in-Chief • **ADAM FORTIER** VP-New Business • **WES HARRIS** VP-Publishing • **LANCE KREITER** VP-Licensing & Merchandising
PHIL BARBARO Director of Finance • **BRYCE CARLSON** Managing Editor • **DAFNA PLEBAN** Editor • **SHANNON WATTERS** Editor • **ERIC HARBURN** Assistant Editor • **ADAM STAFFARONI** Assistant Editor
CHRIS ROSA Assistant Editor • **BRIAN LATIMER** Lead Graphic Designer • **STEPHANIE GONZAGA** Graphic Designer • **DEVIN FUNCHES** Marketing & Sales Assistant • **JASMINE AMIRI** Operations Assistant

SOLDIER ZERO Volume Three — February 2012. Published by BOOM! Studios, a division of Boom Entertainment, Inc. Soldier Zero is Copyright © 2012 Boom Entertainment, Inc. and POW! Entertainment. Originally published in single magazine form as SOLDIER ZERO 9-12. Copyright © 2011 Boom Entertainment, Inc. and POW! Entertainment. All rights reserved. BOOM! Studios™ and the BOOM! Studios logo are trademarks of Boom Entertainment, Inc., registered in various countries and categories. All characters, events, and institutions depicted herein are fictional. Any similarity between any of the names, characters, persons, events, and/or institutions in this publication to actual names, characters, and persons, whether living or dead, events, and/or institutions is unintended and purely coincidental. BOOM! Studios does not read or accept unsolicited submissions of ideas, stories, or artwork.

A catalog record of this book is available from OCLC and from the BOOM! Studios website, www.boom-studios.com, on the Librarians Page.

BOOM! Studios, 6310 San Vicente Boulevard, Suite 107, Los Angeles, CA 90048-5457. Printed in China. First Printing.
ISBN: 978-1-60886-061-6

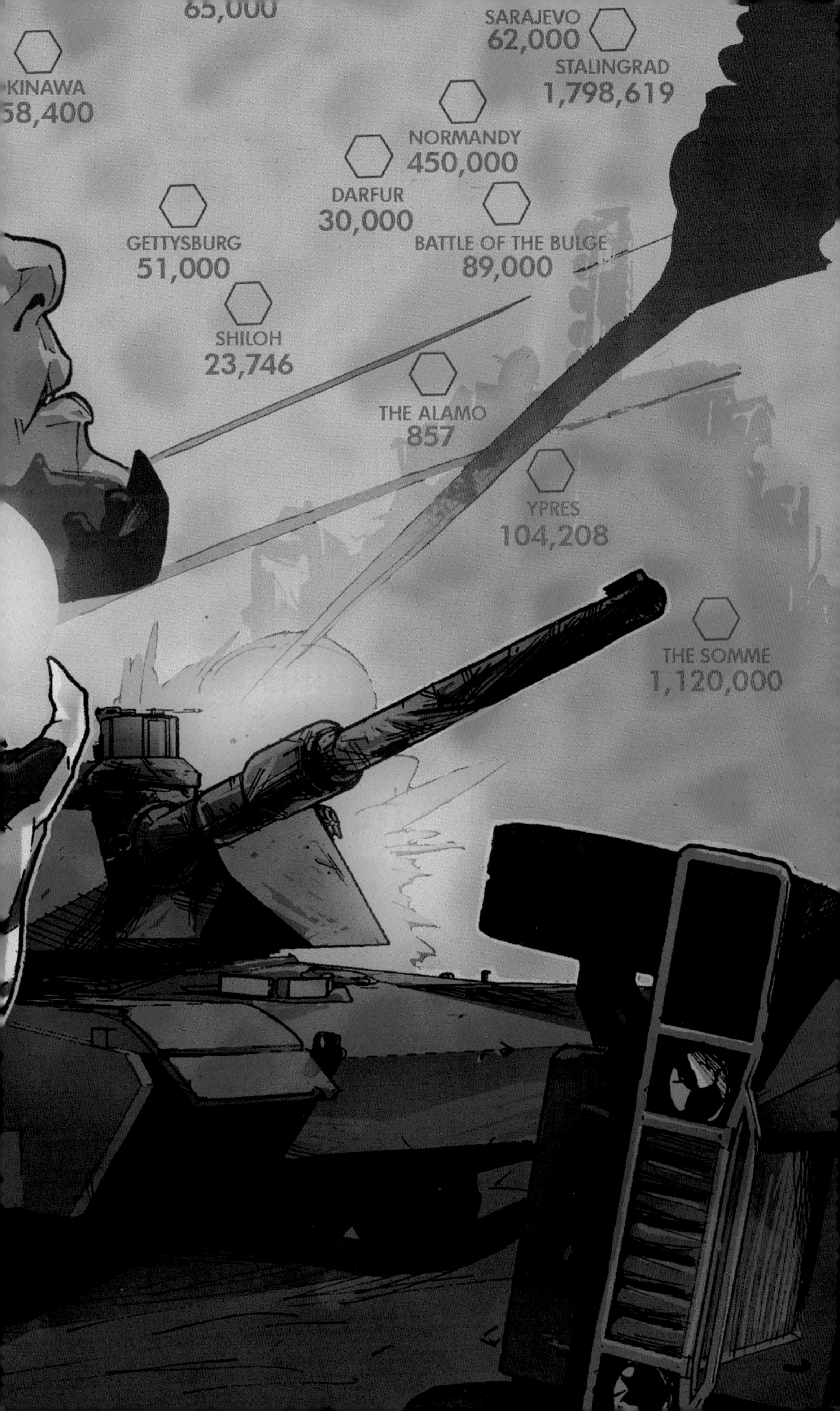
65,000
SARAJEVO
62,000
KINAWA
58,400
STALINGRAD
1,798,619
NORMANDY
450,000
DARFUR
30,000
GETTYSBURG
51,000
BATTLE OF THE BULGE
89,000
SHILOH
23,746
THE ALAMO
857
YPRES
104,208
THE SOMME
1,120,000

GRAND POOBAH
STAN LEE

WRITTEN BY
DAN ABNETT & ANDY LANNING

ART BY
JAVIER PINA & RAMON BACHS

COLORS BY
ARCHIE VAN BUREN

LETTERS BY
ED DUKESHIRE

SOLDIER ZERO
CHARACTER DESIGN
DAVE JOHNSON

COVER
TREVOR HAIRSINE
WITH ARCHIE VAN BUREN

GRAPHIC DESIGNER
BRIAN LATIMER

EDITOR
BRYCE CARLSON

EDITOR-IN-CHIEF
MATT GAGNON

PUBLISHER
ROSS RICHIE

SPECIAL THANKS
GILL CHAMPION

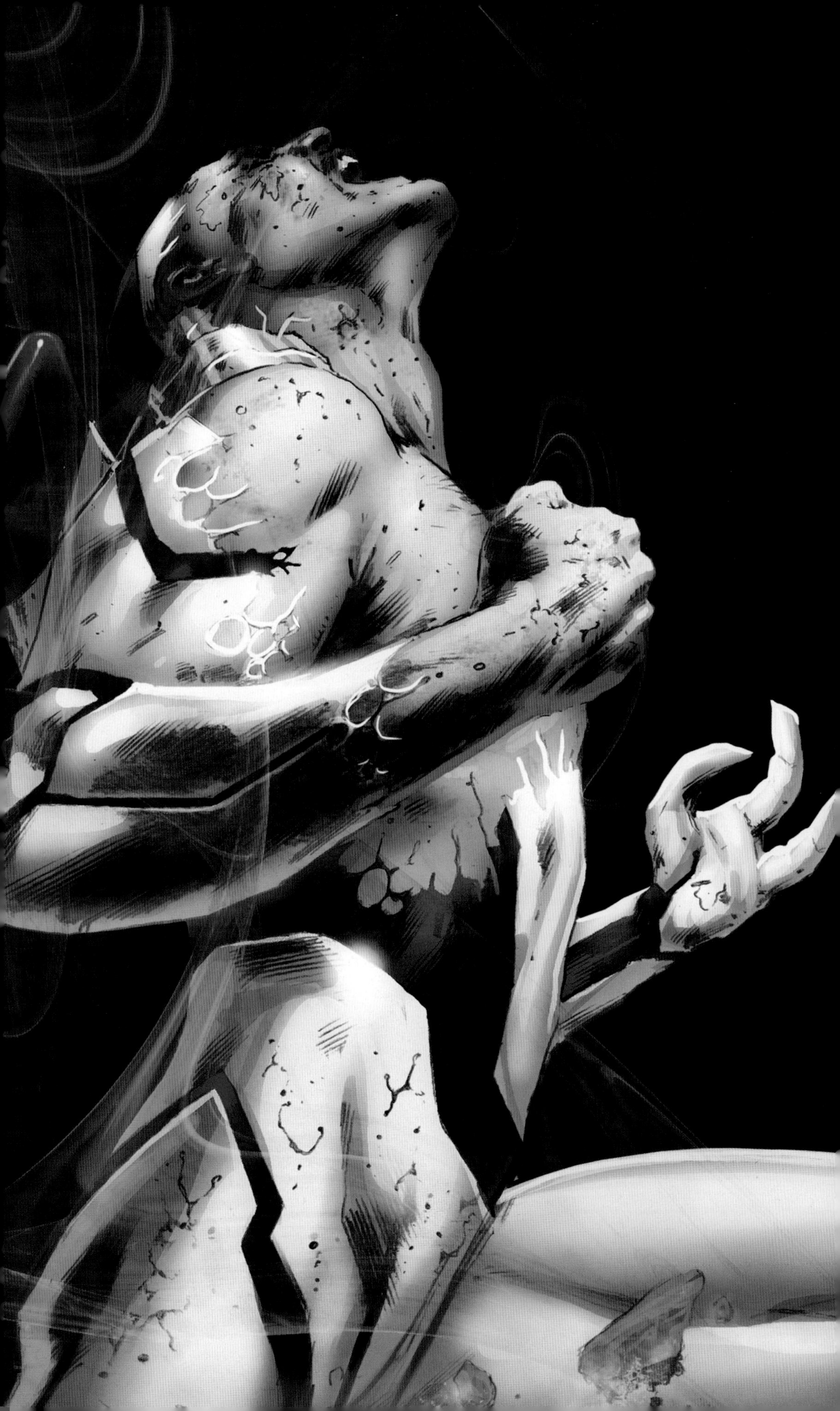

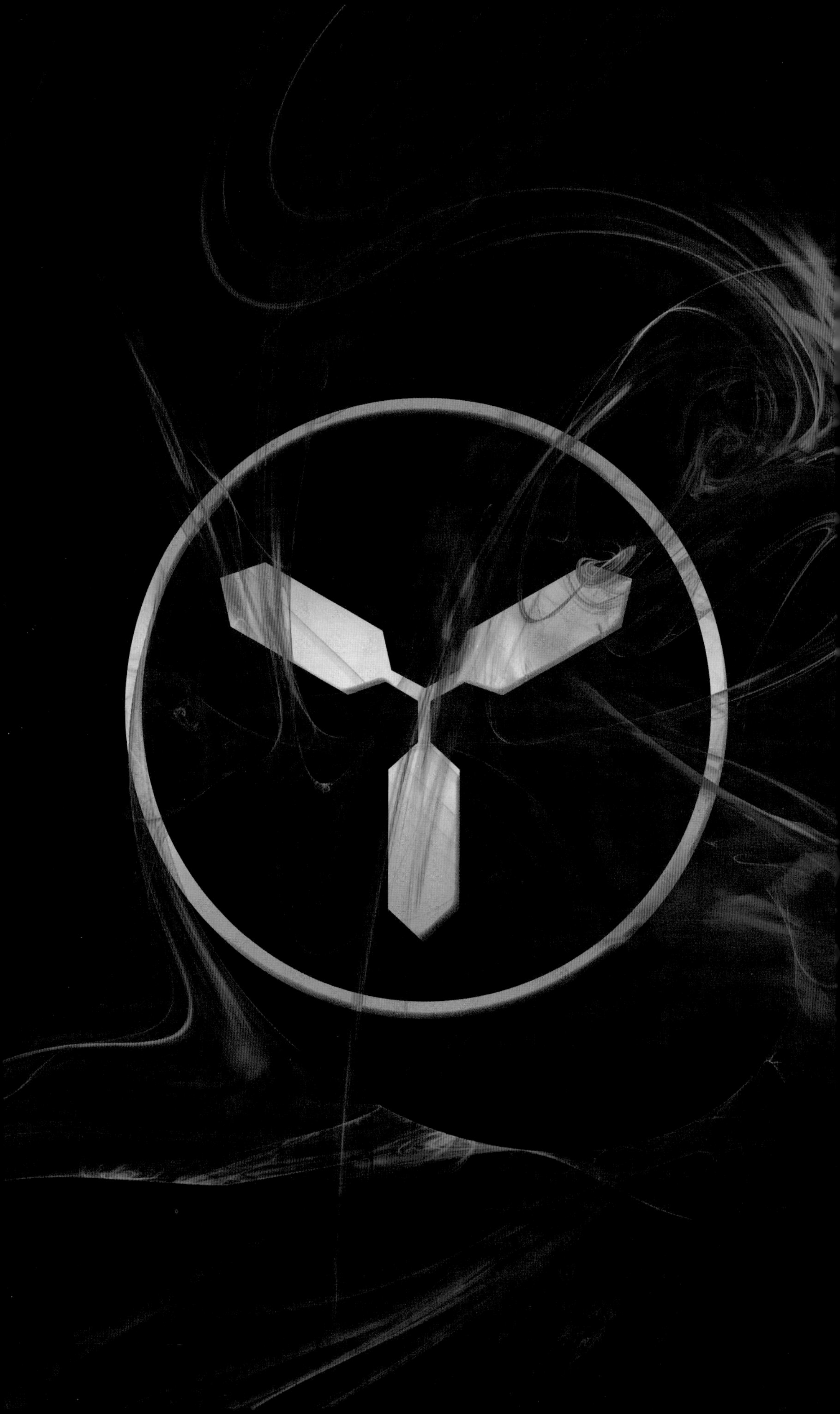

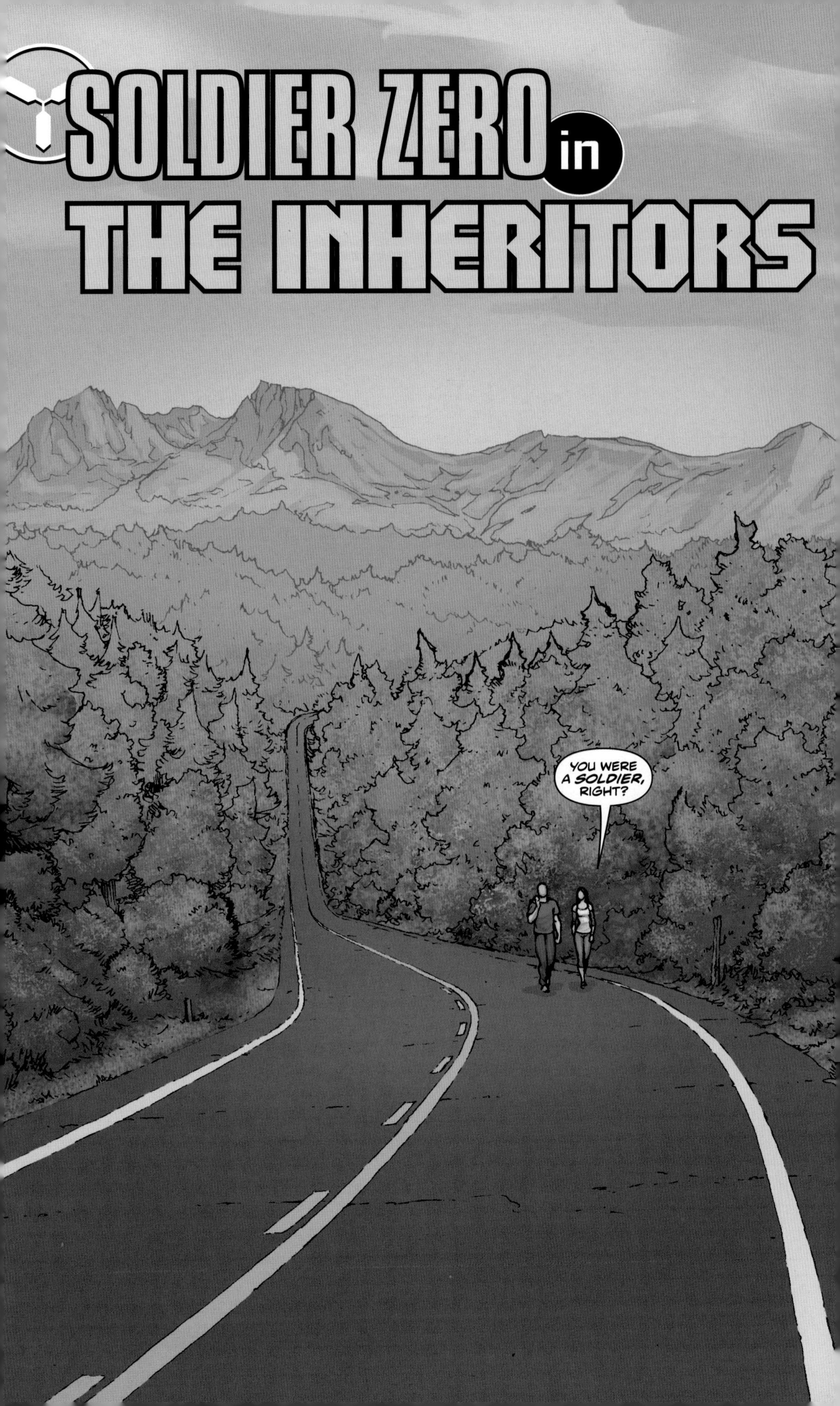
SOLDIER ZERO in
THE INHERITORS
YOU WERE A SOLDIER, RIGHT?

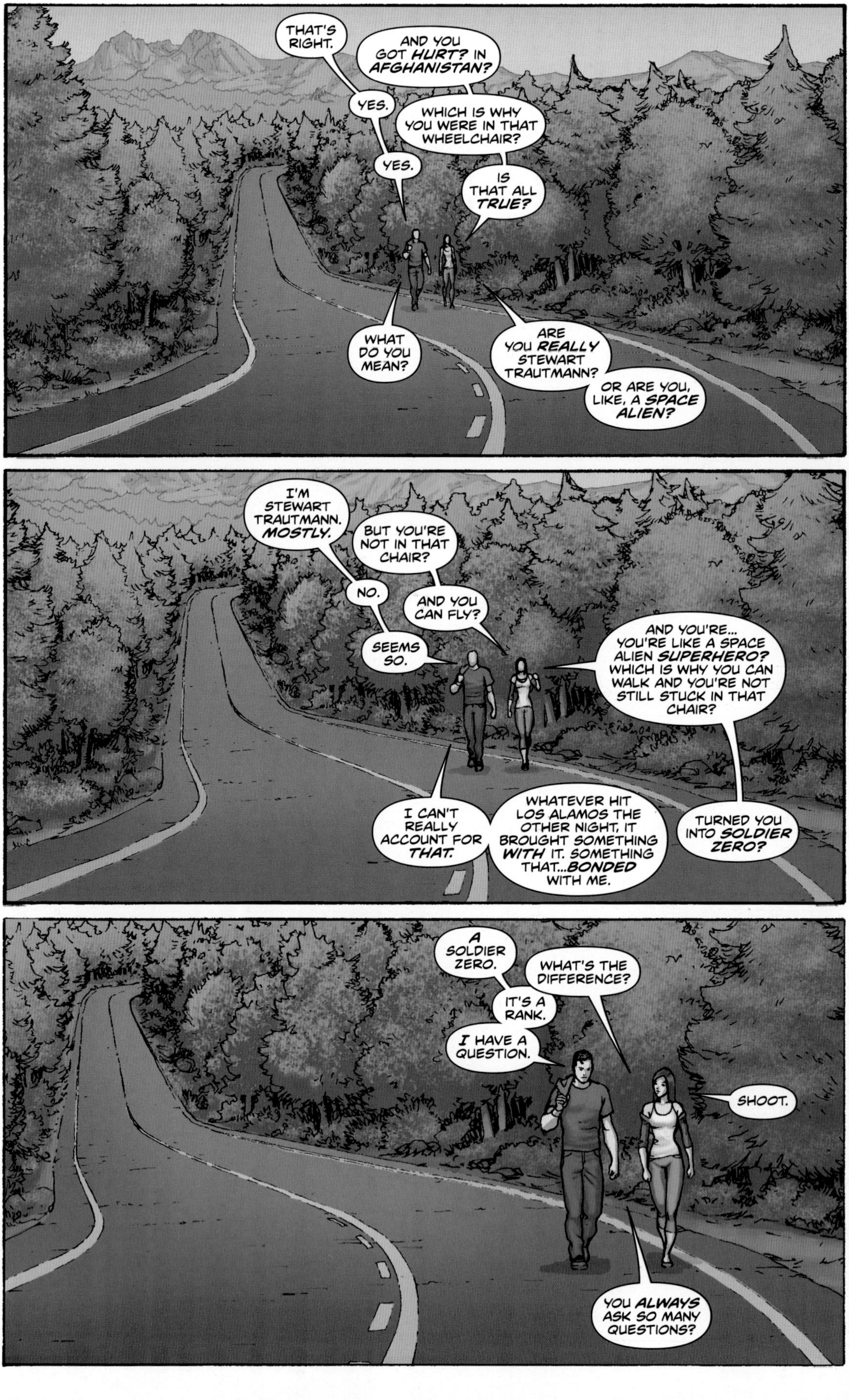
AND YOU GOT HURT? IN AFGHANISTAN?
THAT'S RIGHT.
WHICH IS WHY YOU WERE IN THAT WHEELCHAIR?
YES.
IS THAT ALL TRUE?
YES.
WHAT DO YOU MEAN?
ARE YOU REALLY STEWART TRAUTMANN?
OR ARE YOU, LIKE, A SPACE ALIEN?
I'M STEWART TRAUTMANN. MOSTLY.
BUT YOU'RE NOT IN THAT CHAIR?
NO.
AND YOU CAN FLY?
SEEMS SO.
AND YOU'RE... YOU'RE LIKE A SPACE ALIEN SUPERHERO? WHICH IS WHY YOU CAN WALK AND YOU'RE NOT STILL STUCK IN THAT CHAIR?
I CAN'T REALLY ACCOUNT FOR THAT.
WHATEVER HIT LOS ALAMOS THE OTHER NIGHT, IT BROUGHT SOMETHING WITH IT. SOMETHING THAT...BONDED WITH ME.
TURNED YOU INTO SOLDIER ZERO?
A SOLDIER ZERO.
WHAT'S THE DIFFERENCE?
IT'S A RANK.
I HAVE A QUESTION.
SHOOT.
YOU ALWAYS ASK SO MANY QUESTIONS?

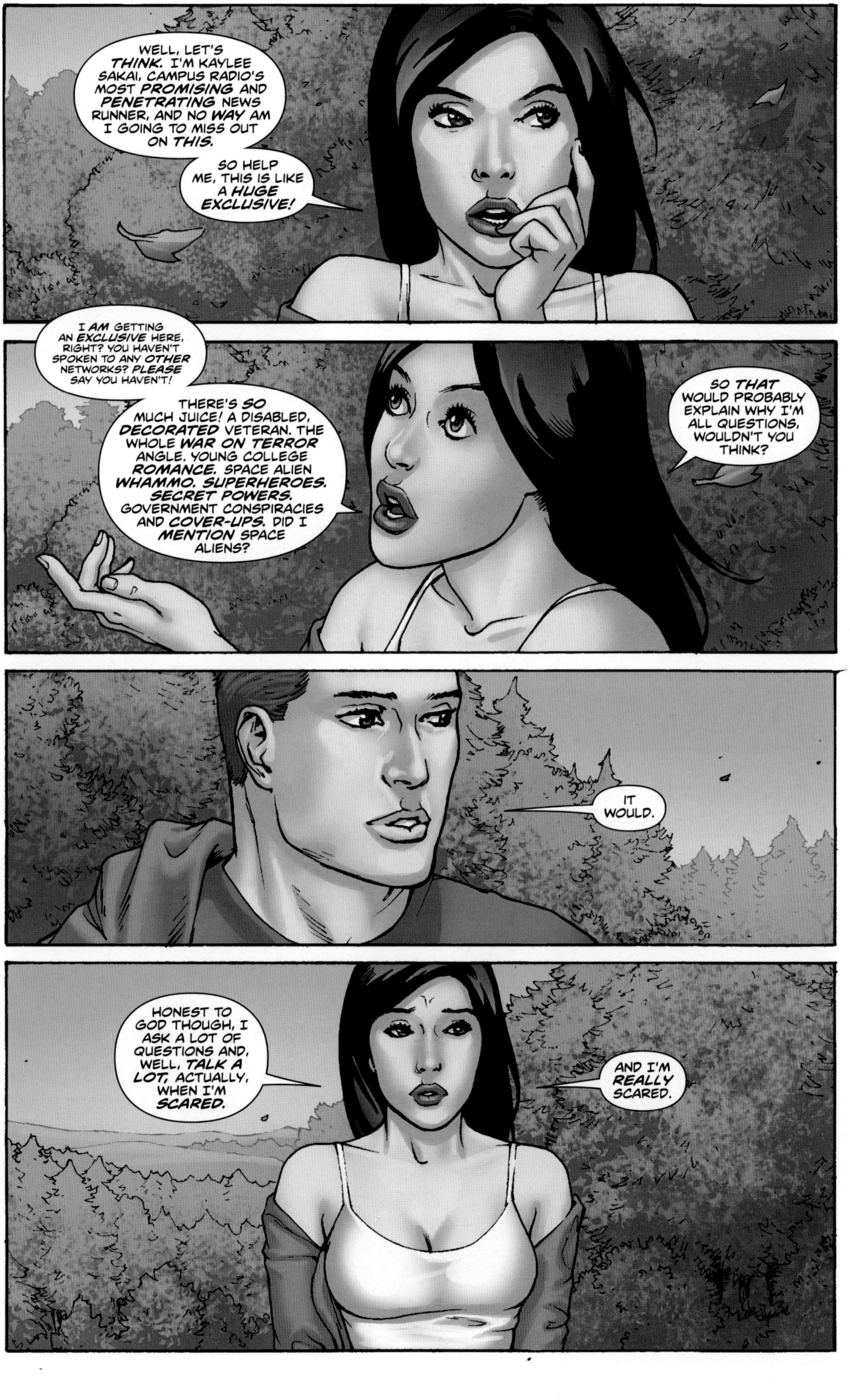
WELL, LET'S THINK. I'M KAYLEE SAKAI, CAMPUS RADIO'S MOST PROMISING AND PENETRATING NEWS RUNNER, AND NO WAY AM I GOING TO MISS OUT ON THIS.
SO HELP ME, THIS IS LIKE A HUGE EXCLUSIVE!
I AM GETTING AN EXCLUSIVE HERE, RIGHT? YOU HAVEN'T SPOKEN TO ANY OTHER NETWORKS? PLEASE SAY YOU HAVEN'T!
THERE'S SO MUCH JUICE! A DISABLED, DECORATED VETERAN. THE WHOLE WAR ON TERROR ANGLE. YOUNG COLLEGE ROMANCE. SPACE ALIEN WHAMMO. SUPERHEROES. SECRET POWERS. GOVERNMENT CONSPIRACIES AND COVER-UPS. DID I MENTION SPACE ALIENS?
SO THAT WOULD PROBABLY EXPLAIN WHY I'M ALL QUESTIONS, WOULDN'T YOU THINK?
IT WOULD.
HONEST TO GOD THOUGH, I ASK A LOT OF QUESTIONS AND, WELL, TALK A LOT, ACTUALLY, WHEN I'M SCARED.
AND I'M REALLY SCARED.

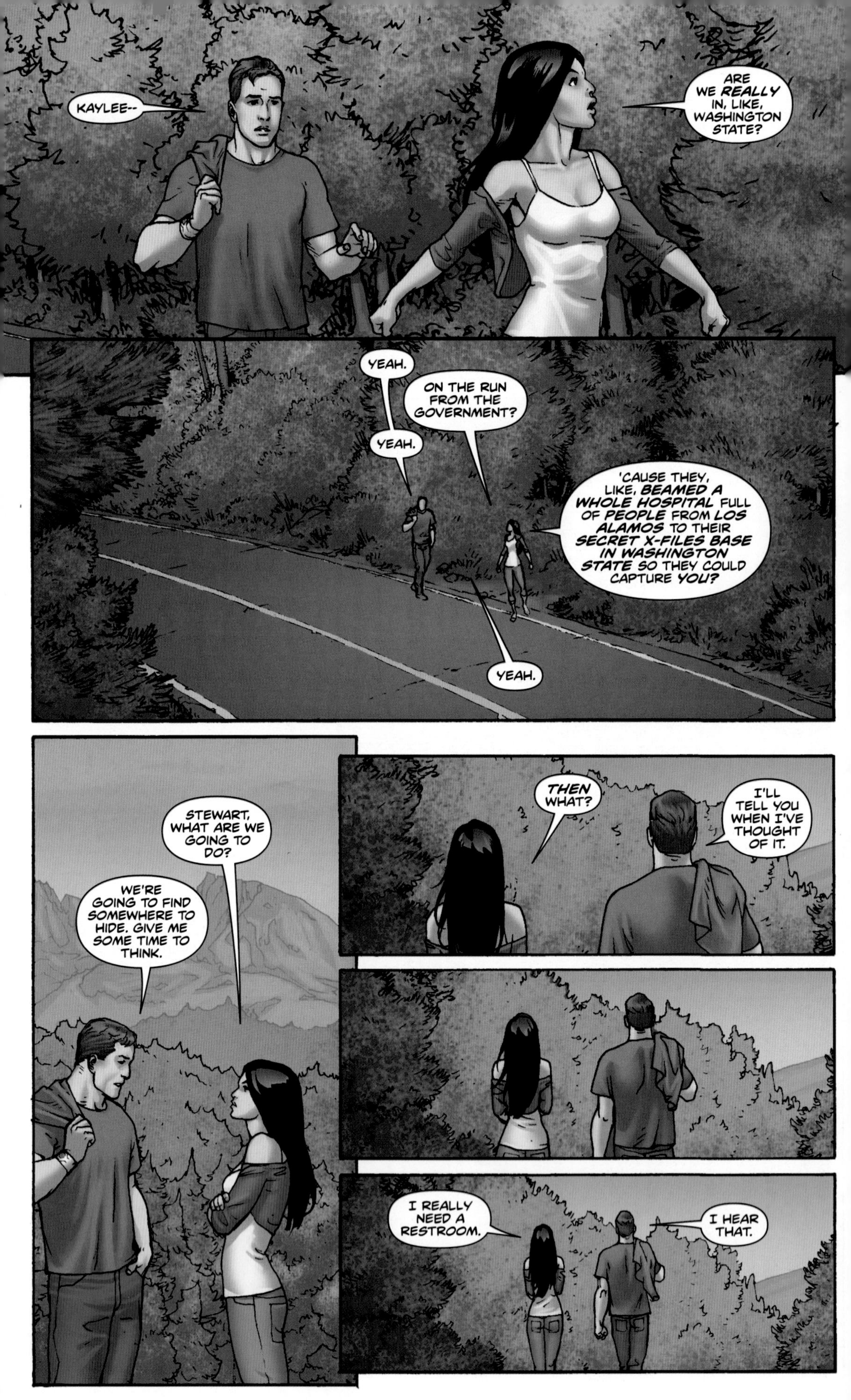
KAYLEE--
ARE WE REALLY IN, LIKE, WASHINGTON STATE?
YEAH.
ON THE RUN FROM THE GOVERNMENT?
YEAH.
'CAUSE THEY, LIKE, BEAMED A WHOLE HOSPITAL FULL OF PEOPLE FROM LOS ALAMOS TO THEIR SECRET X-FILES BASE IN WASHINGTON STATE SO THEY COULD CAPTURE YOU?
YEAH.
STEWART, WHAT ARE WE GOING TO DO?
WE'RE GOING TO FIND SOMEWHERE TO HIDE. GIVE ME SOME TIME TO THINK.
THEN WHAT?
I'LL TELL YOU WHEN I'VE THOUGHT OF IT.
I REALLY NEED A RESTROOM.
I HEAR THAT.

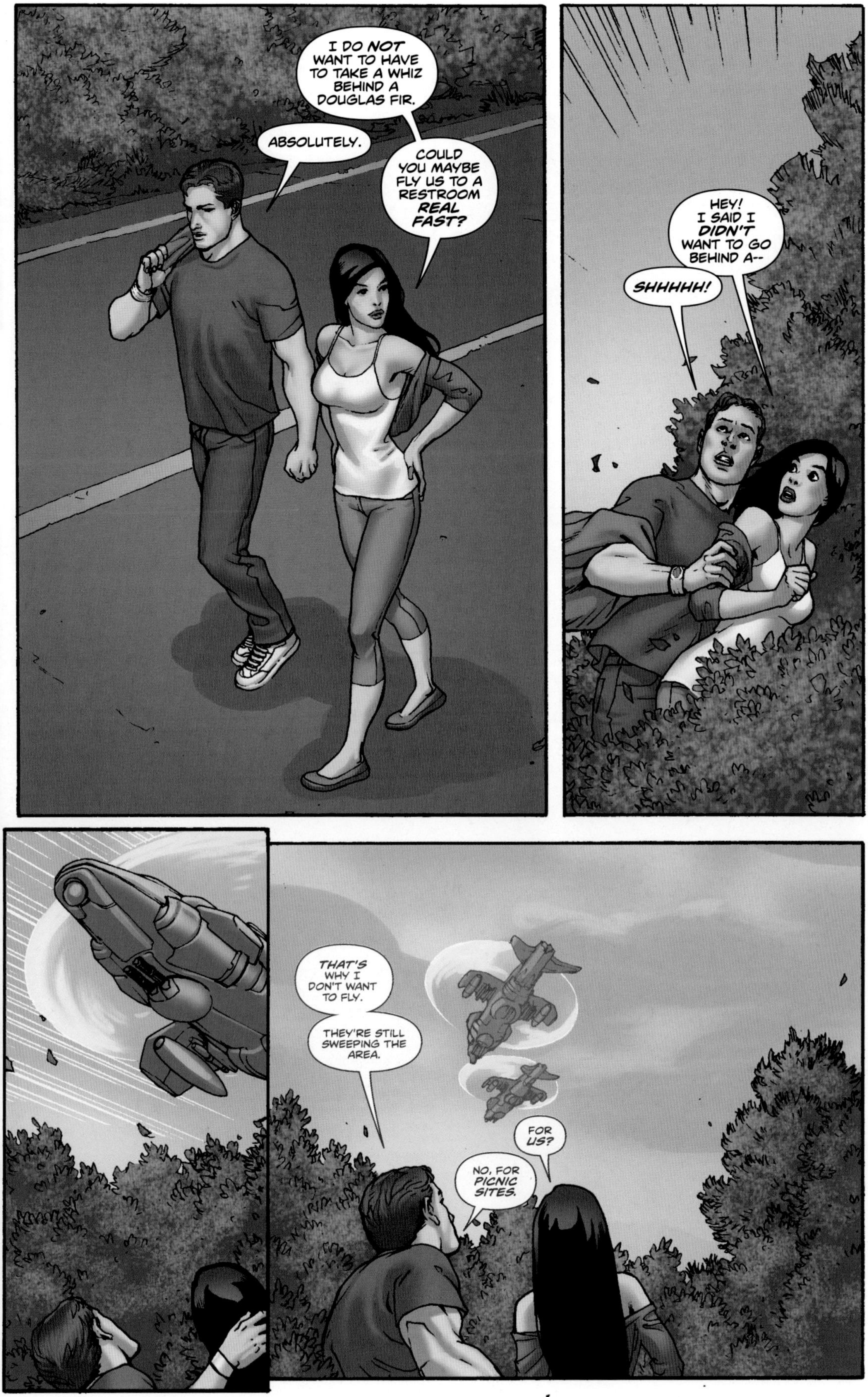

I DO NOT WANT TO HAVE TO TAKE A WHIZ BEHIND A DOUGLAS FIR.
ABSOLUTELY.
COULD YOU MAYBE FLY US TO A RESTROOM REAL FAST?
HEY! I SAID I DIDN'T WANT TO GO BEHIND A--
SHHHHH!
THAT'S WHY I DON'T WANT TO FLY.
THEY'RE STILL SWEEPING THE AREA.
FOR US?
NO, FOR PICNIC SITES.

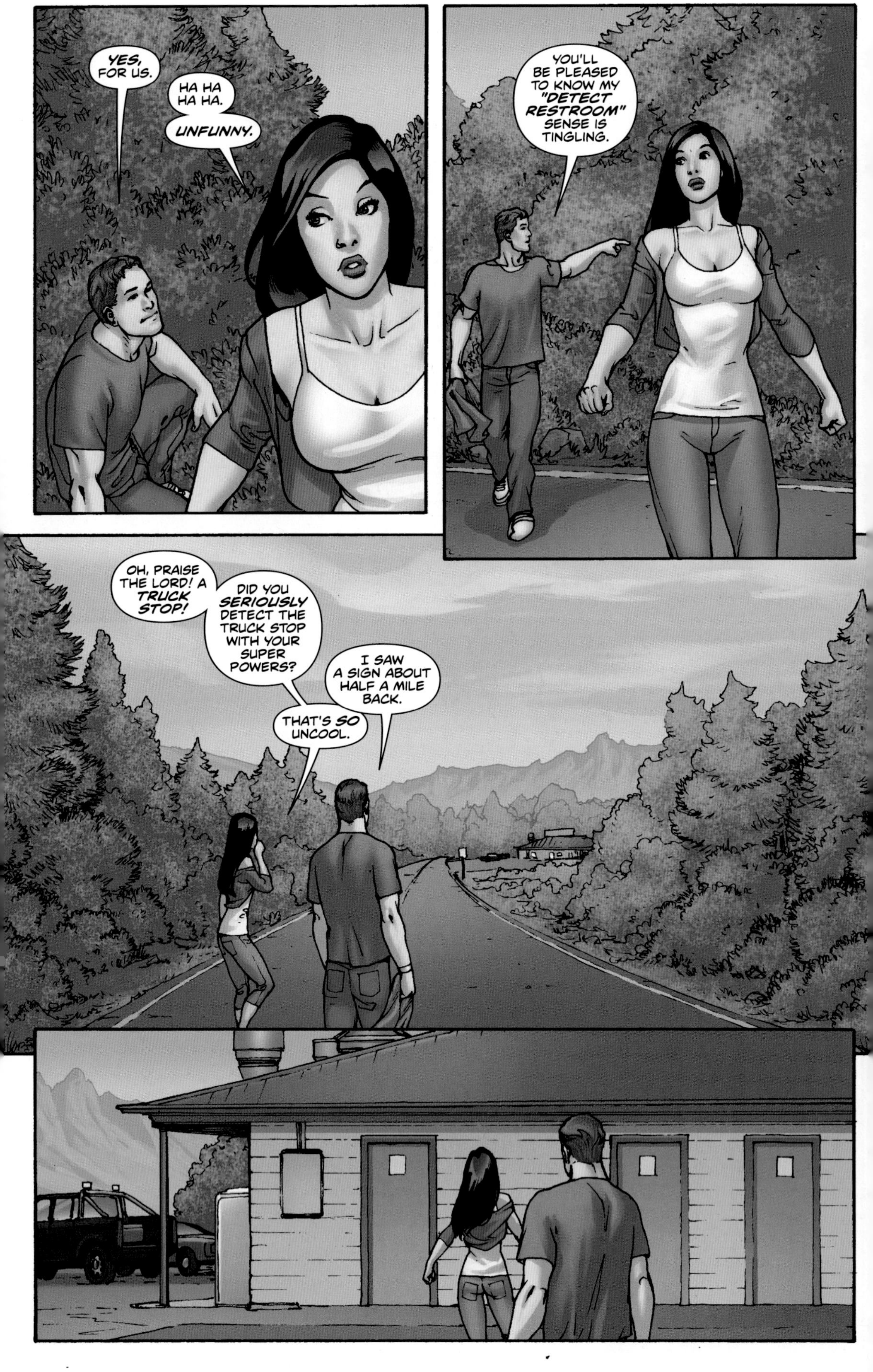

YES, FOR US.
HA HA HA HA.
UNFUNNY.
YOU'LL BE PLEASED TO KNOW MY "DETECT RESTROOM" SENSE IS TINGLING.
OH, PRAISE THE LORD! A TRUCK STOP!
DID YOU SERIOUSLY DETECT THE TRUCK STOP WITH YOUR SUPER POWERS?
I SAW A SIGN ABOUT HALF A MILE BACK.
THAT'S SO UNCOOL.

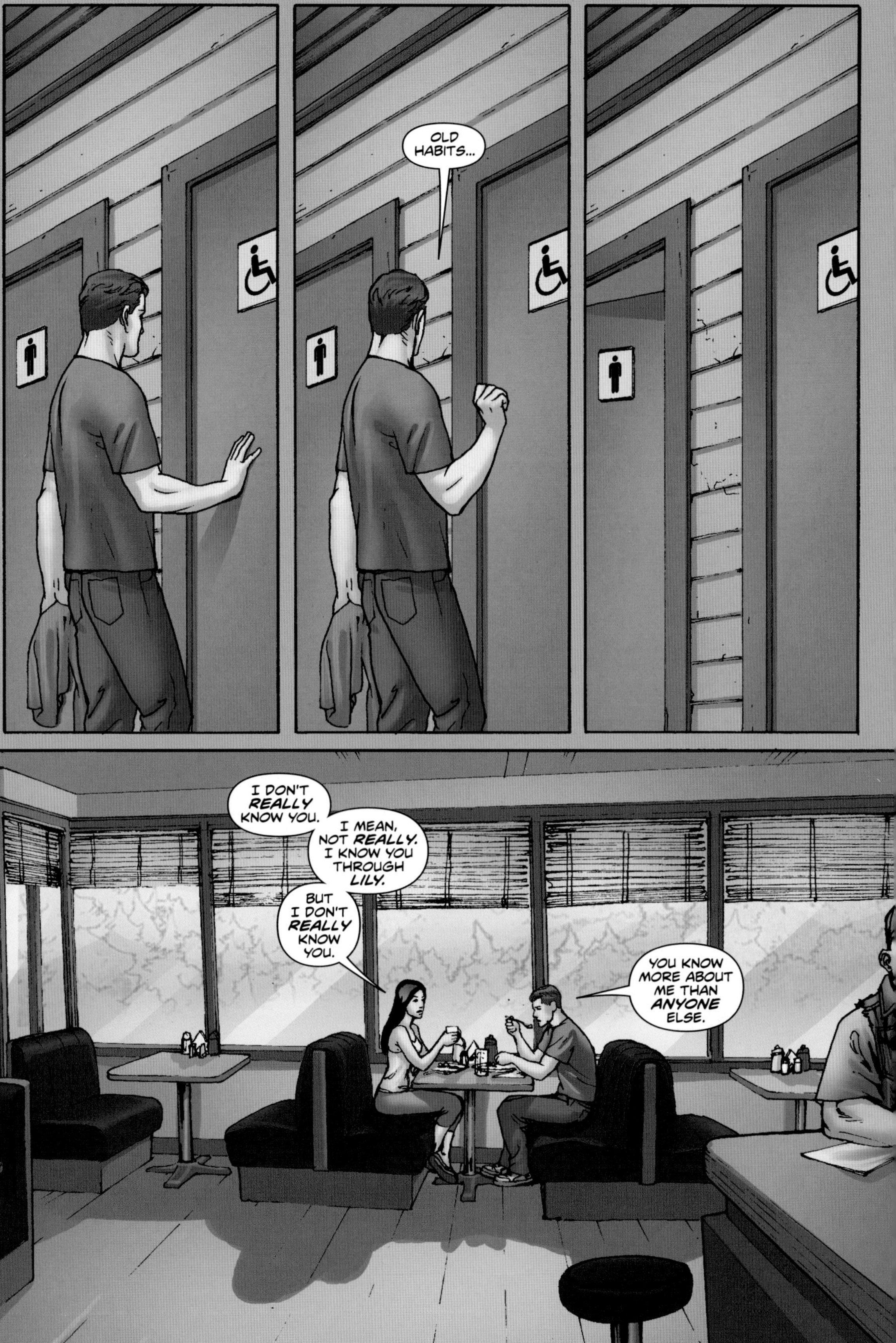
OLD HABITS...
I DON'T REALLY KNOW YOU.
I MEAN, NOT REALLY. I KNOW YOU THROUGH LILY.
BUT I DON'T REALLY KNOW YOU.
YOU KNOW MORE ABOUT ME THAN ANYONE ELSE.

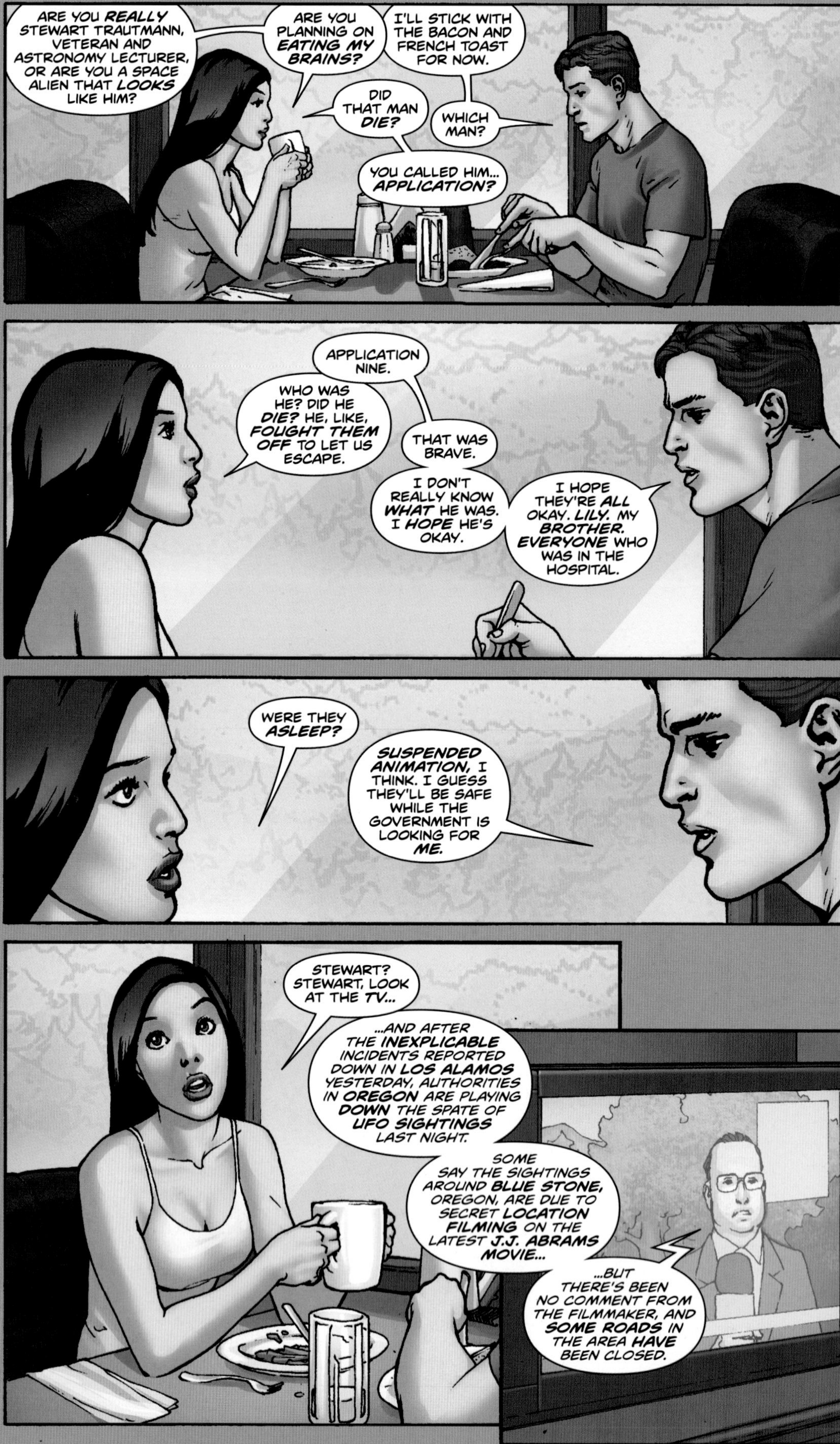
ARE YOU REALLY STEWART TRAUTMANN, VETERAN AND ASTRONOMY LECTURER, OR ARE YOU A SPACE ALIEN THAT LOOKS LIKE HIM?
ARE YOU PLANNING ON EATING MY BRAINS?
I'LL STICK WITH THE BACON AND FRENCH TOAST FOR NOW.
DID THAT MAN DIE?
WHICH MAN?
YOU CALLED HIM... APPLICATION?
APPLICATION NINE.
WHO WAS HE? DID HE DIE? HE, LIKE, FOUGHT THEM OFF TO LET US ESCAPE.
THAT WAS BRAVE.
I DON'T REALLY KNOW WHAT HE WAS. I HOPE HE'S OKAY.
I HOPE THEY'RE ALL OKAY. LILY. MY BROTHER. EVERYONE WHO WAS IN THE HOSPITAL.
WERE THEY ASLEEP?
SUSPENDED ANIMATION, I THINK. I GUESS THEY'LL BE SAFE WHILE THE GOVERNMENT IS LOOKING FOR ME.
STEWART? STEWART, LOOK AT THE TV...
...AND AFTER THE INEXPLICABLE INCIDENTS REPORTED DOWN IN LOS ALAMOS YESTERDAY, AUTHORITIES IN OREGON ARE PLAYING DOWN THE SPATE OF UFO SIGHTINGS LAST NIGHT.
SOME SAY THE SIGHTINGS AROUND BLUE STONE, OREGON, ARE DUE TO SECRET LOCATION FILMING ON THE LATEST J.J. ABRAMS MOVIE...
...BUT THERE'S BEEN NO COMMENT FROM THE FILMMAKER, AND SOME ROADS IN THE AREA HAVE BEEN CLOSED.

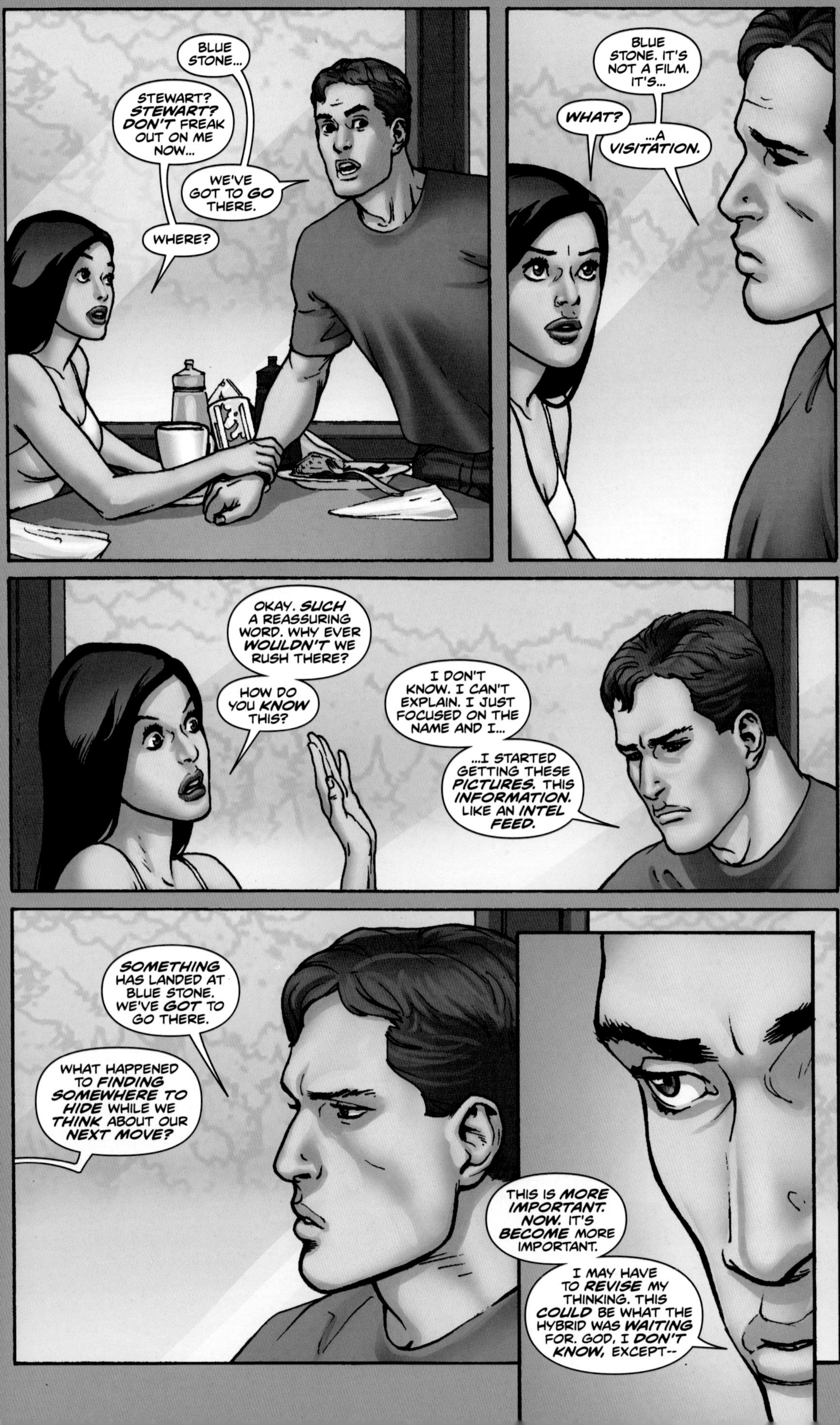
BLUE STONE...
STEWART? STEWART? DON'T FREAK OUT ON ME NOW...
WE'VE GOT TO GO THERE.
WHERE?
BLUE STONE. IT'S NOT A FILM. IT'S...
WHAT?
...A VISITATION.
OKAY. SUCH A REASSURING WORD. WHY EVER WOULDN'T WE RUSH THERE?
HOW DO YOU KNOW THIS?
I DON'T KNOW. I CAN'T EXPLAIN. I JUST FOCUSED ON THE NAME AND I...
...I STARTED GETTING THESE PICTURES. THIS INFORMATION. LIKE AN INTEL FEED.
SOMETHING HAS LANDED AT BLUE STONE. WE'VE GOT TO GO THERE.
WHAT HAPPENED TO FINDING SOMEWHERE TO HIDE WHILE WE THINK ABOUT OUR NEXT MOVE?
THIS IS MORE IMPORTANT. NOW. IT'S BECOME MORE IMPORTANT.
I MAY HAVE TO REVISE MY THINKING. THIS COULD BE WHAT THE HYBRID WAS WAITING FOR. GOD, I DON'T KNOW, EXCEPT--

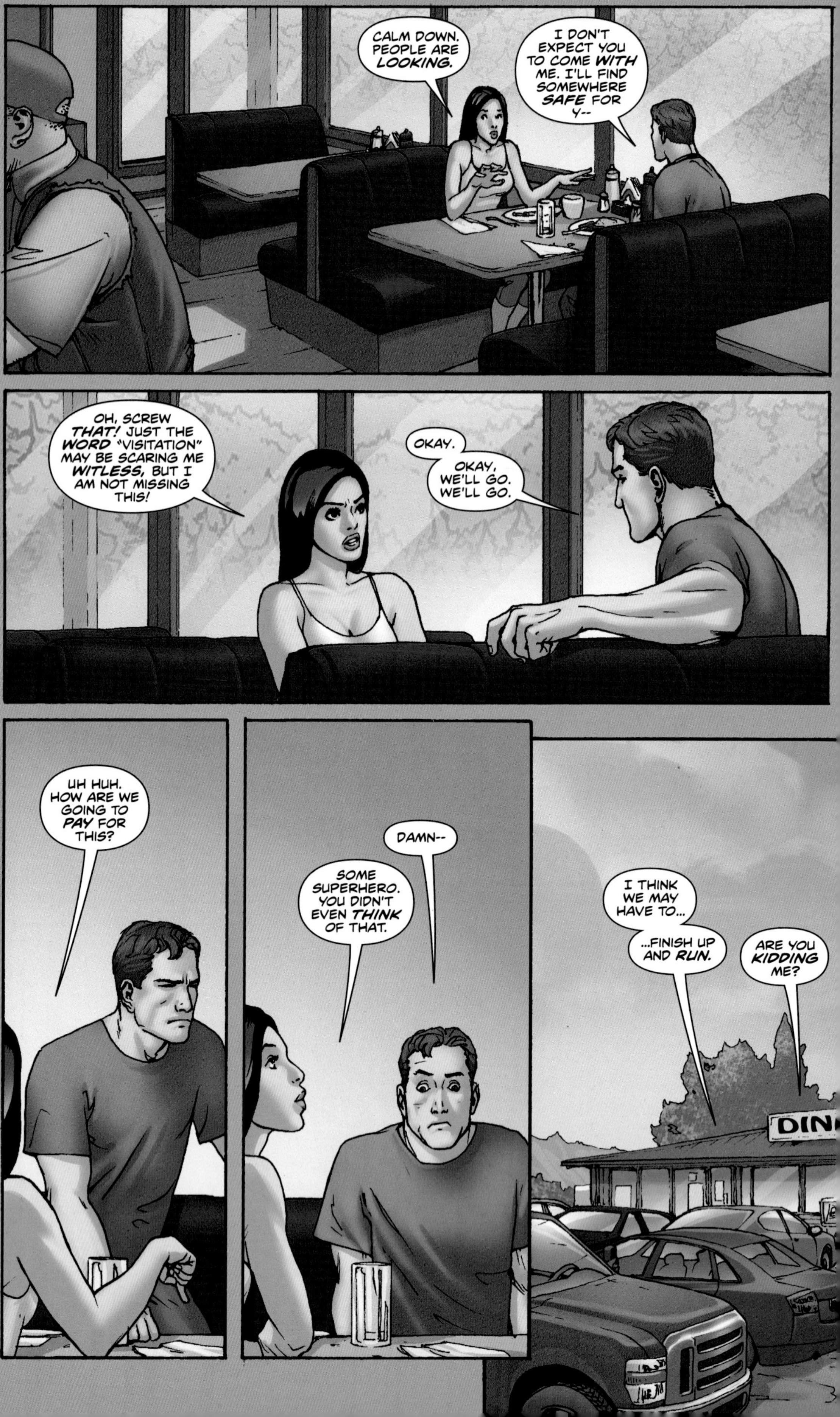

CALM DOWN. PEOPLE ARE LOOKING.
I DON'T EXPECT YOU TO COME WITH ME. I'LL FIND SOMEWHERE SAFE FOR Y--
OH, SCREW THAT! JUST THE WORD "VISITATION" MAY BE SCARING ME WITLESS, BUT I AM NOT MISSING THIS!
OKAY.
OKAY, WE'LL GO. WE'LL GO.
UH HUH. HOW ARE WE GOING TO PAY FOR THIS?
DAMN--
SOME SUPERHERO. YOU DIDN'T EVEN THINK OF THAT.
I THINK WE MAY HAVE TO...
...FINISH UP AND RUN.
ARE YOU KIDDING ME?
DIN

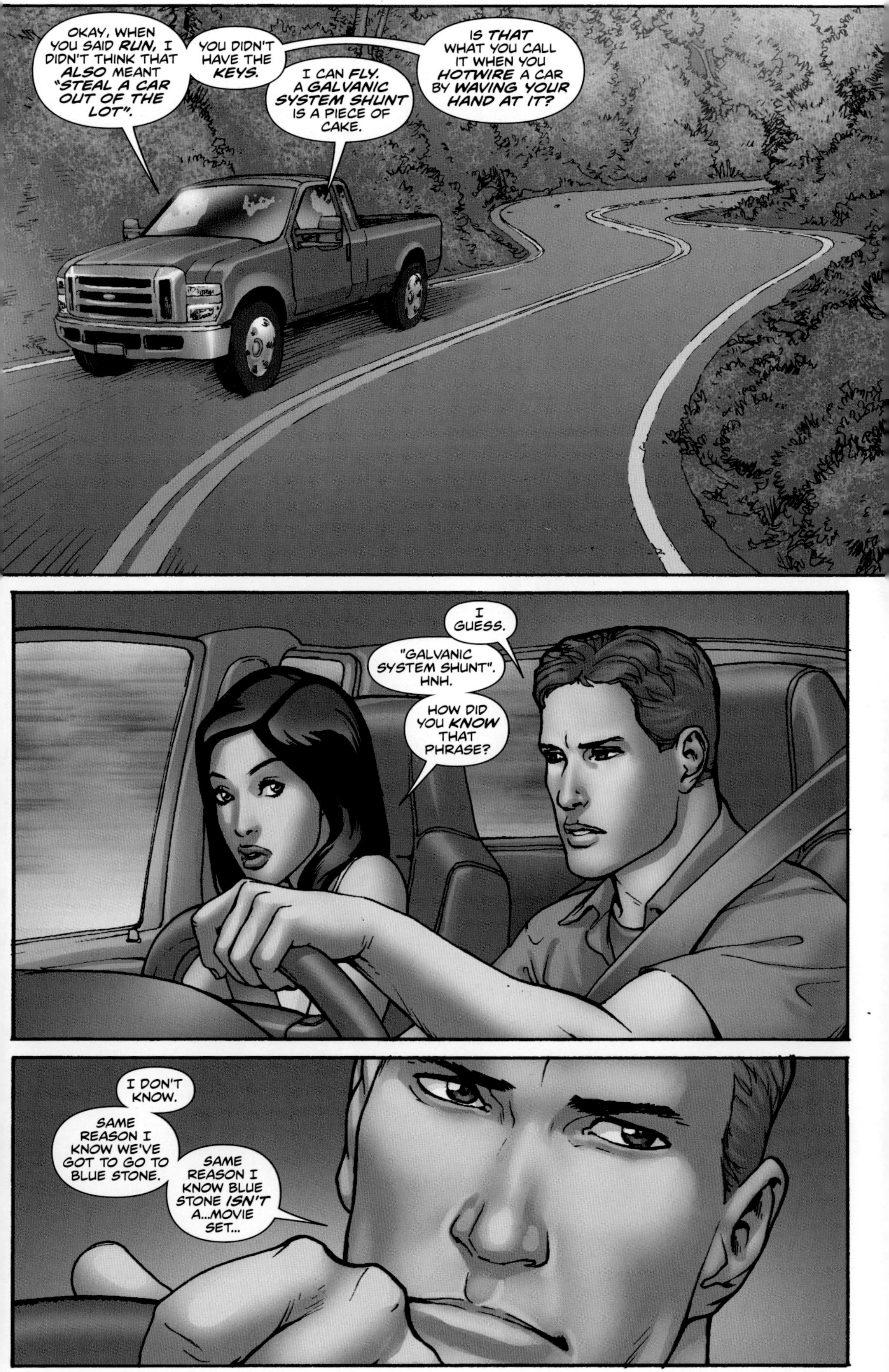
OKAY, WHEN YOU SAID RUN, I DIDN'T THINK THAT ALSO MEANT "STEAL A CAR OUT OF THE LOT".
YOU DIDN'T HAVE THE KEYS.
I CAN FLY. A GALVANIC SYSTEM SHUNT IS A PIECE OF CAKE.
IS THAT WHAT YOU CALL IT WHEN YOU HOTWIRE A CAR BY WAVING YOUR HAND AT IT?
I GUESS.
"GALVANIC SYSTEM SHUNT". HNH.
HOW DID YOU KNOW THAT PHRASE?
I DON'T KNOW.
SAME REASON I KNOW WE'VE GOT TO GO TO BLUE STONE.
SAME REASON I KNOW BLUE STONE ISN'T A...MOVIE SET...

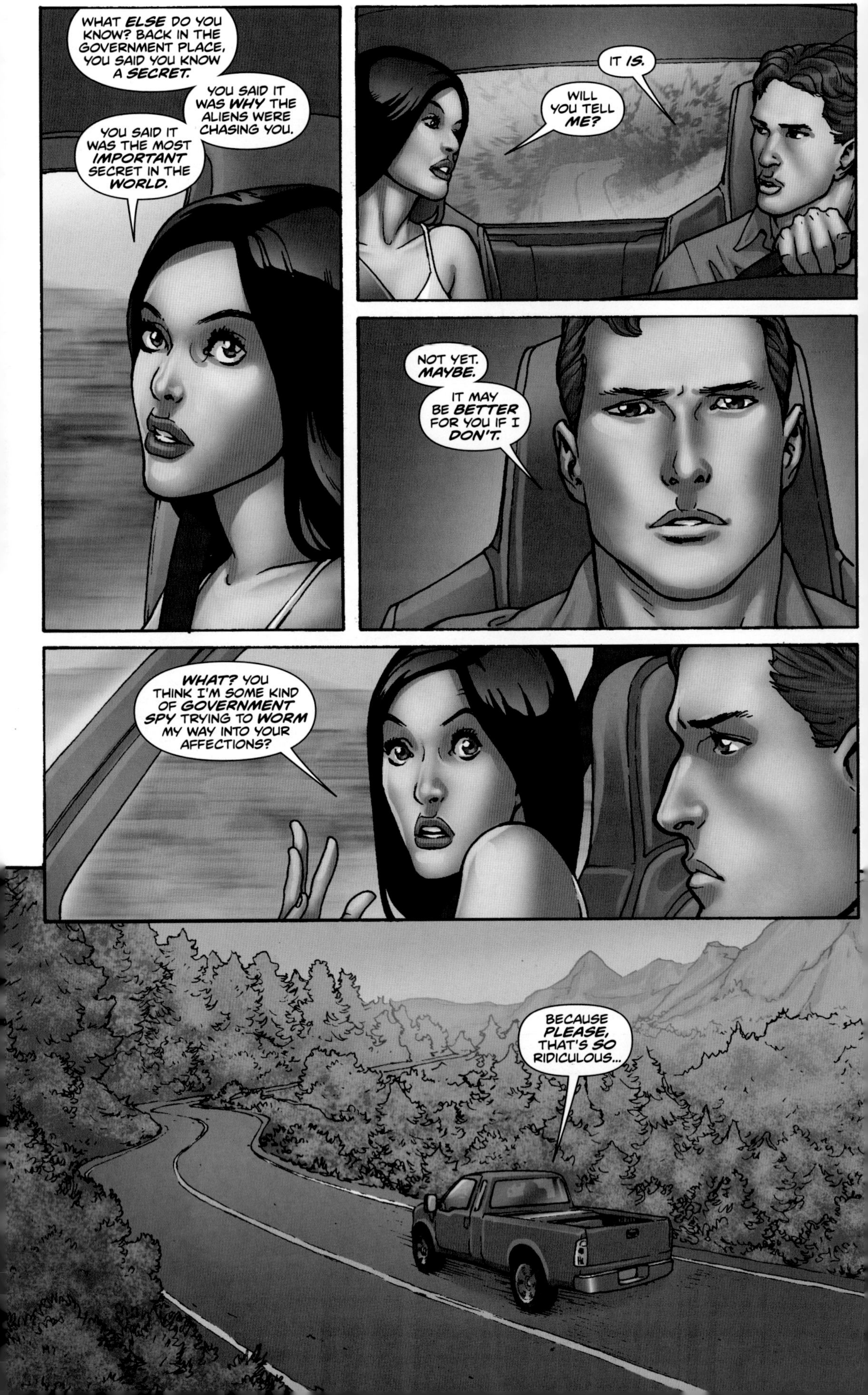

WHAT ELSE DO YOU KNOW? BACK IN THE GOVERNMENT PLACE, YOU SAID YOU KNOW A SECRET.
YOU SAID IT WAS WHY THE ALIENS WERE CHASING YOU.
YOU SAID IT WAS THE MOST IMPORTANT SECRET IN THE WORLD.
IT IS.
WILL YOU TELL ME?
NOT YET. MAYBE.
IT MAY BE BETTER FOR YOU IF I DON'T.
WHAT? YOU THINK I'M SOME KIND OF GOVERNMENT SPY TRYING TO WORM MY WAY INTO YOUR AFFECTIONS?
BECAUSE PLEASE, THAT'S SO RIDICULOUS...

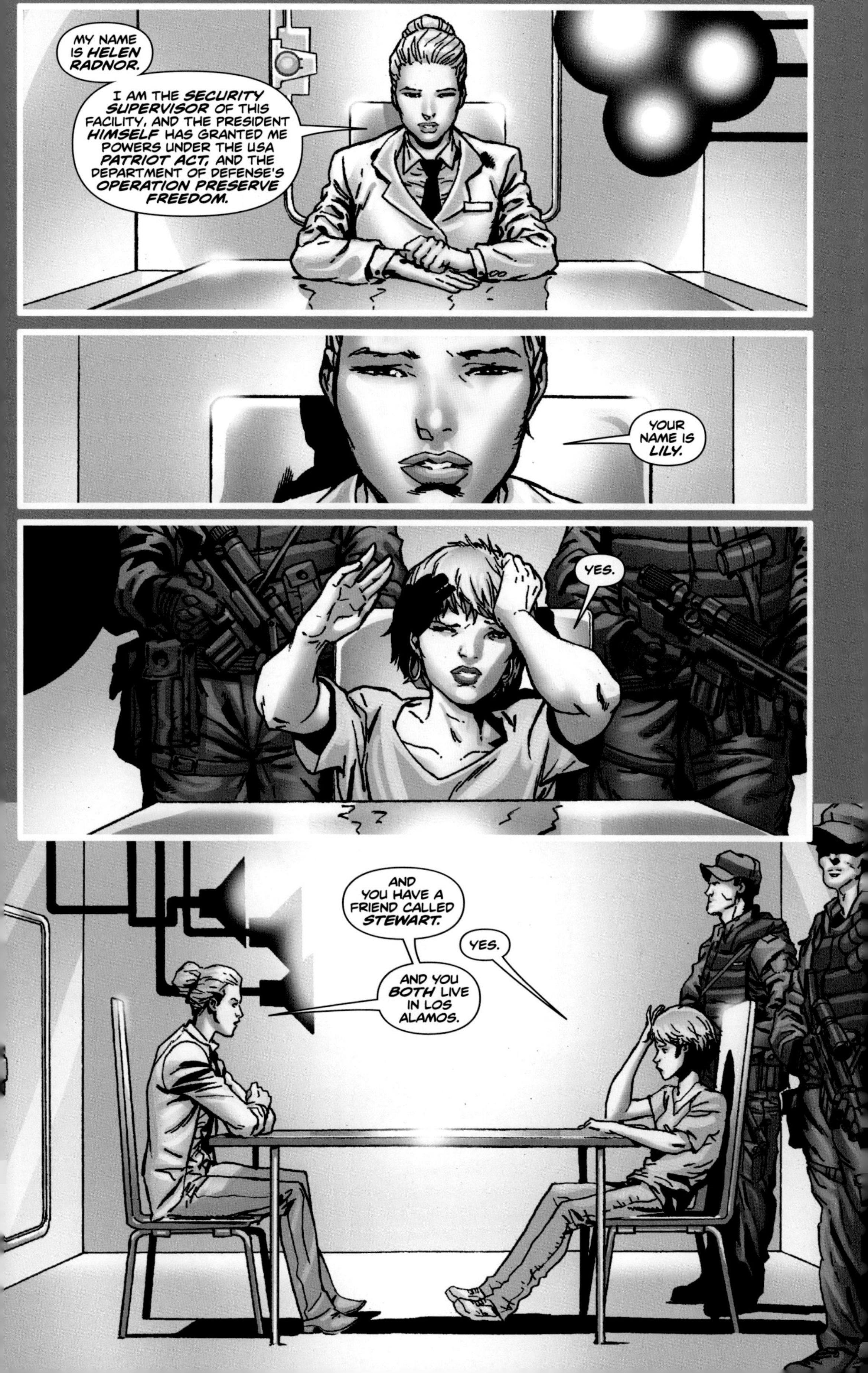

MY NAME IS HELEN RADNOR.
I AM THE SECURITY SUPERVISOR OF THIS FACILITY, AND THE PRESIDENT HIMSELF HAS GRANTED ME POWERS UNDER THE USA PATRIOT ACT, AND THE DEPARTMENT OF DEFENSE'S OPERATION PRESERVE FREEDOM.
YOUR NAME IS LILY.
YES.
AND YOU HAVE A FRIEND CALLED STEWART.
YES.
AND YOU BOTH LIVE IN LOS ALAMOS.

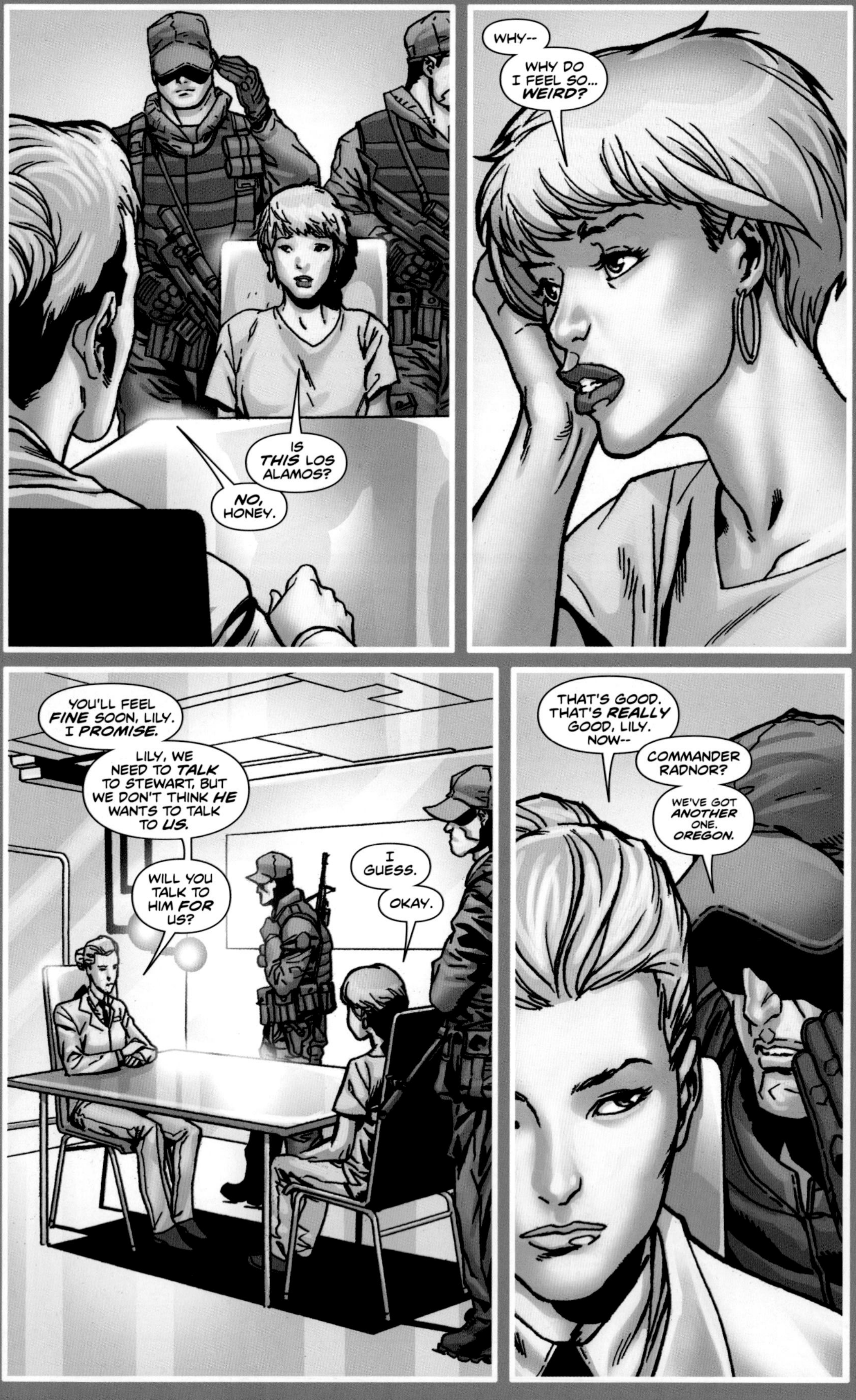
IS THIS LOS ALAMOS?
NO, HONEY.
WHY--
WHY DO I FEEL SO... WEIRD?
YOU'LL FEEL FINE SOON, LILY. I PROMISE.
LILY, WE NEED TO TALK TO STEWART, BUT WE DON'T THINK HE WANTS TO TALK TO US.
WILL YOU TALK TO HIM FOR US?
I GUESS.
OKAY.
THAT'S GOOD. THAT'S REALLY GOOD, LILY. NOW--
COMMANDER RADNOR?
WE'VE GOT ANOTHER ONE. OREGON.

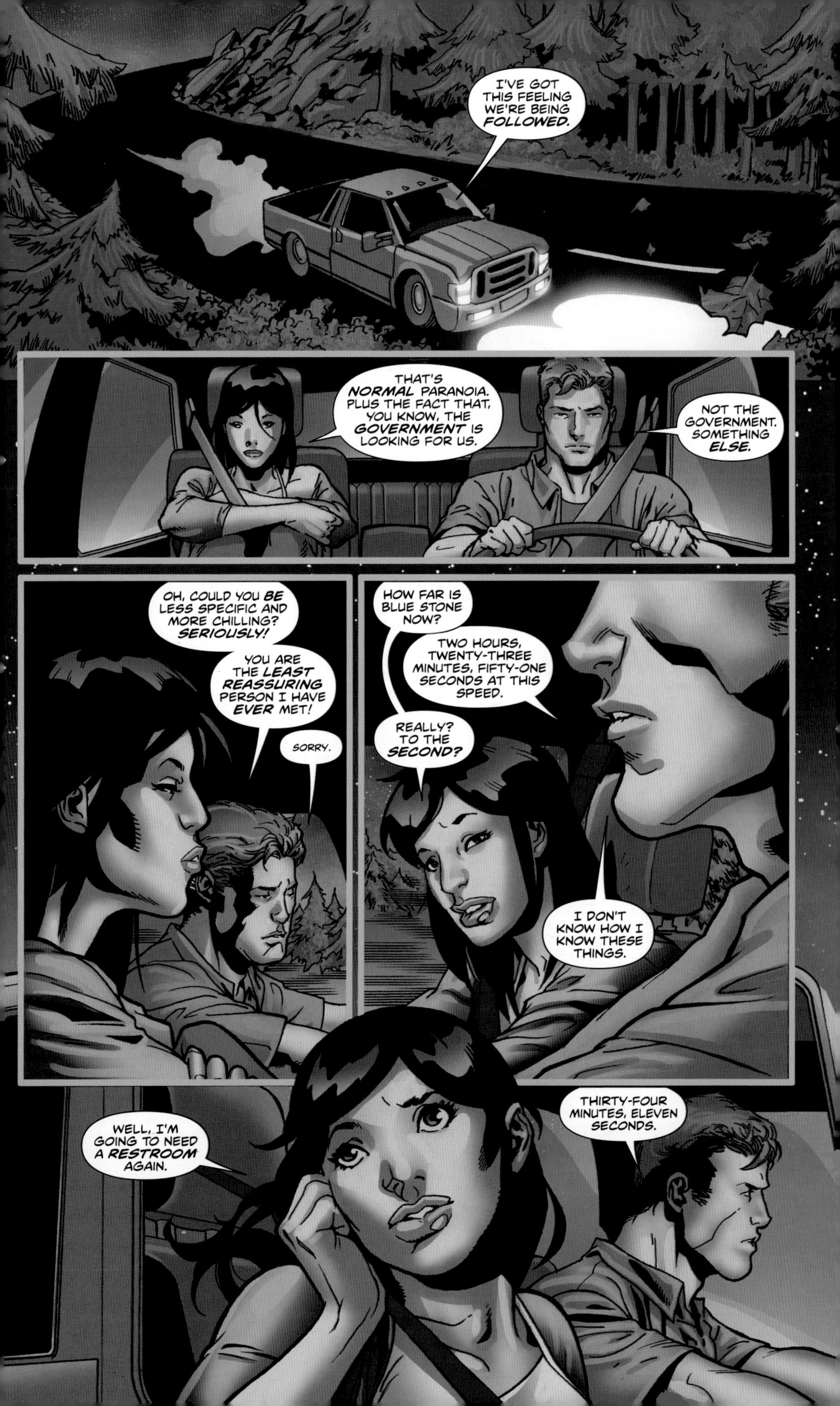

I'VE GOT THIS FEELING WE'RE BEING FOLLOWED.
THAT'S NORMAL PARANOIA. PLUS THE FACT THAT, YOU KNOW, THE GOVERNMENT IS LOOKING FOR US.
NOT THE GOVERNMENT. SOMETHING ELSE.
OH, COULD YOU BE LESS SPECIFIC AND MORE CHILLING? SERIOUSLY!
YOU ARE THE LEAST REASSURING PERSON I HAVE EVER MET!
SORRY.
HOW FAR IS BLUE STONE NOW?
TWO HOURS, TWENTY-THREE MINUTES, FIFTY-ONE SECONDS AT THIS SPEED.
REALLY? TO THE SECOND?
I DON'T KNOW HOW I KNOW THESE THINGS.
WELL, I'M GOING TO NEED A RESTROOM AGAIN.
THIRTY-FOUR MINUTES, ELEVEN SECONDS.

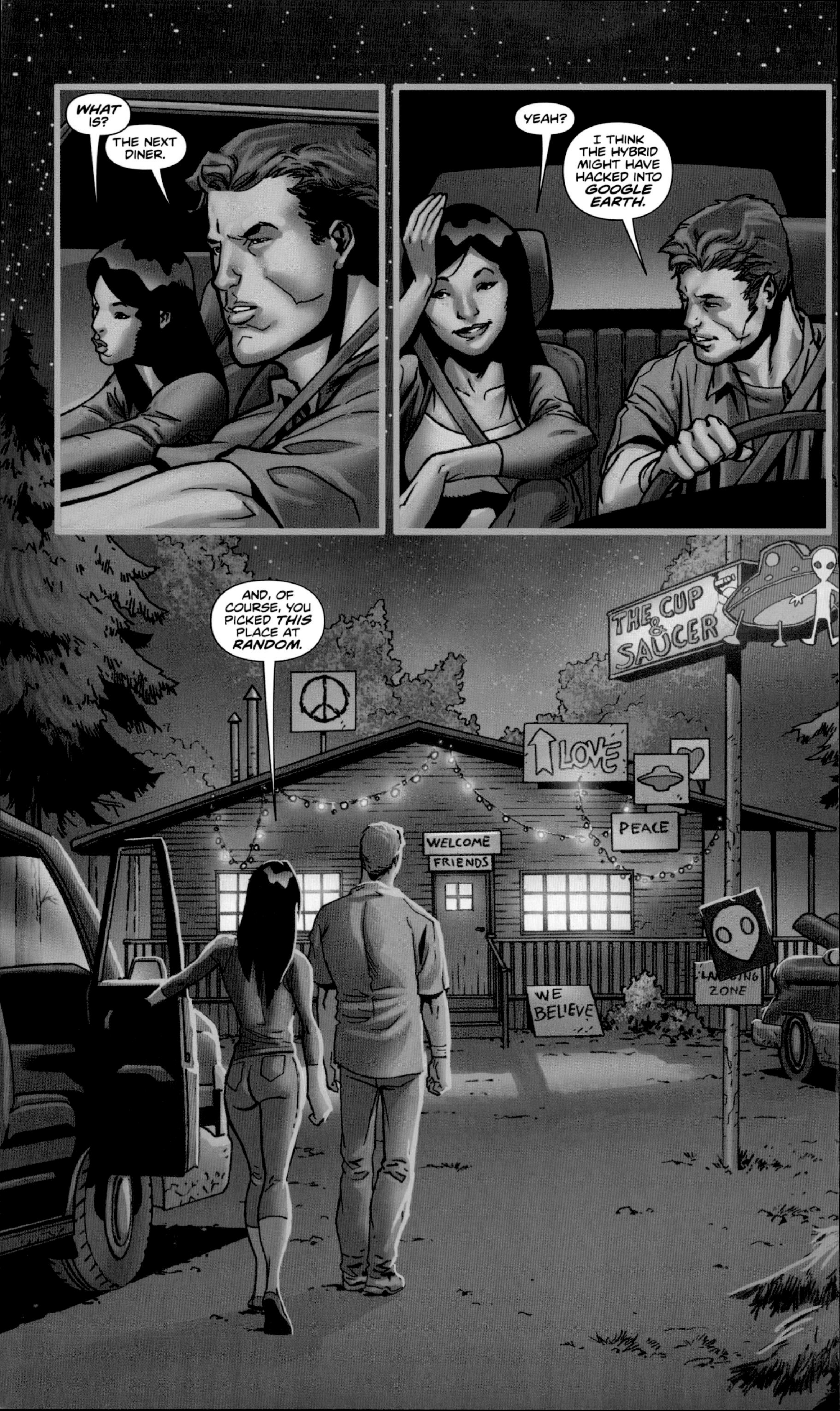
WHAT IS?
THE NEXT DINER.
YEAH?
I THINK THE HYBRID MIGHT HAVE HACKED INTO GOOGLE EARTH.
AND, OF COURSE, YOU PICKED THIS PLACE AT RANDOM.
THE CUP & SAUCER
LOVE
PEACE
WELCOME
FRIENDS
WE BELIEVE
ZONE

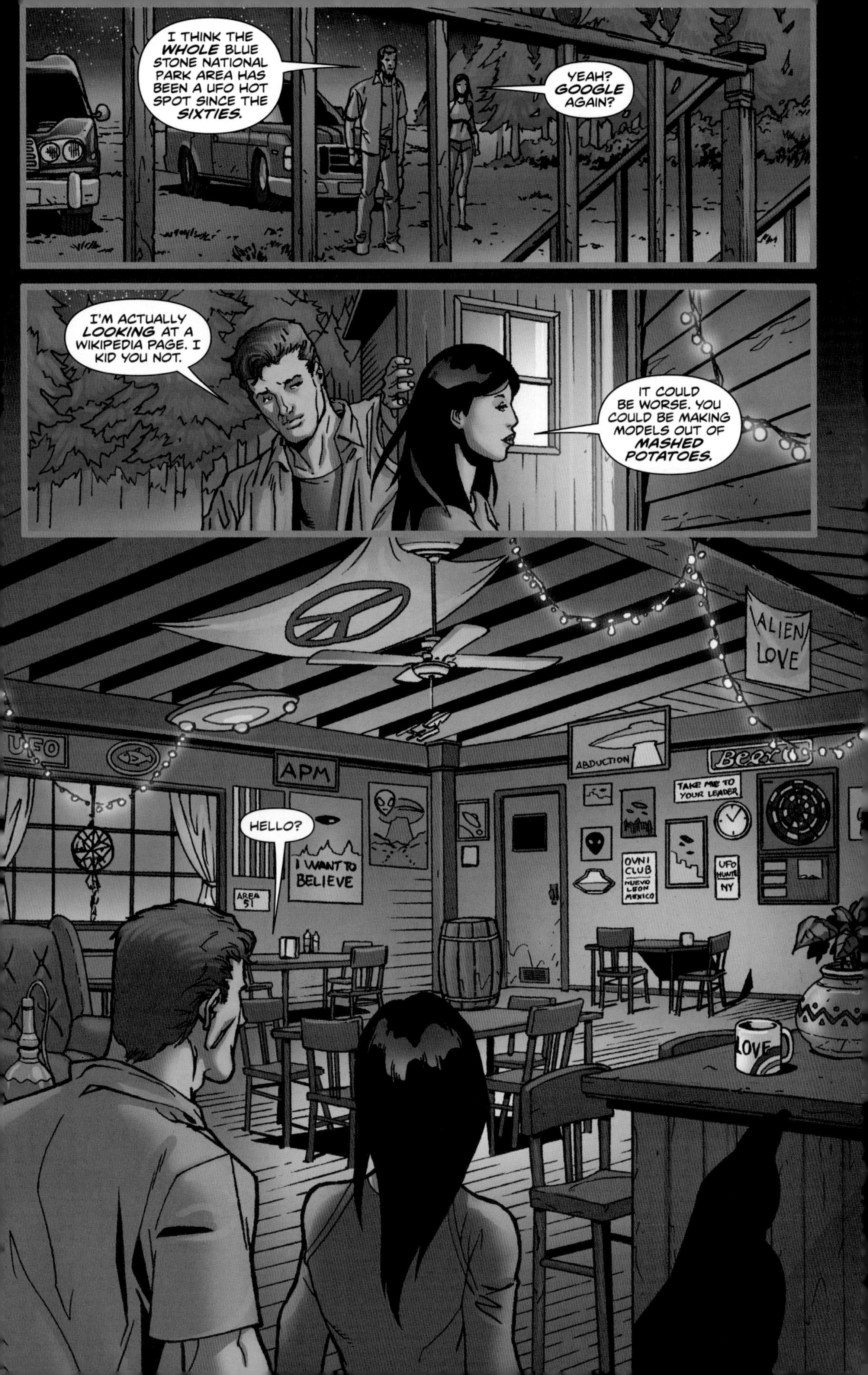
I THINK THE WHOLE BLUE STONE NATIONAL PARK AREA HAS BEEN A UFO HOT SPOT SINCE THE SIXTIES.
YEAH? GOOGLE AGAIN?
I'M ACTUALLY LOOKING AT A WIKIPEDIA PAGE. I KID YOU NOT.
IT COULD BE WORSE. YOU COULD BE MAKING MODELS OUT OF MASHED POTATOES.
ALIEN LOVE
UFO
APM
ABDUCTION
TAKE ME TO YOUR LEADER
HELLO?
I WANT TO BELIEVE
AREA 51
OVNI CLUB
NUEVO LEON MEXICO
UFO HUNTE
NY
LOVE

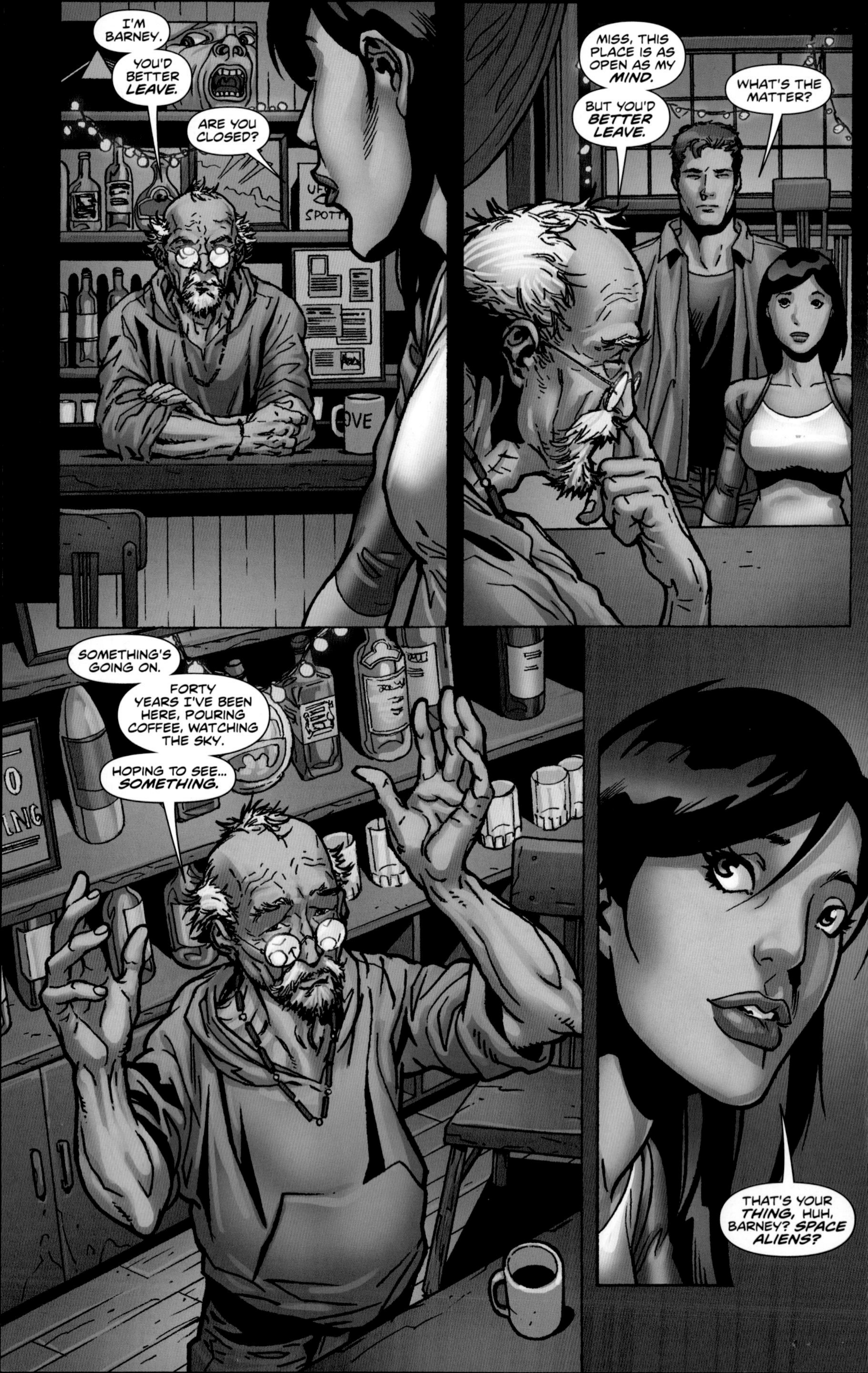
I'M BARNEY.
YOU'D BETTER *LEAVE.*
ARE YOU CLOSED?
MISS, THIS PLACE IS AS OPEN AS MY *MIND.*
BUT YOU'D *BETTER LEAVE.*
WHAT'S THE MATTER?
SOMETHING'S GOING ON.
FORTY YEARS I'VE BEEN HERE, POURING COFFEE, WATCHING THE SKY.
HOPING TO SEE... ***SOMETHING.***
THAT'S YOUR *THING,* HUH, BARNEY? *SPACE ALIENS?*

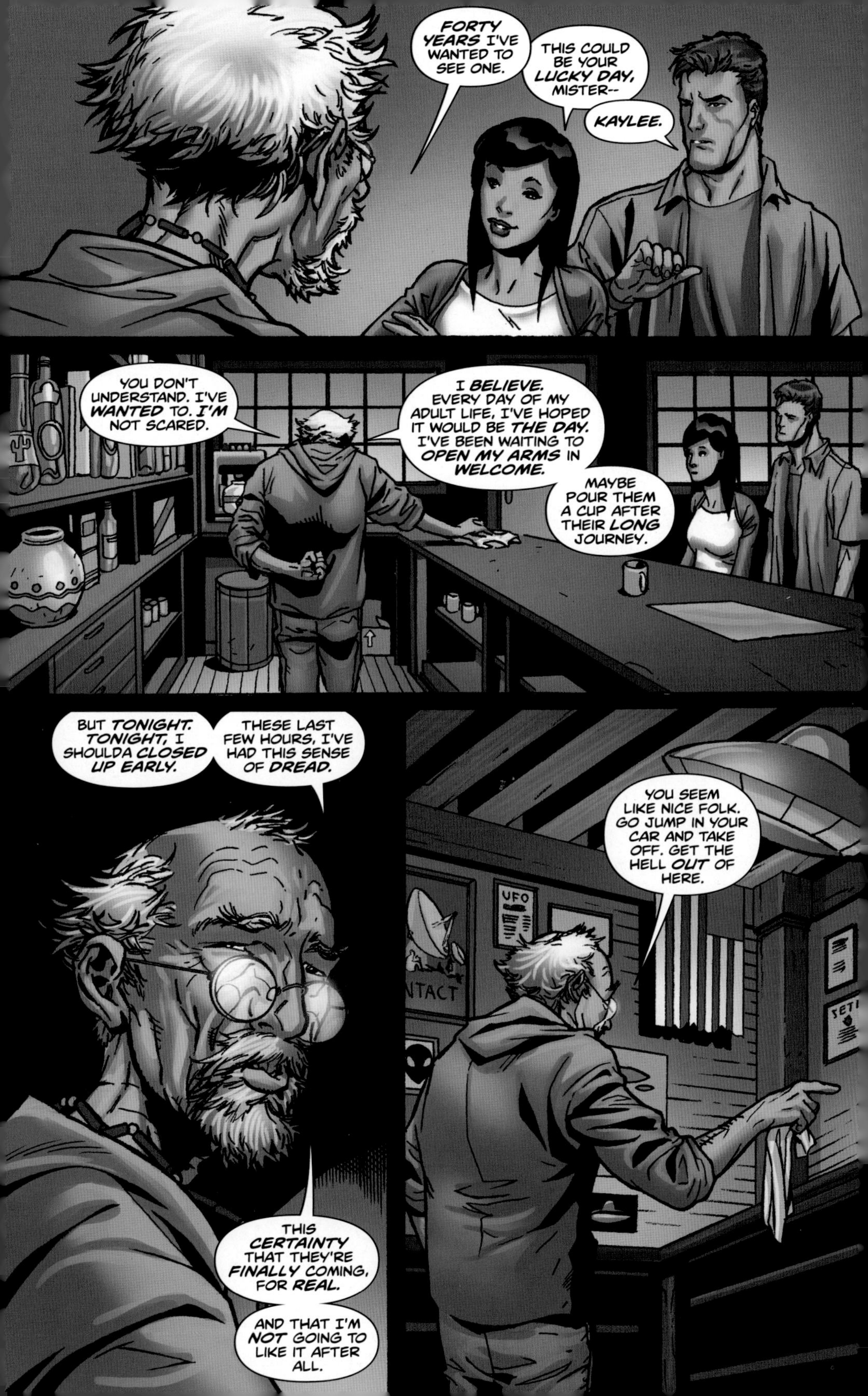
FORTY YEARS I'VE WANTED TO SEE ONE.
THIS COULD BE YOUR LUCKY DAY, MISTER--
KAYLEE.
YOU DON'T UNDERSTAND. I'VE WANTED TO. I'M NOT SCARED.
I BELIEVE. EVERY DAY OF MY ADULT LIFE, I'VE HOPED IT WOULD BE THE DAY. I'VE BEEN WAITING TO OPEN MY ARMS IN WELCOME.
MAYBE POUR THEM A CUP AFTER THEIR LONG JOURNEY.
BUT TONIGHT. TONIGHT, I SHOULDA CLOSED UP EARLY.
THESE LAST FEW HOURS, I'VE HAD THIS SENSE OF DREAD.
THIS CERTAINTY THAT THEY'RE FINALLY COMING, FOR REAL.
AND THAT I'M NOT GOING TO LIKE IT AFTER ALL.
YOU SEEM LIKE NICE FOLK. GO JUMP IN YOUR CAR AND TAKE OFF. GET THE HELL OUT OF HERE.
UFO
SETI

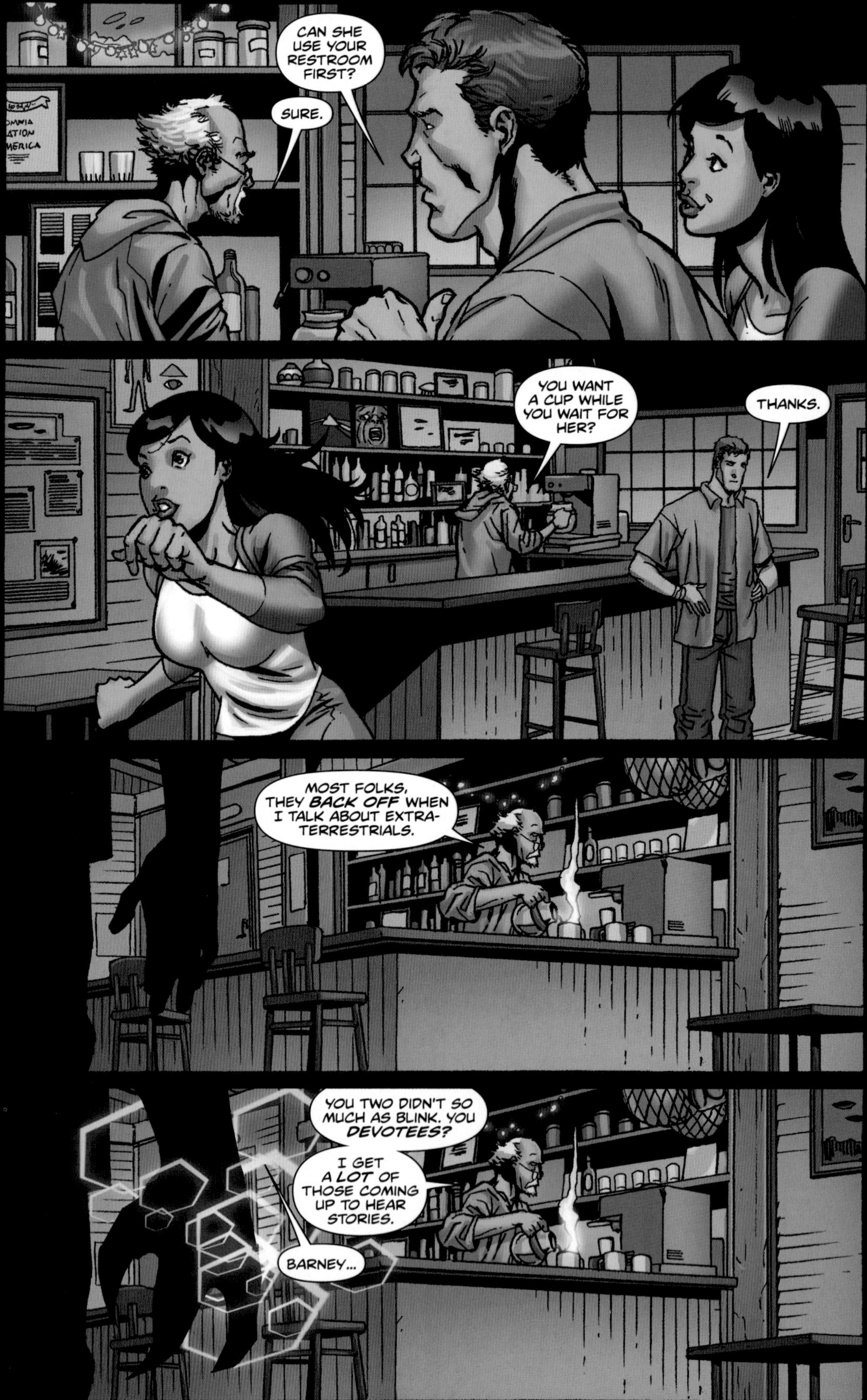
CAN SHE USE YOUR RESTROOM FIRST?
SURE.
YOU WANT A CUP WHILE YOU WAIT FOR HER?
THANKS.
MOST FOLKS, THEY BACK OFF WHEN I TALK ABOUT EXTRA-TERRESTRIALS.
YOU TWO DIDN'T SO MUCH AS BLINK. YOU DEVOTEES?
I GET A LOT OF THOSE COMING UP TO HEAR STORIES.
BARNEY...

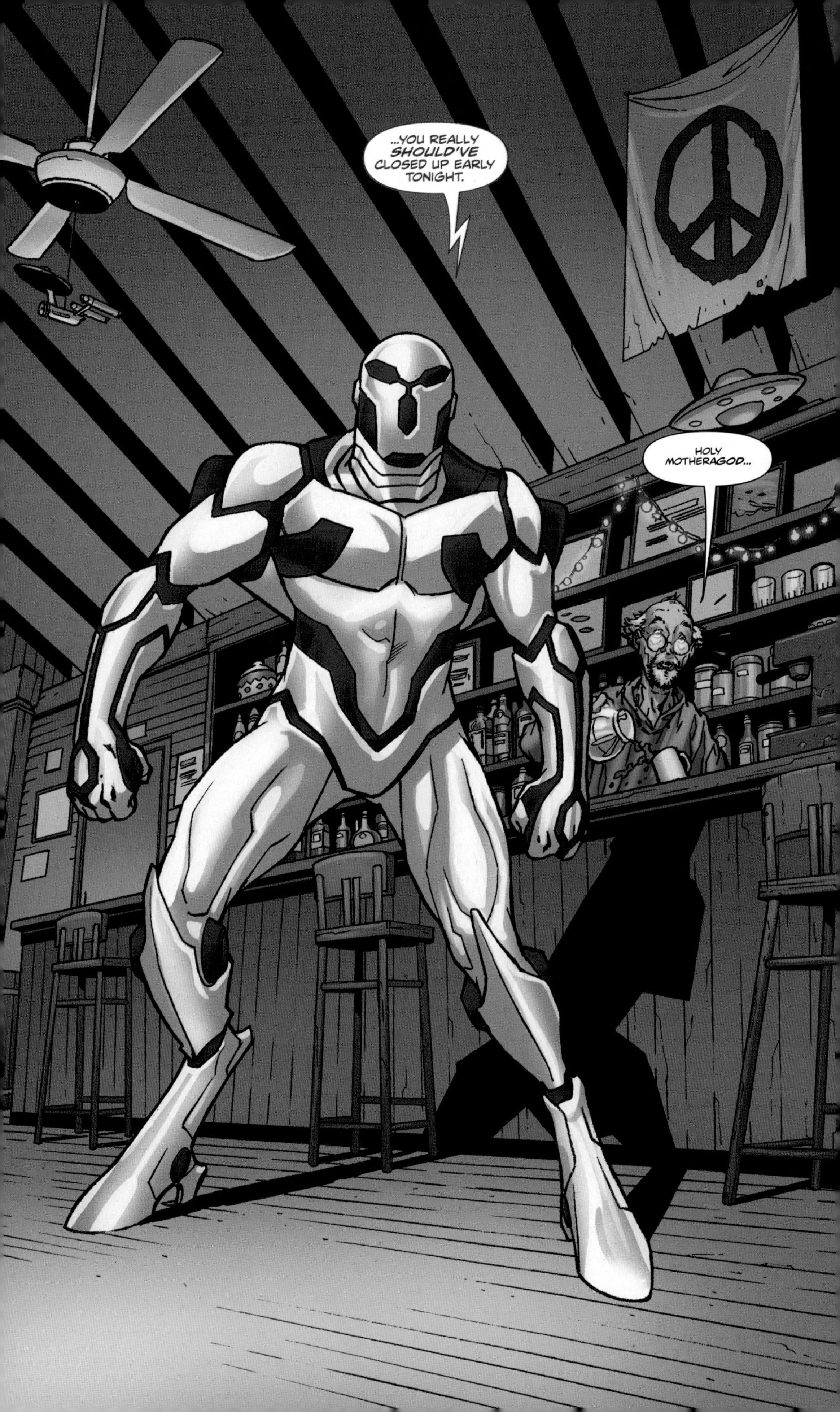
...YOU REALLY SHOULD'VE CLOSED UP EARLY TONIGHT.
HOLY MOTHERAGOD...

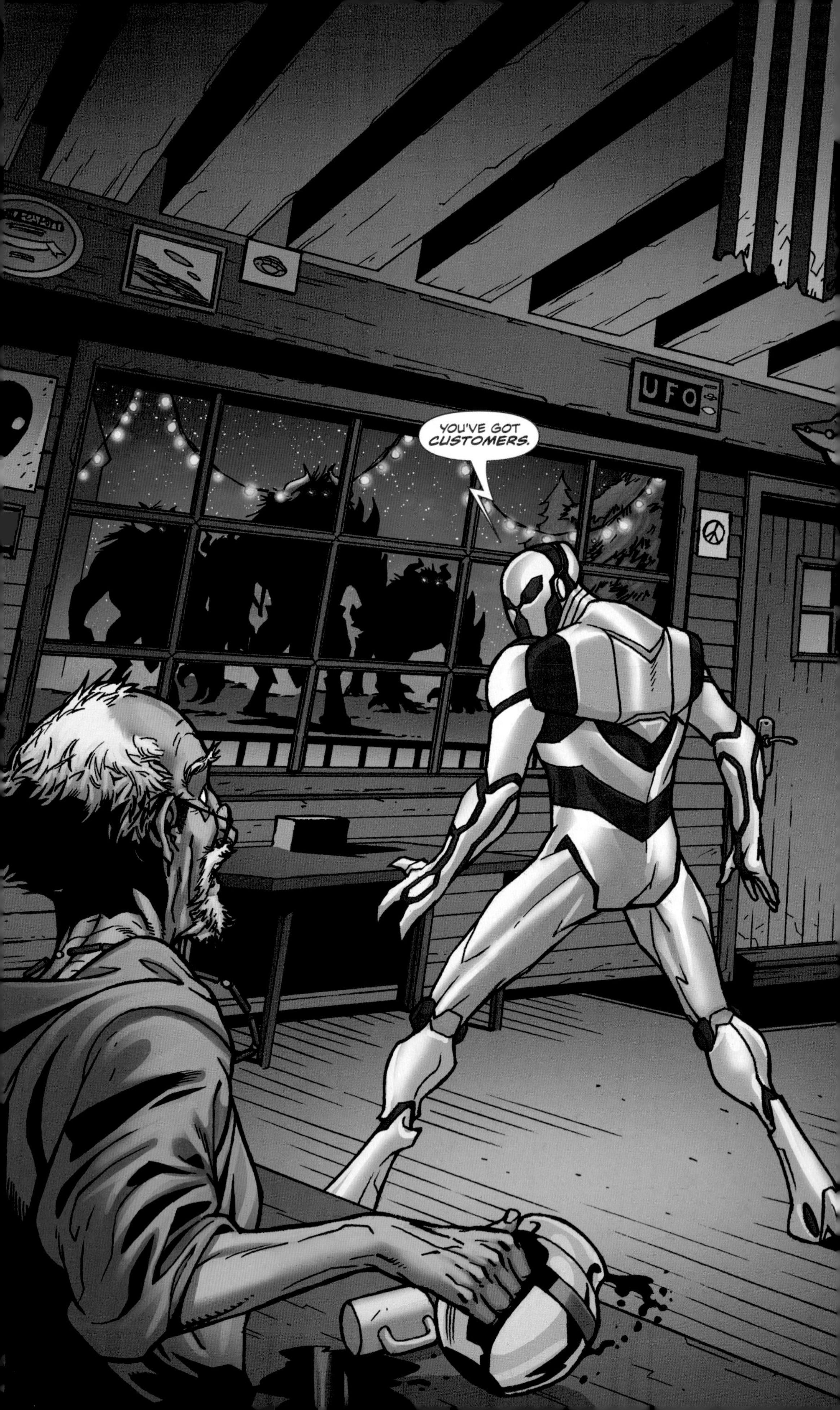
UFO
YOU'VE GOT CUSTOMERS.

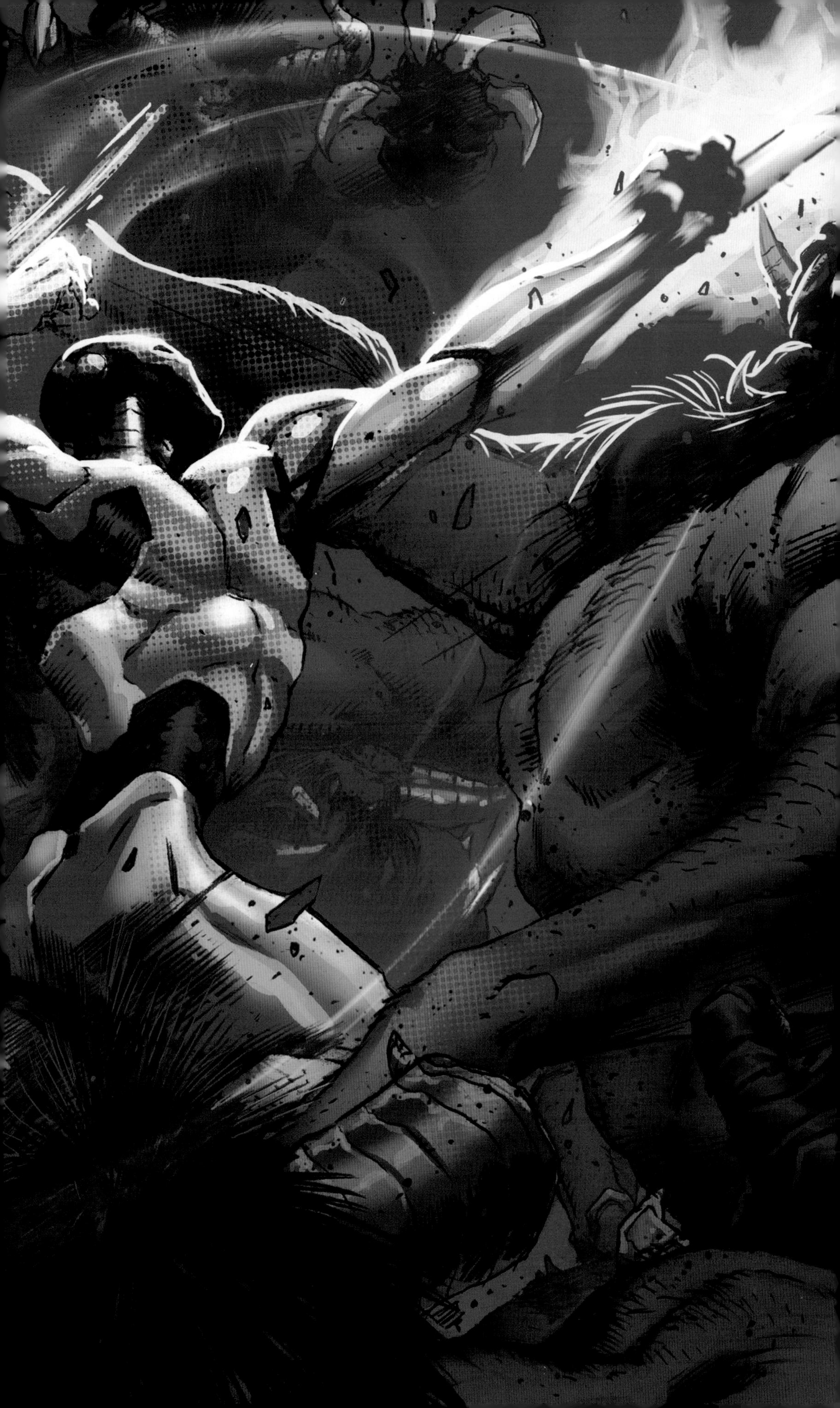

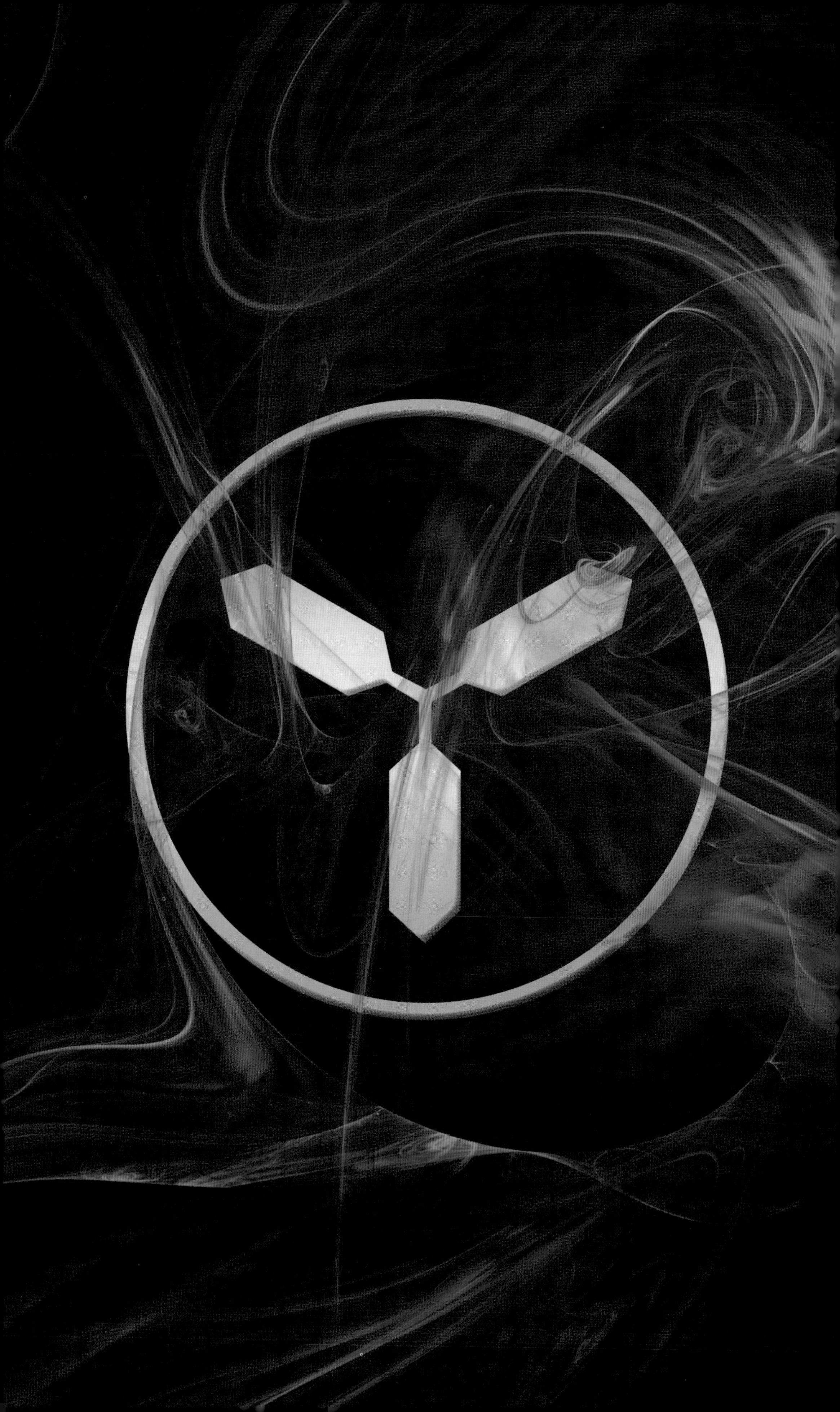

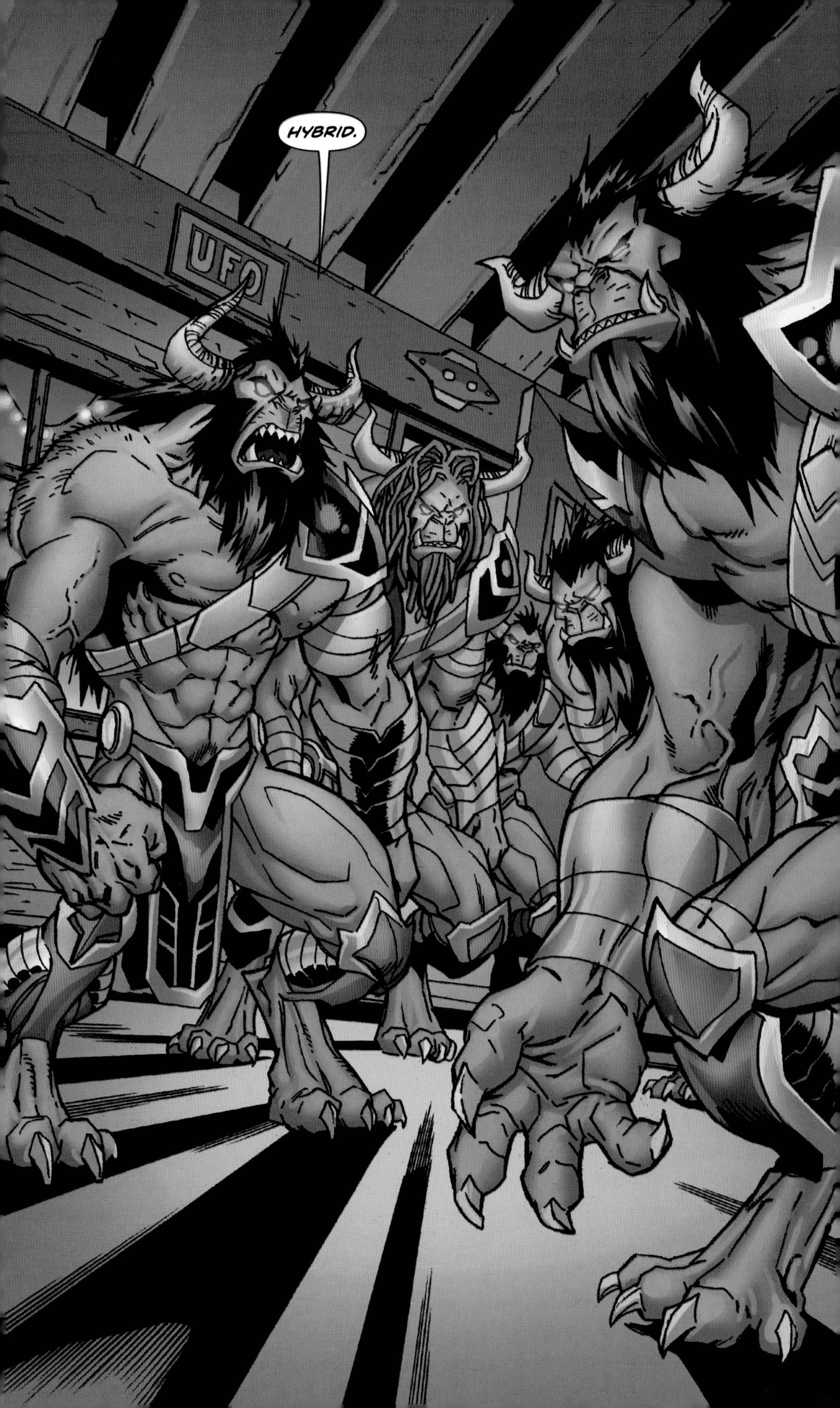
HYBRID.
UFO

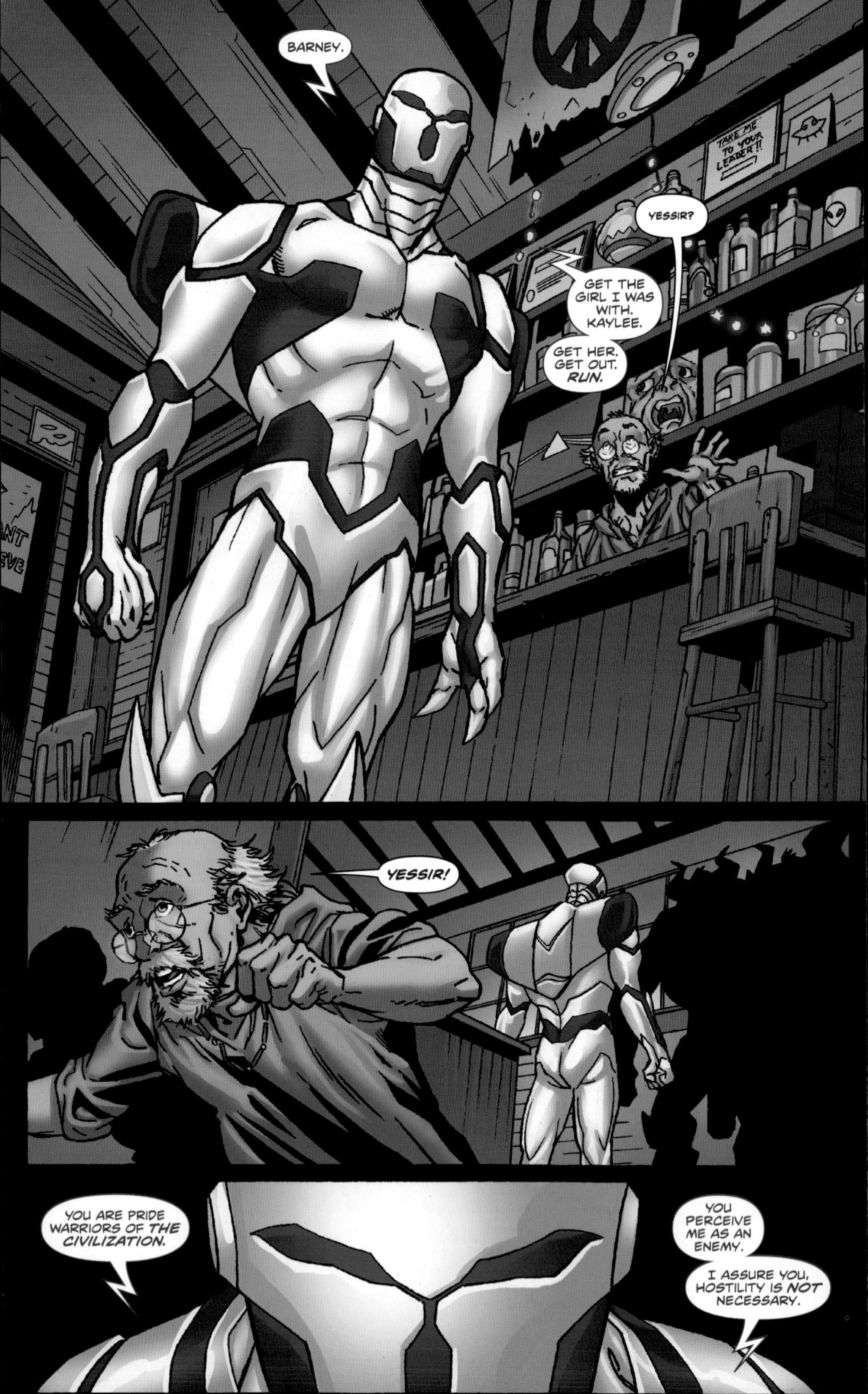
BARNEY.
YESSIR?
GET THE GIRL I WAS WITH. KAYLEE.
GET HER. GET OUT. *RUN.*
TAKE ME TO YOUR LEADER!!
YESSIR!
YOU ARE PRIDE WARRIORS OF *THE CIVILIZATION.*
YOU PERCEIVE ME AS AN ENEMY.
I ASSURE YOU, HOSTILITY IS *NOT* NECESSARY.

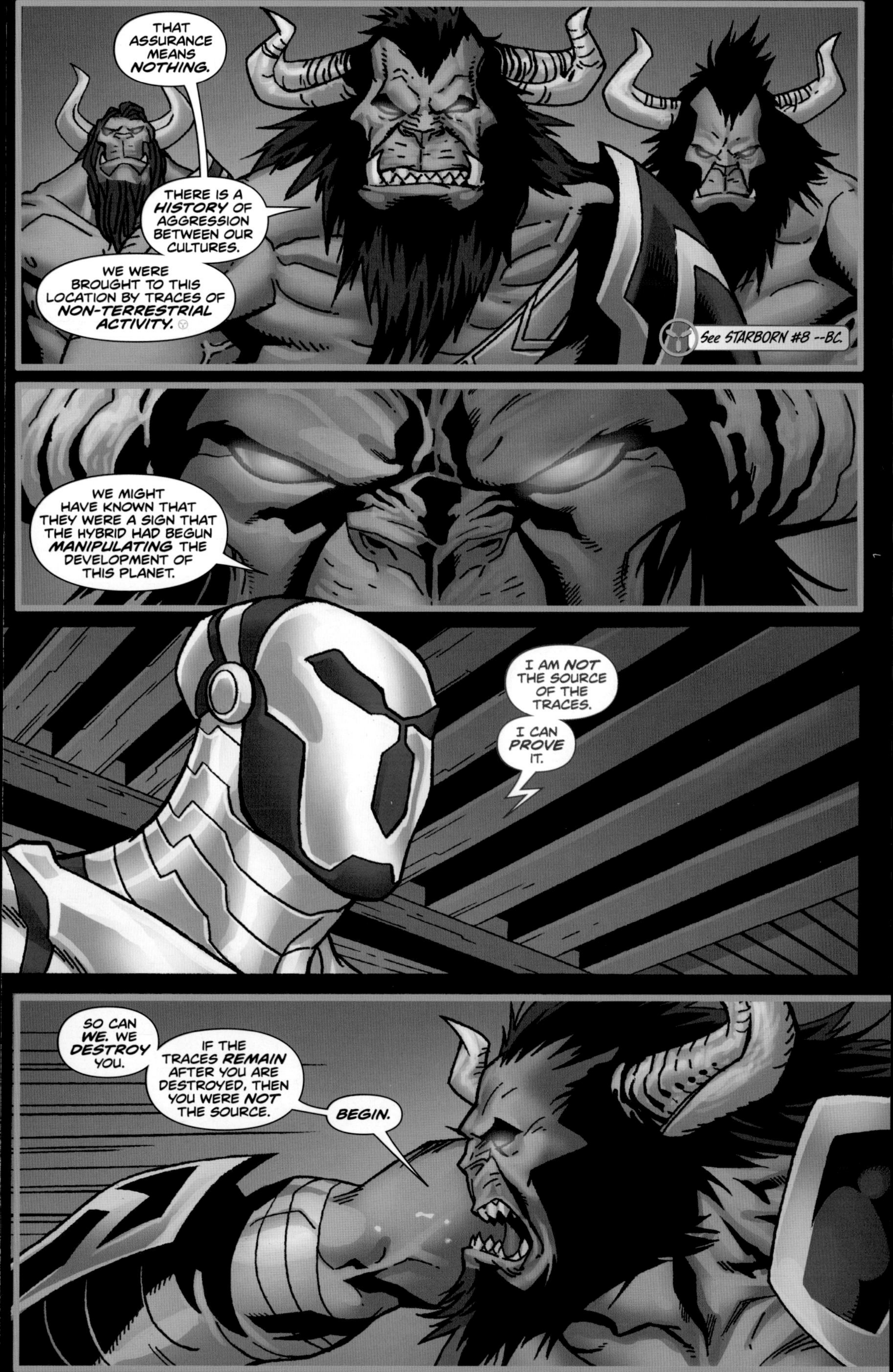
THAT ASSURANCE MEANS NOTHING.
THERE IS A HISTORY OF AGGRESSION BETWEEN OUR CULTURES.
WE WERE BROUGHT TO THIS LOCATION BY TRACES OF NON-TERRESTRIAL ACTIVITY.
See STARBORN #8 --BC.
WE MIGHT HAVE KNOWN THAT THEY WERE A SIGN THAT THE HYBRID HAD BEGUN MANIPULATING THE DEVELOPMENT OF THIS PLANET.
I AM NOT THE SOURCE OF THE TRACES.
I CAN PROVE IT.
SO CAN WE. WE DESTROY YOU.
IF THE TRACES REMAIN AFTER YOU ARE DESTROYED, THEN YOU WERE NOT THE SOURCE.
BEGIN.

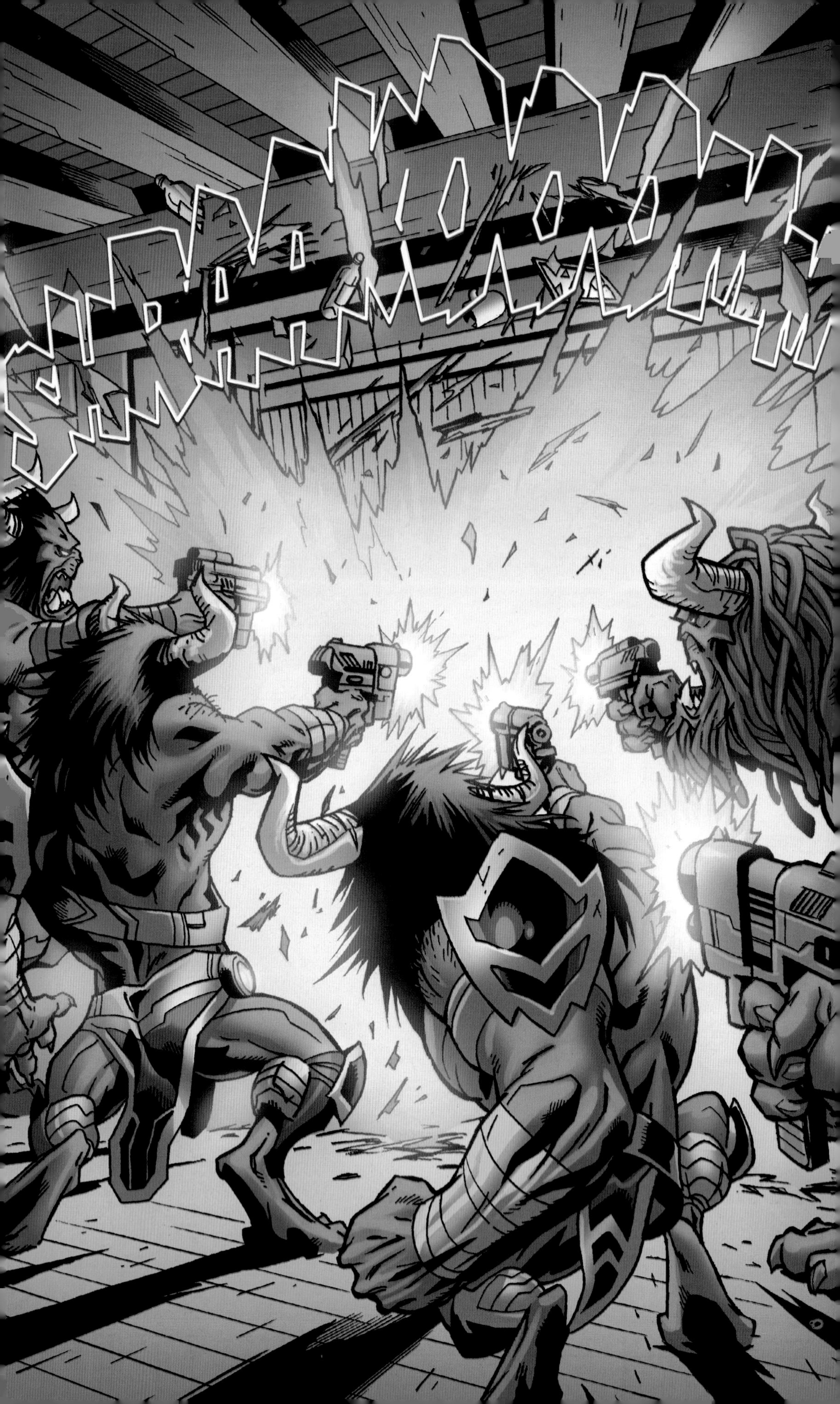

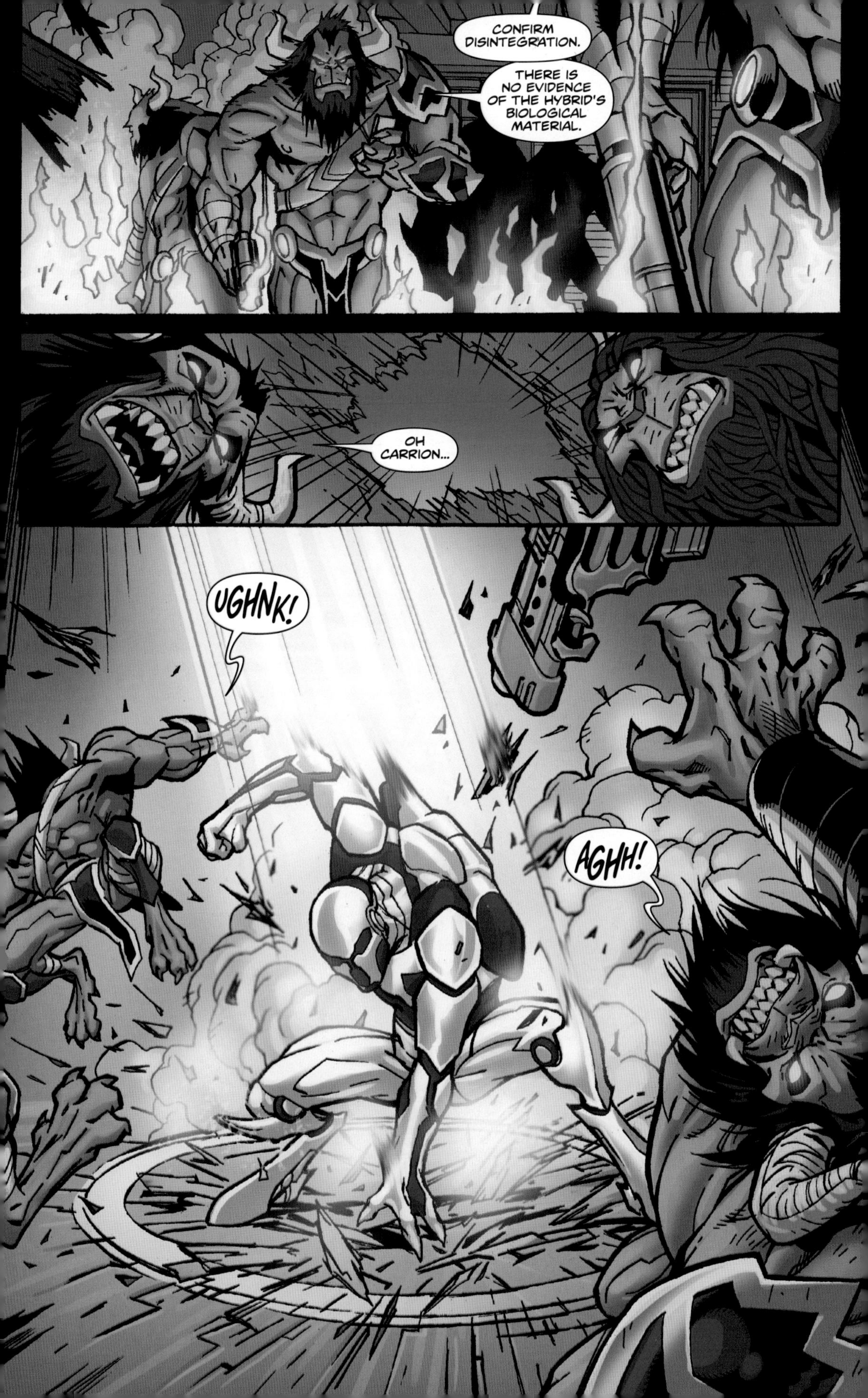
CONFIRM DISINTEGRATION.
THERE IS NO EVIDENCE OF THE HYBRID'S BIOLOGICAL MATERIAL.
OH CARRION...
UGHNK!
AGHH!

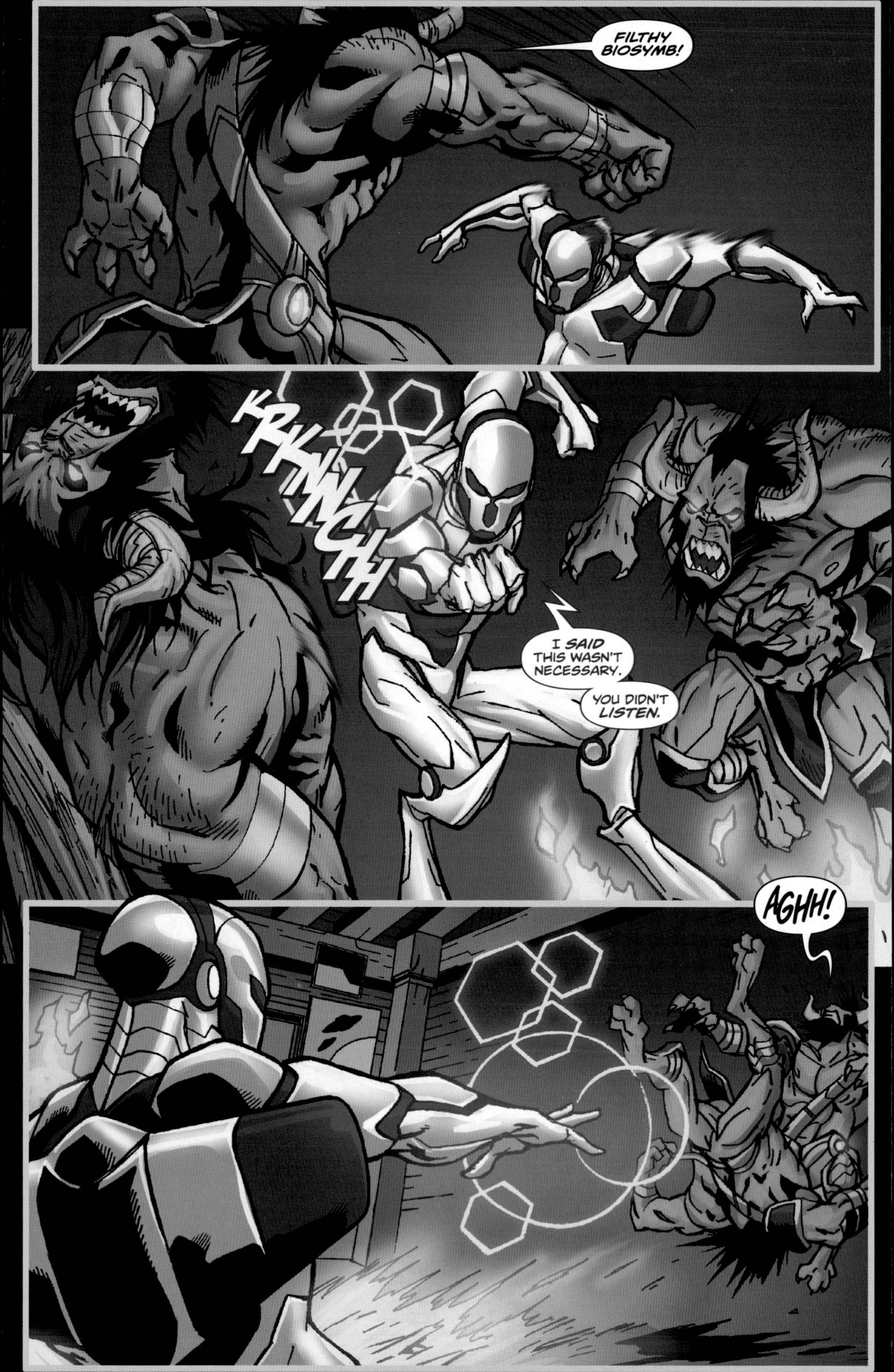
FILTHY BIOSYMB!
KRKNCHH
I SAID THIS WASN'T NECESSARY.
YOU DIDN'T LISTEN.
AGHH!

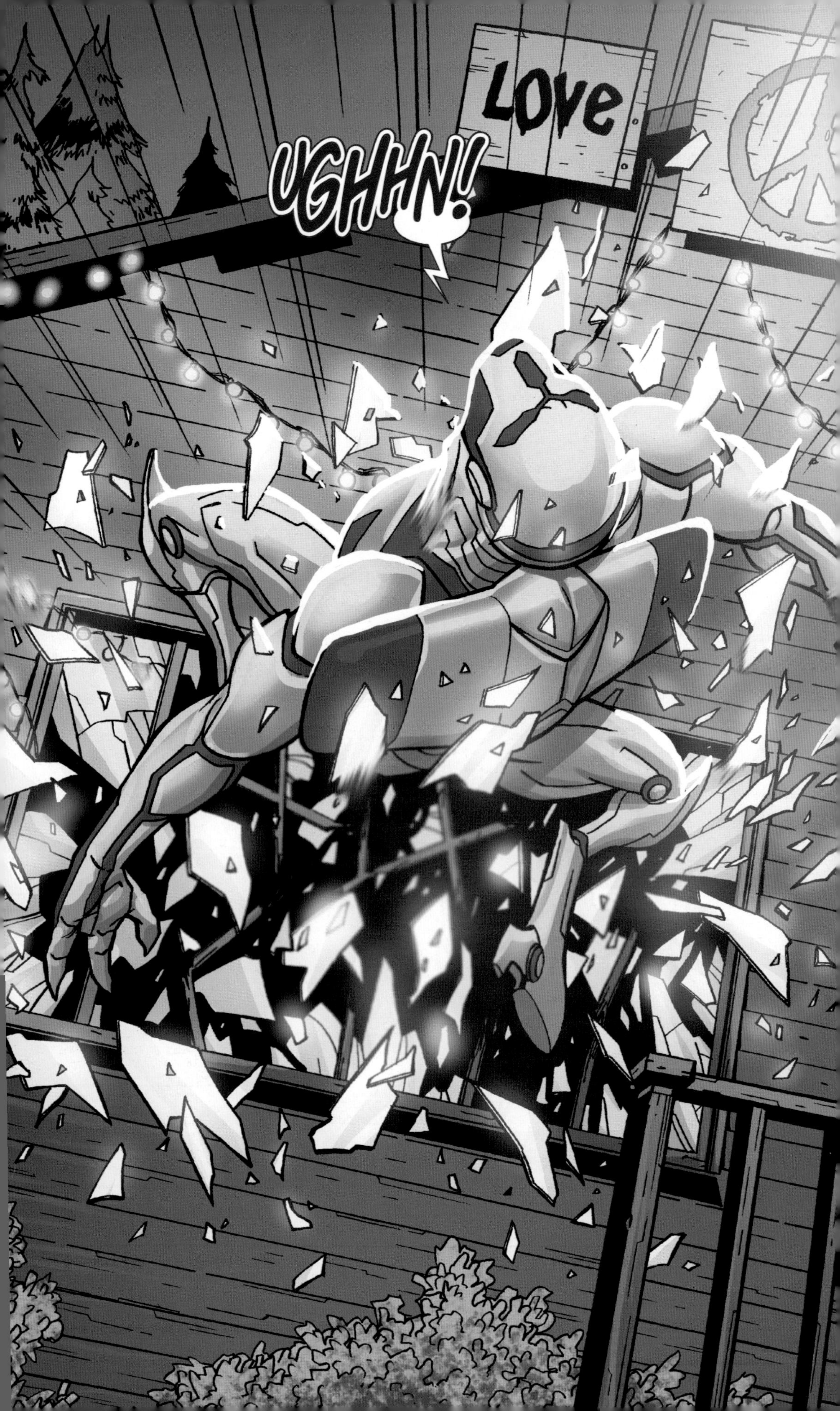
LOVE
UGHHN!

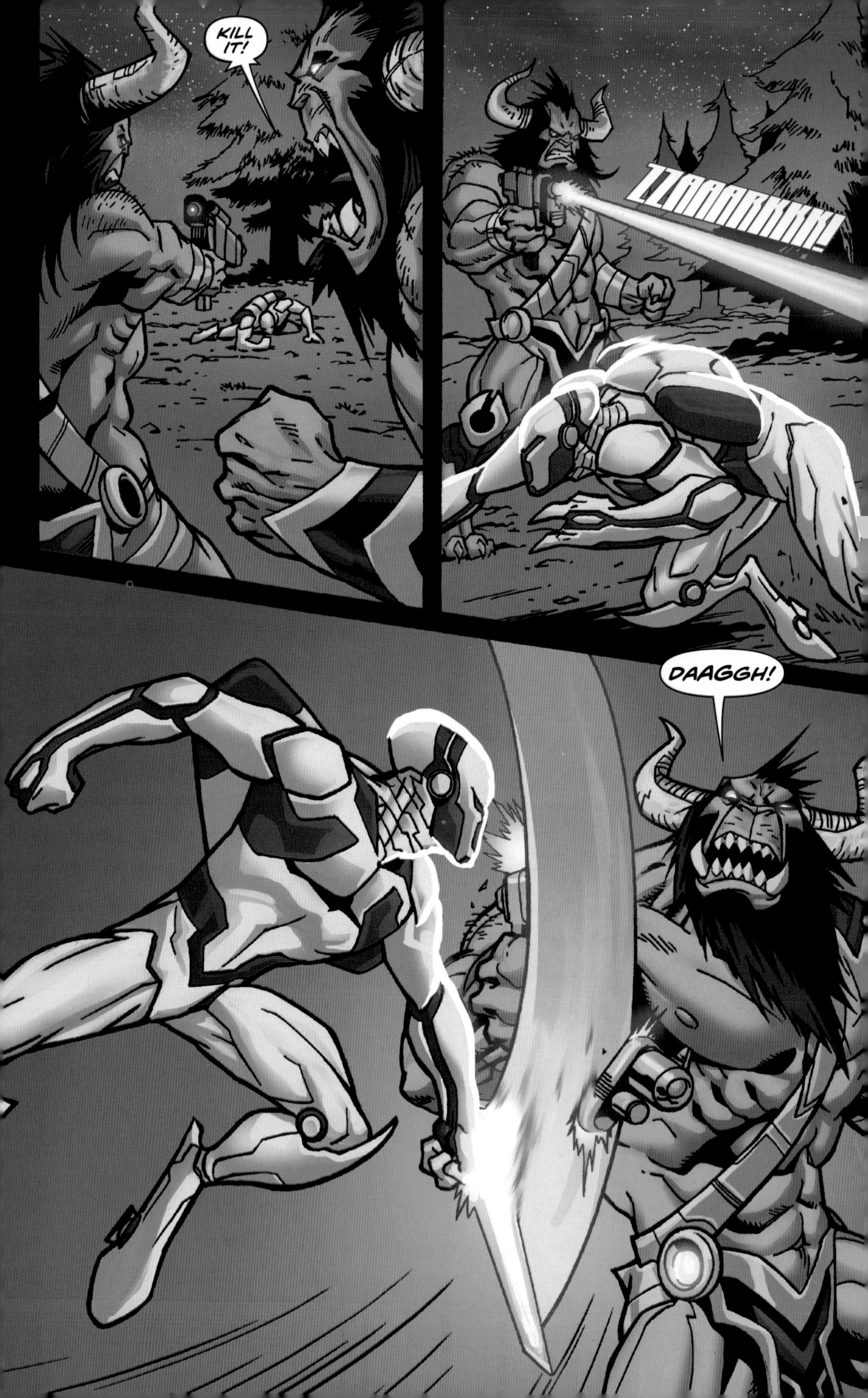
KILL IT!
ZZAAARKKK!
DAAGGH!

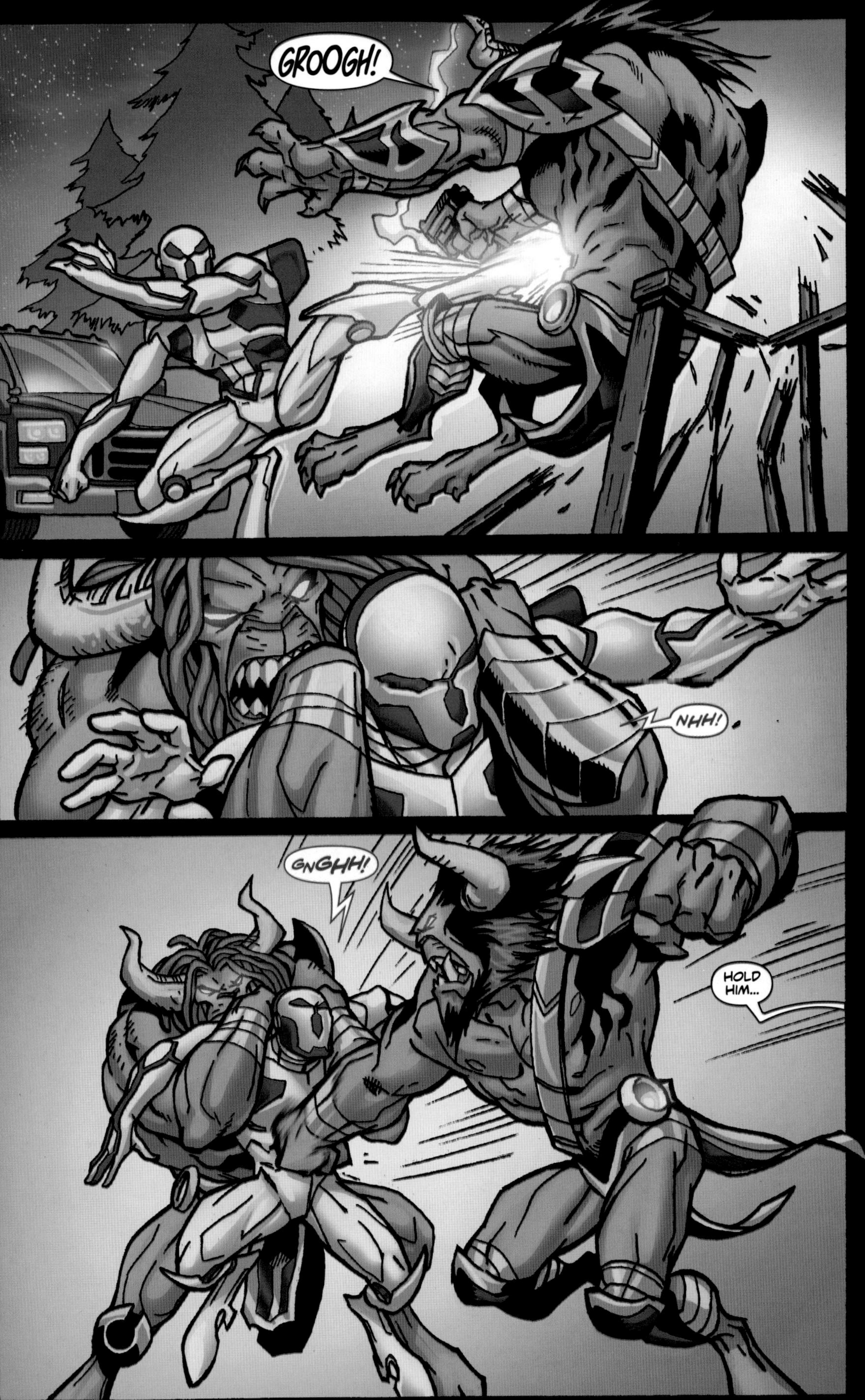
GROOGH!
NHH!
GNGHH!
HOLD HIM...

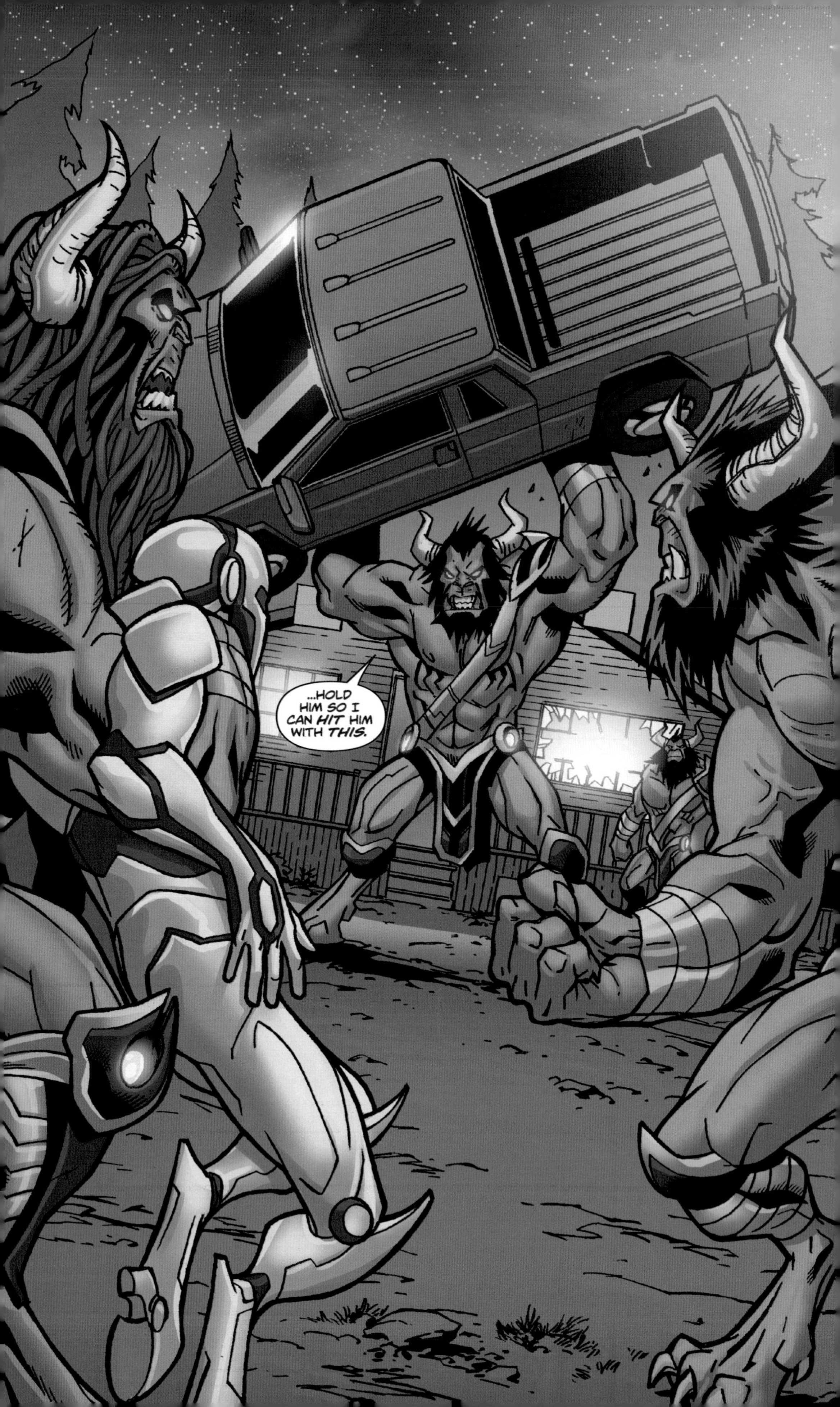
...HOLD HIM SO I CAN *HIT* HIM WITH *THIS*.

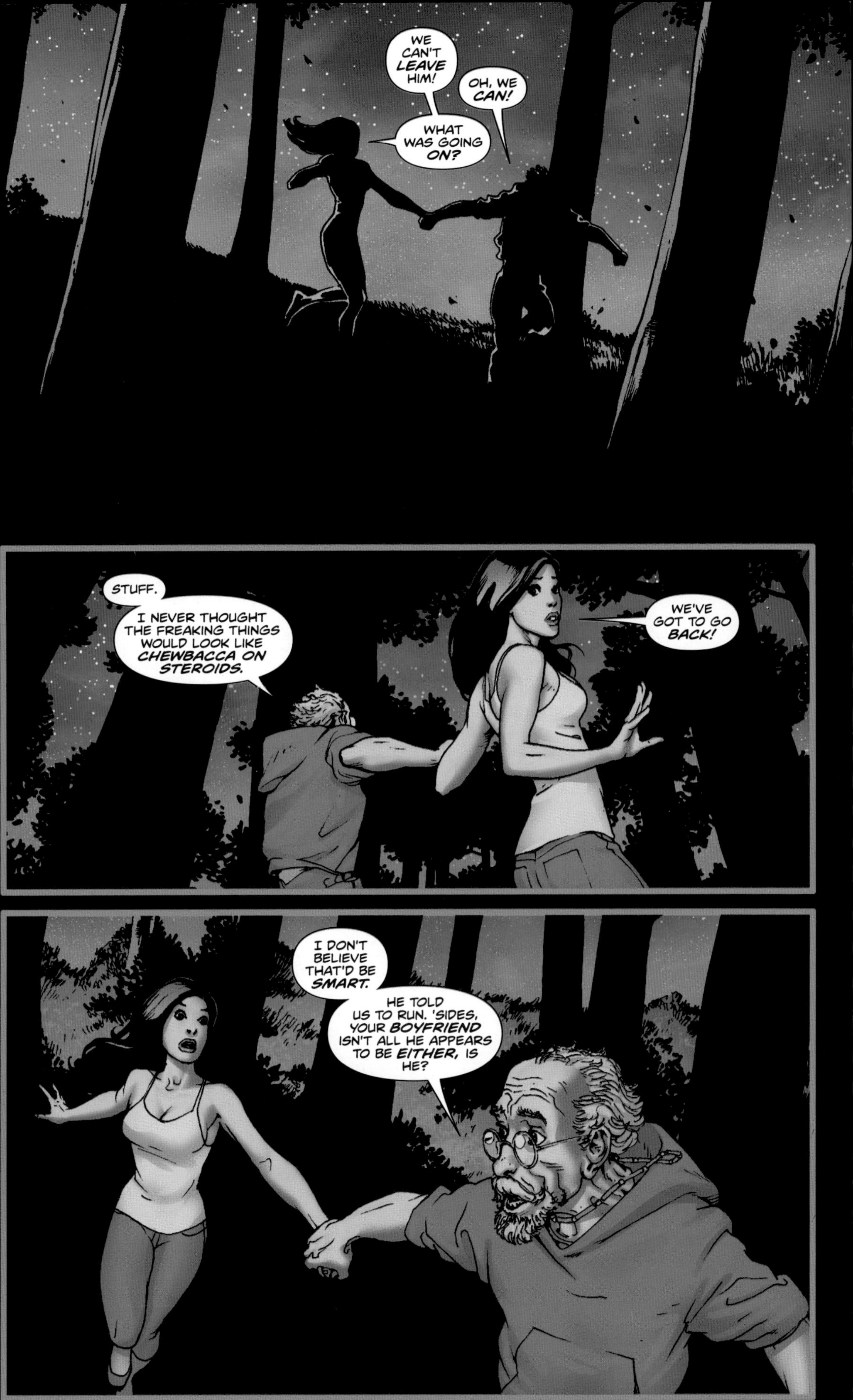
WE CAN'T LEAVE HIM!
WHAT WAS GOING ON?
OH, WE CAN!
STUFF.
I NEVER THOUGHT THE FREAKING THINGS WOULD LOOK LIKE CHEWBACCA ON STEROIDS.
WE'VE GOT TO GO BACK!
I DON'T BELIEVE THAT'D BE SMART.
HE TOLD US TO RUN. 'SIDES, YOUR BOYFRIEND ISN'T ALL HE APPEARS TO BE EITHER, IS HE?

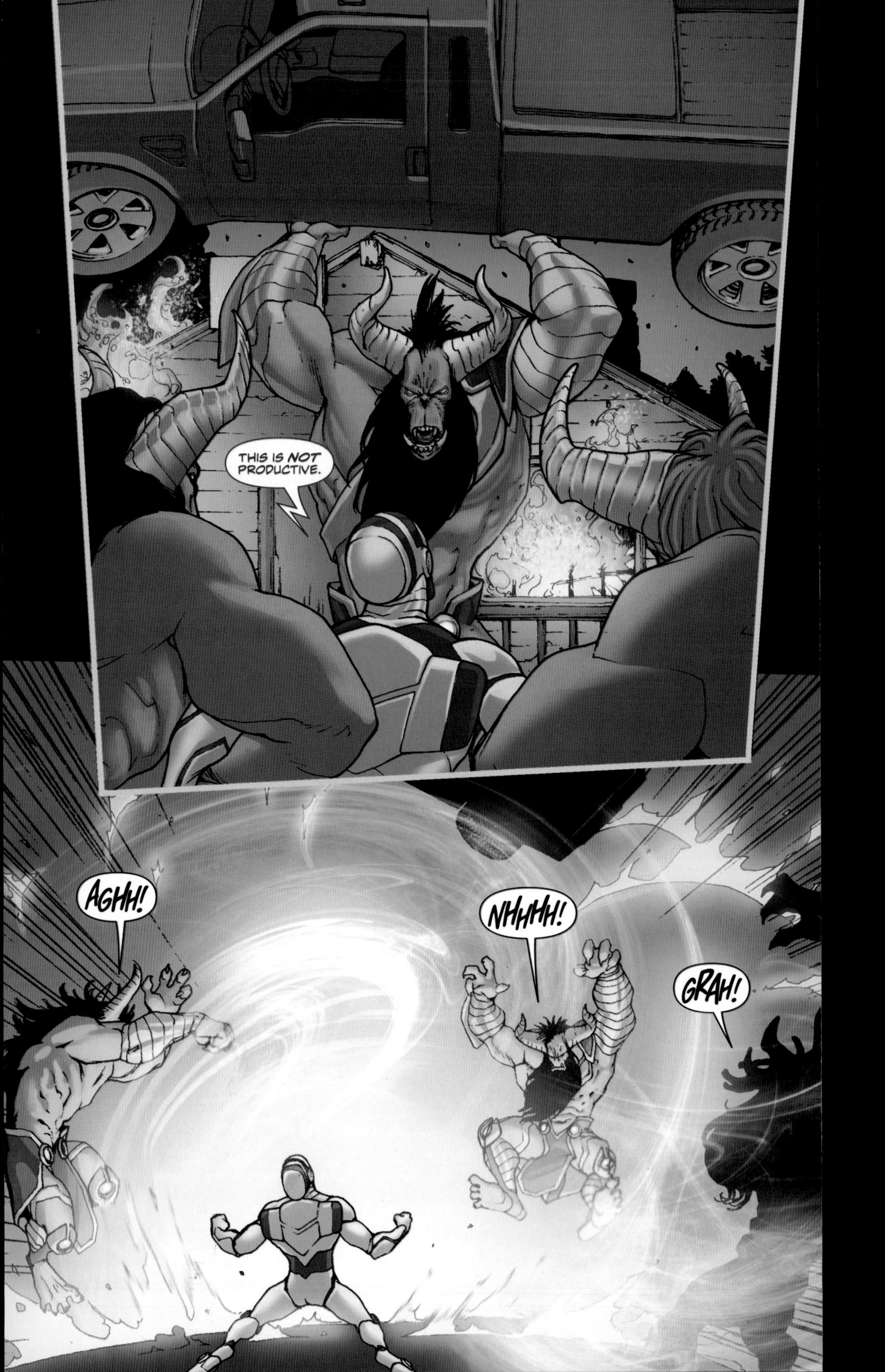
THIS IS NOT PRODUCTIVE.
AGHH!
NHHHH!
GRAH!

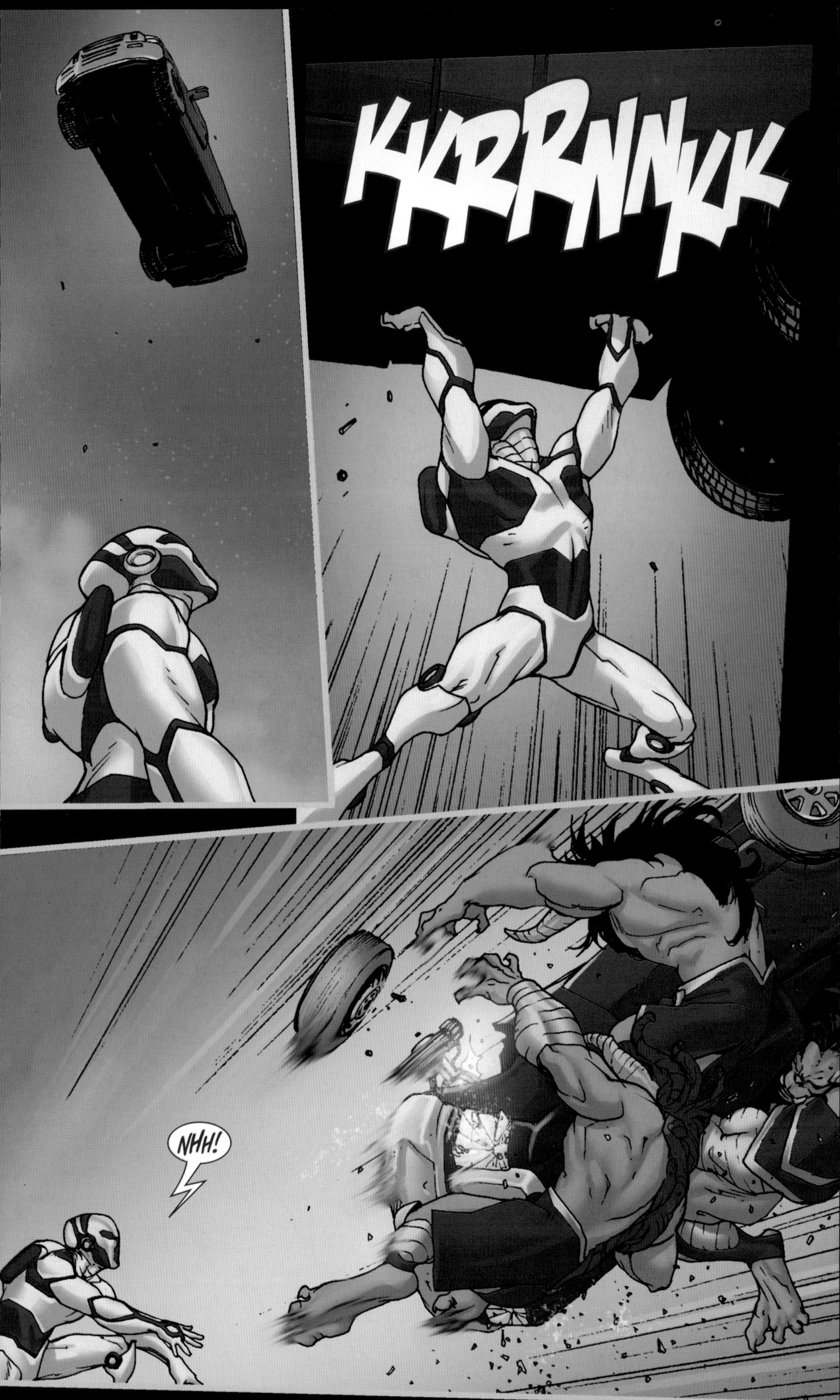
KKRRNNKK
NHH!

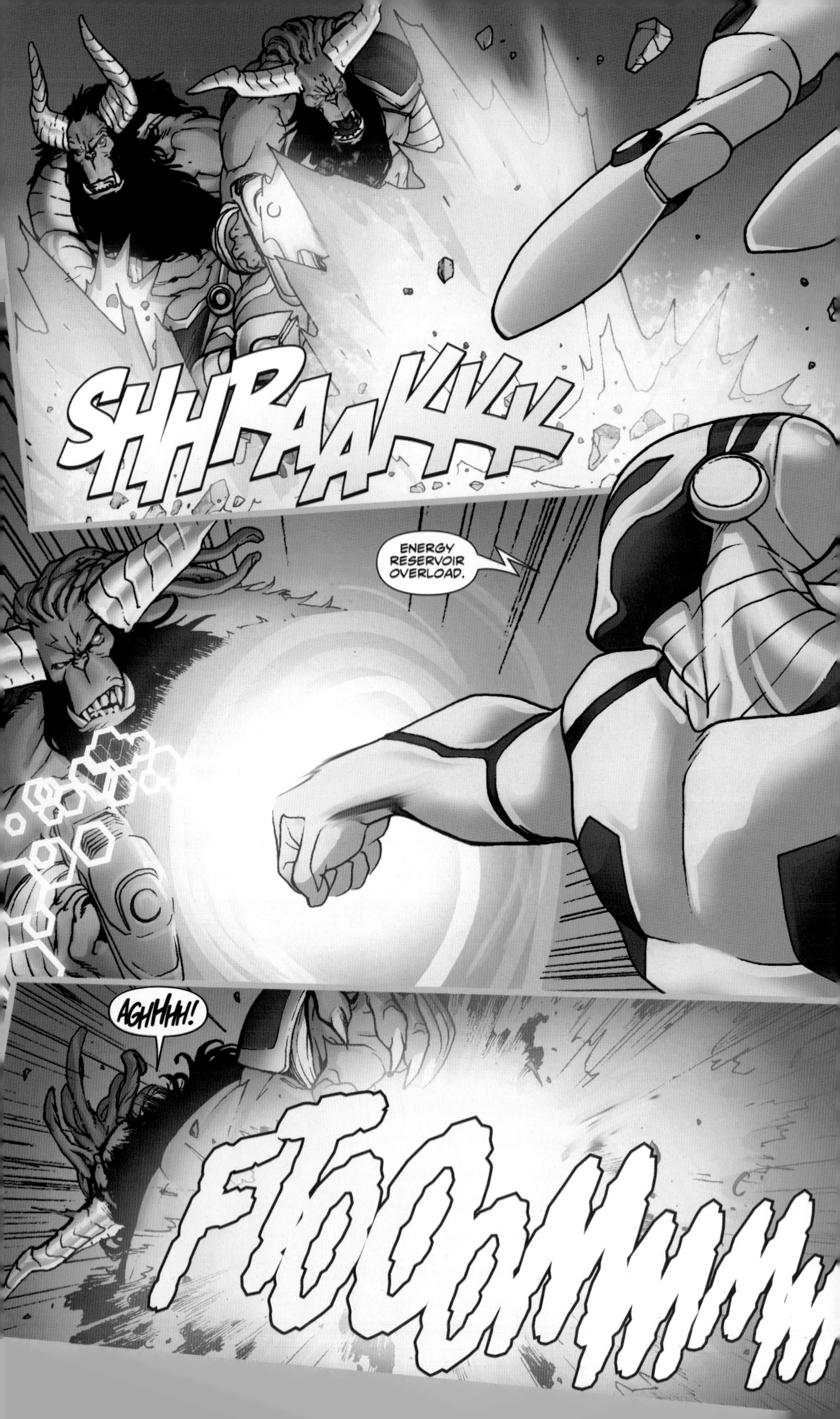
SHHRAAKKKK
ENERGY RESERVOIR OVERLOAD.
AGHHHH!
FTOOOMMMM

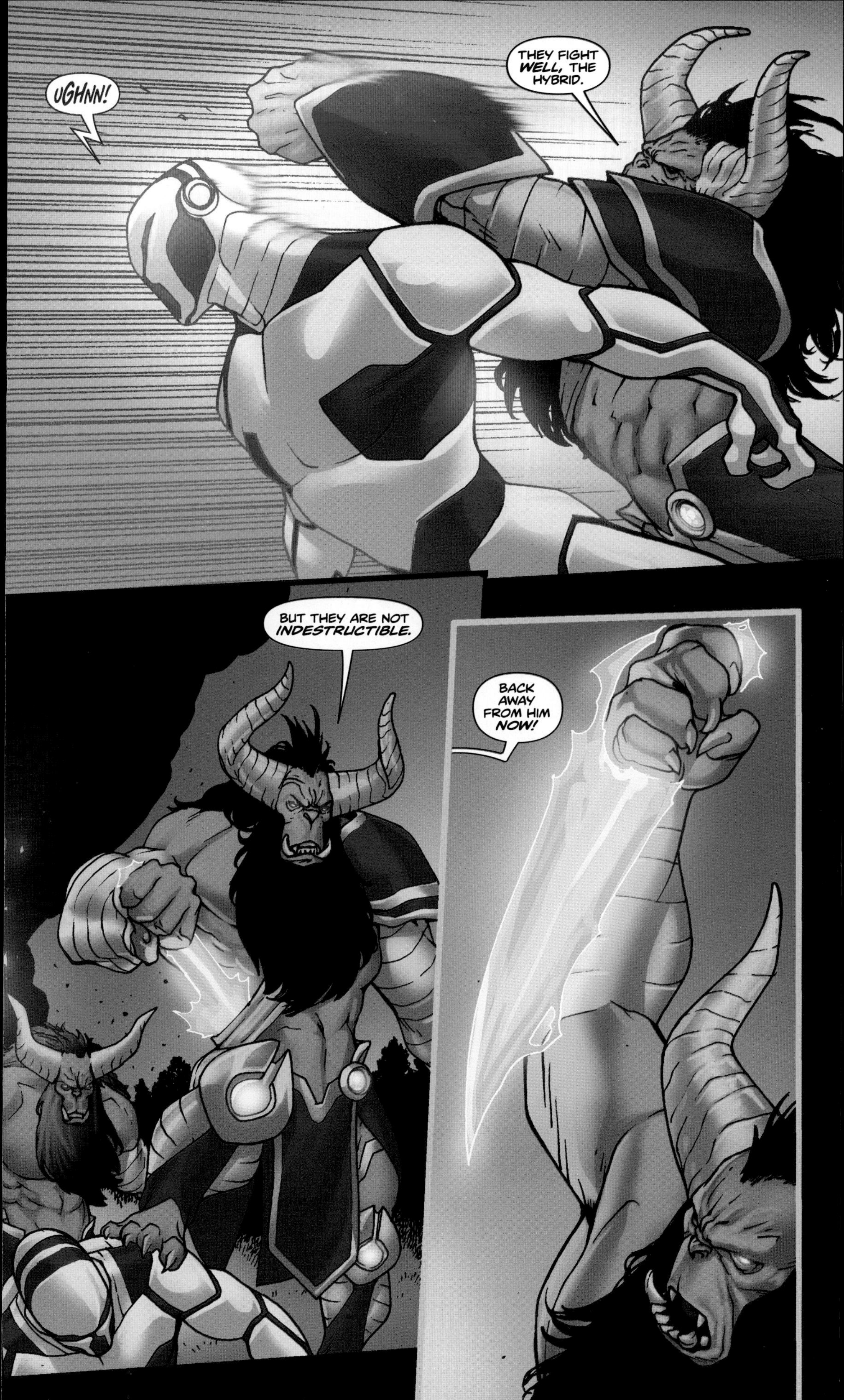
UGHNN!
THEY FIGHT WELL, THE HYBRID.
BUT THEY ARE NOT INDESTRUCTIBLE.
BACK AWAY FROM HIM NOW!

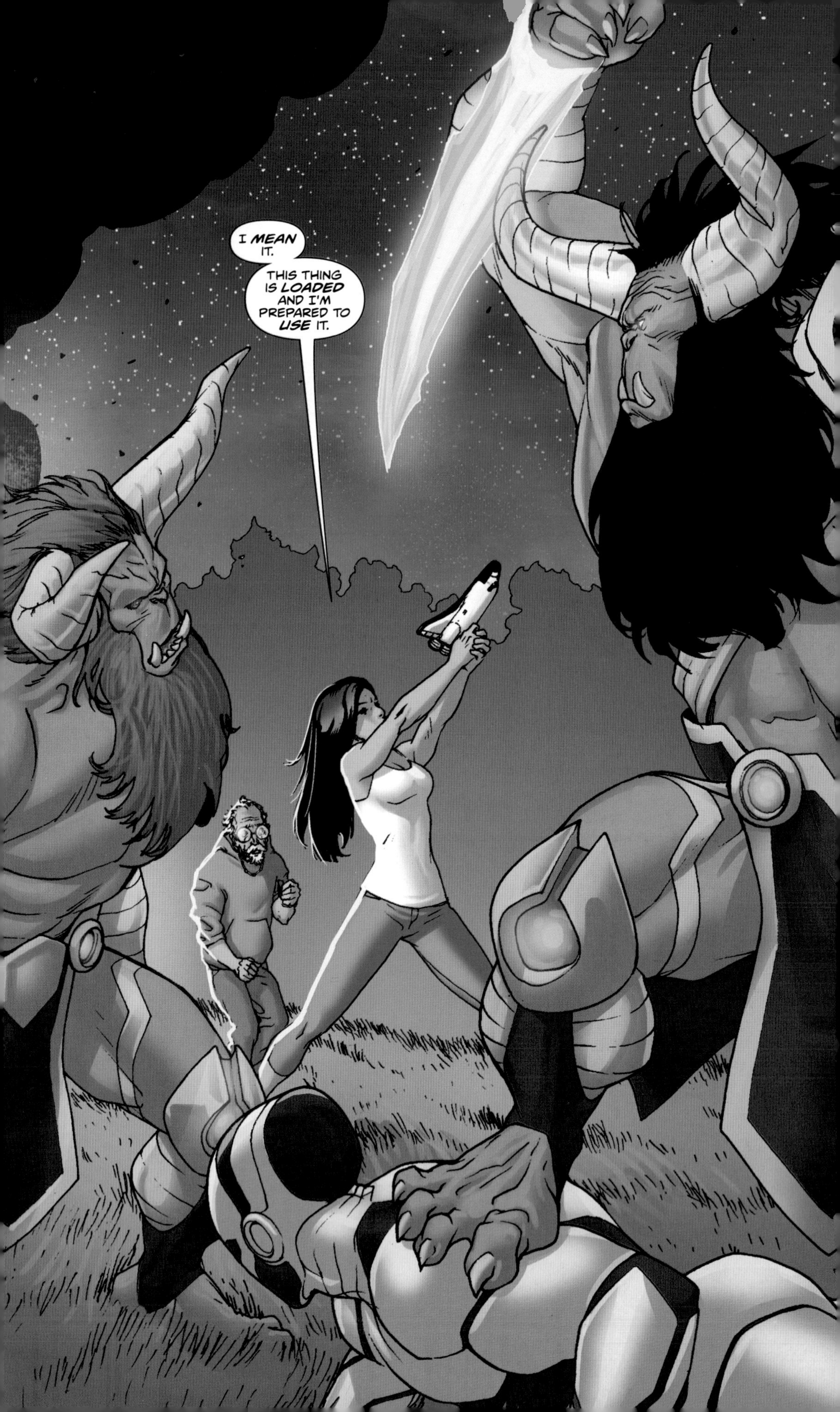
I MEAN IT.
THIS THING IS LOADED AND I'M PREPARED TO USE IT.

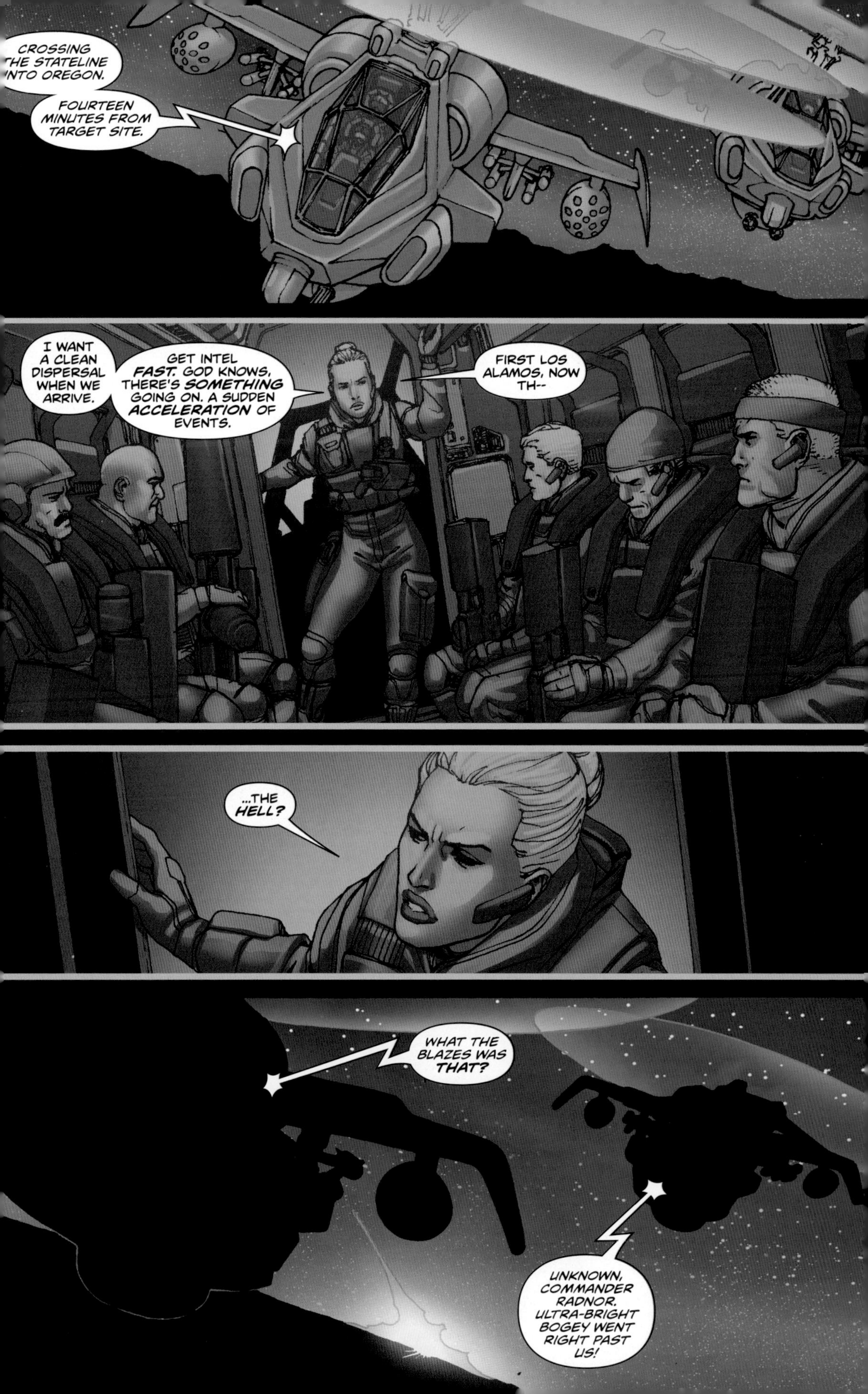
CROSSING THE STATELINE INTO OREGON.
FOURTEEN MINUTES FROM TARGET SITE.
I WANT A CLEAN DISPERSAL WHEN WE ARRIVE.
GET INTEL FAST. GOD KNOWS, THERE'S SOMETHING GOING ON. A SUDDEN ACCELERATION OF EVENTS.
FIRST LOS ALAMOS, NOW TH--
...THE HELL?
WHAT THE BLAZES WAS THAT?
UNKNOWN, COMMANDER RADNOR. ULTRA-BRIGHT BOGEY WENT RIGHT PAST US!

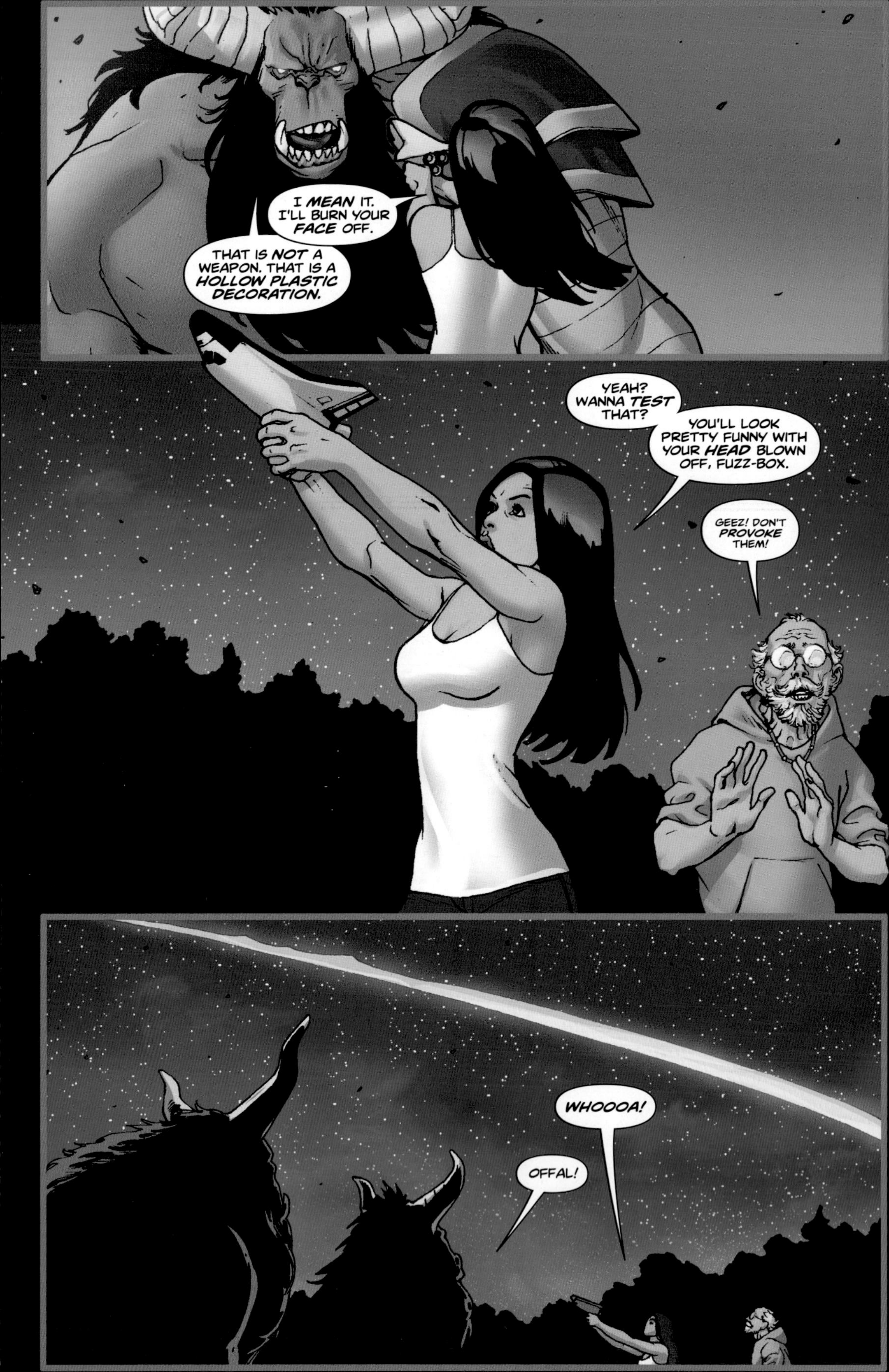
I MEAN IT. I'LL BURN YOUR FACE OFF.
THAT IS NOT A WEAPON. THAT IS A HOLLOW PLASTIC DECORATION.
YEAH? WANNA TEST THAT?
YOU'LL LOOK PRETTY FUNNY WITH YOUR HEAD BLOWN OFF, FUZZ-BOX.
GEEZ! DON'T PROVOKE THEM!
WHOOOA!
OFFAL!

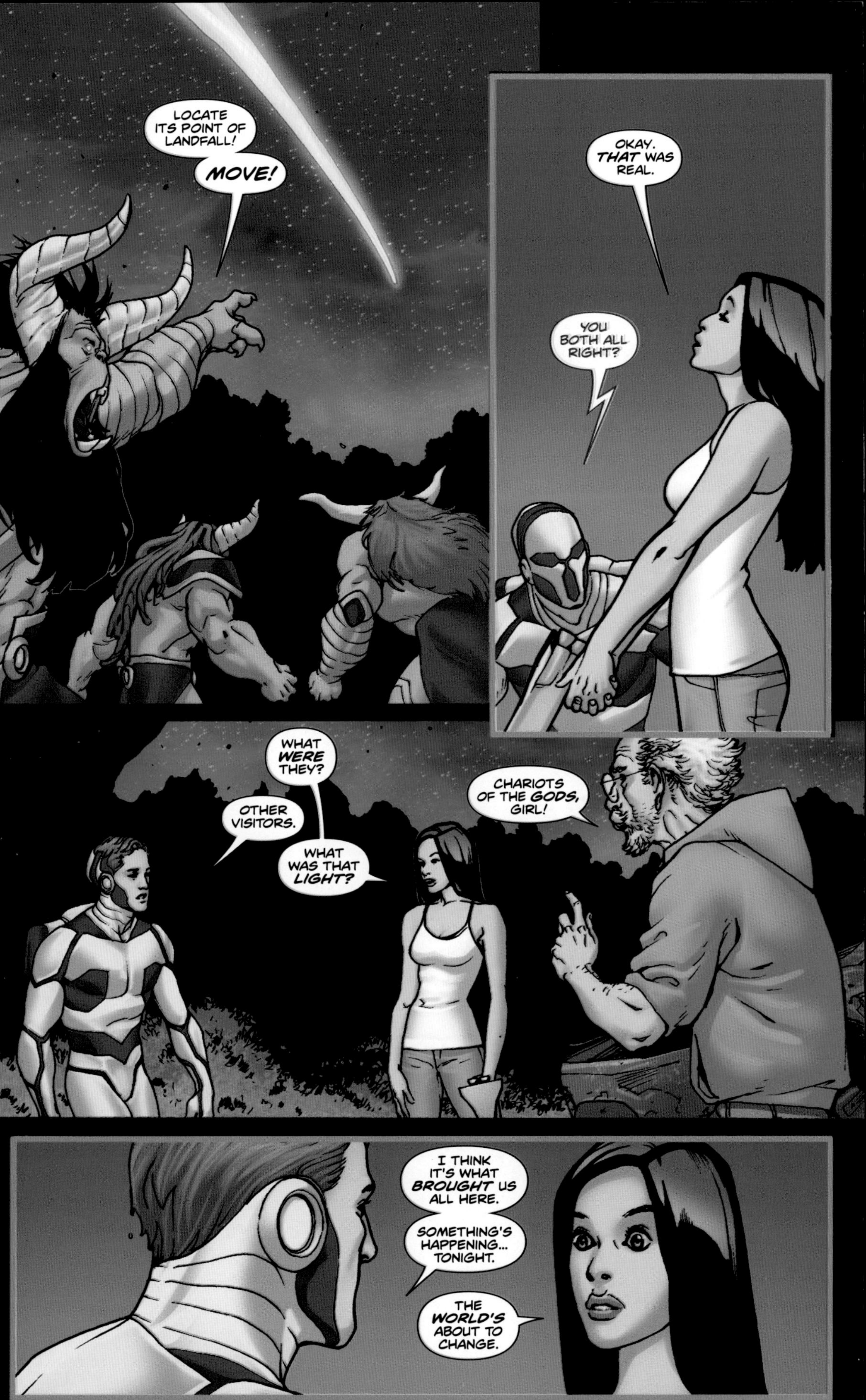
LOCATE ITS POINT OF LANDFALL!
MOVE!
OKAY. THAT WAS REAL.
YOU BOTH ALL RIGHT?
WHAT WERE THEY?
OTHER VISITORS.
CHARIOTS OF THE GODS, GIRL!
WHAT WAS THAT LIGHT?
I THINK IT'S WHAT BROUGHT US ALL HERE.
SOMETHING'S HAPPENING... TONIGHT.
THE WORLD'S ABOUT TO CHANGE.

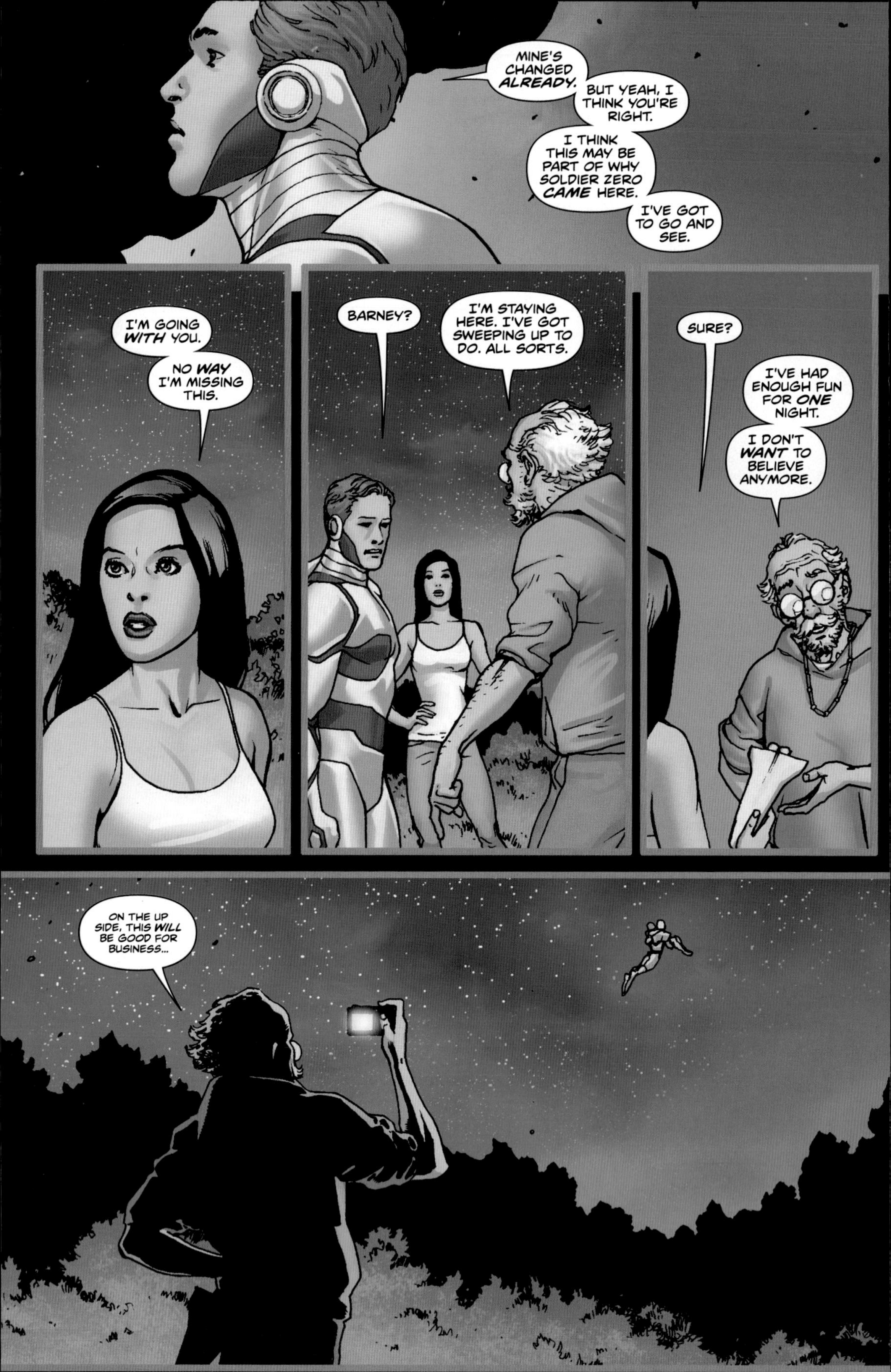
MINE'S CHANGED ALREADY.
BUT YEAH, I THINK YOU'RE RIGHT.
I THINK THIS MAY BE PART OF WHY SOLDIER ZERO CAME HERE.
I'VE GOT TO GO AND SEE.
I'M GOING WITH YOU.
NO WAY I'M MISSING THIS.
BARNEY?
I'M STAYING HERE. I'VE GOT SWEEPING UP TO DO. ALL SORTS.
SURE?
I'VE HAD ENOUGH FUN FOR ONE NIGHT.
I DON'T WANT TO BELIEVE ANYMORE.
ON THE UP SIDE, THIS WILL BE GOOD FOR BUSINESS...

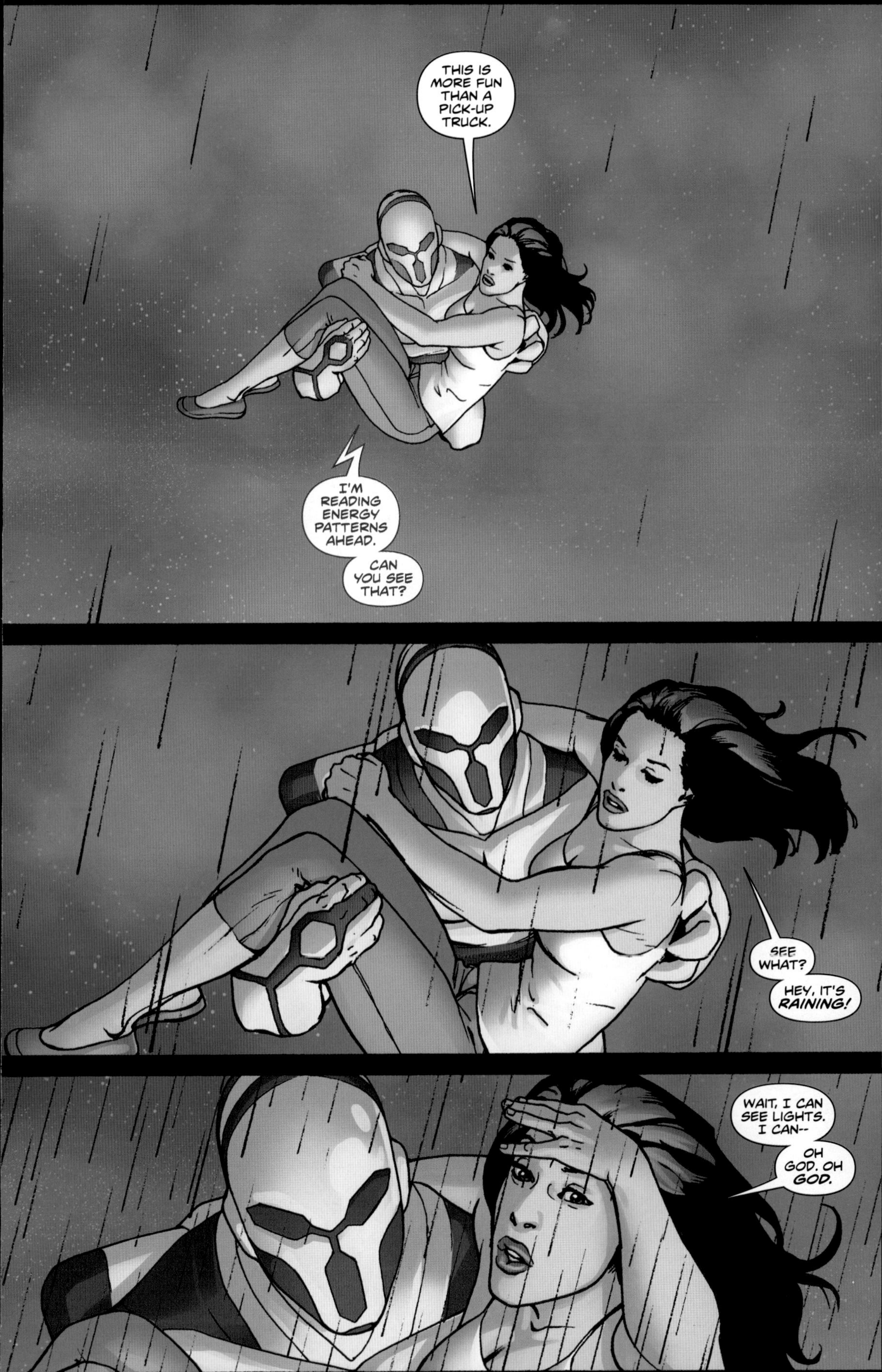
THIS IS MORE FUN THAN A PICK-UP TRUCK.
I'M READING ENERGY PATTERNS AHEAD.
CAN YOU SEE THAT?
SEE WHAT?
HEY, IT'S *RAINING!*
WAIT, I CAN SEE LIGHTS. I CAN--
OH GOD. OH *GOD.*

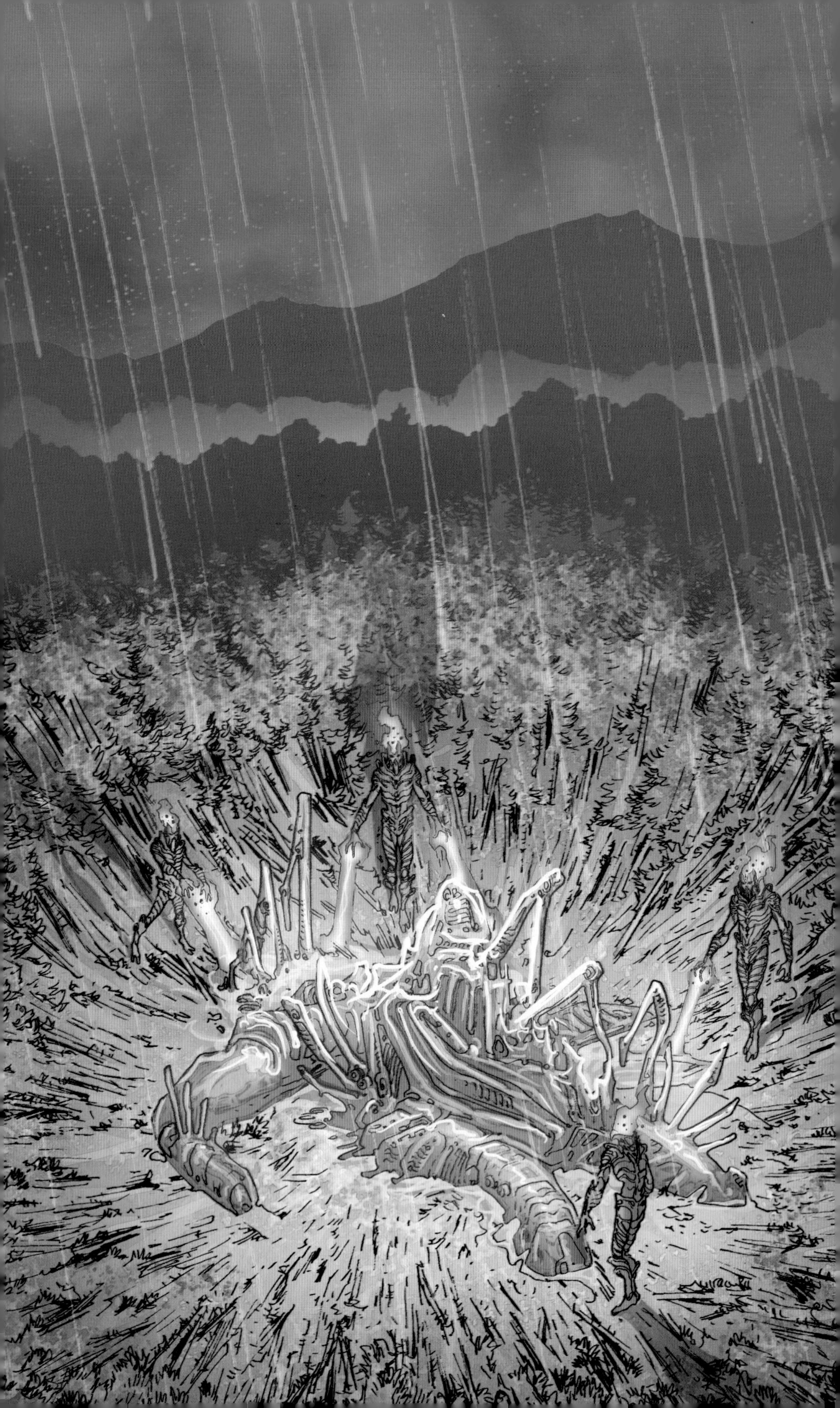

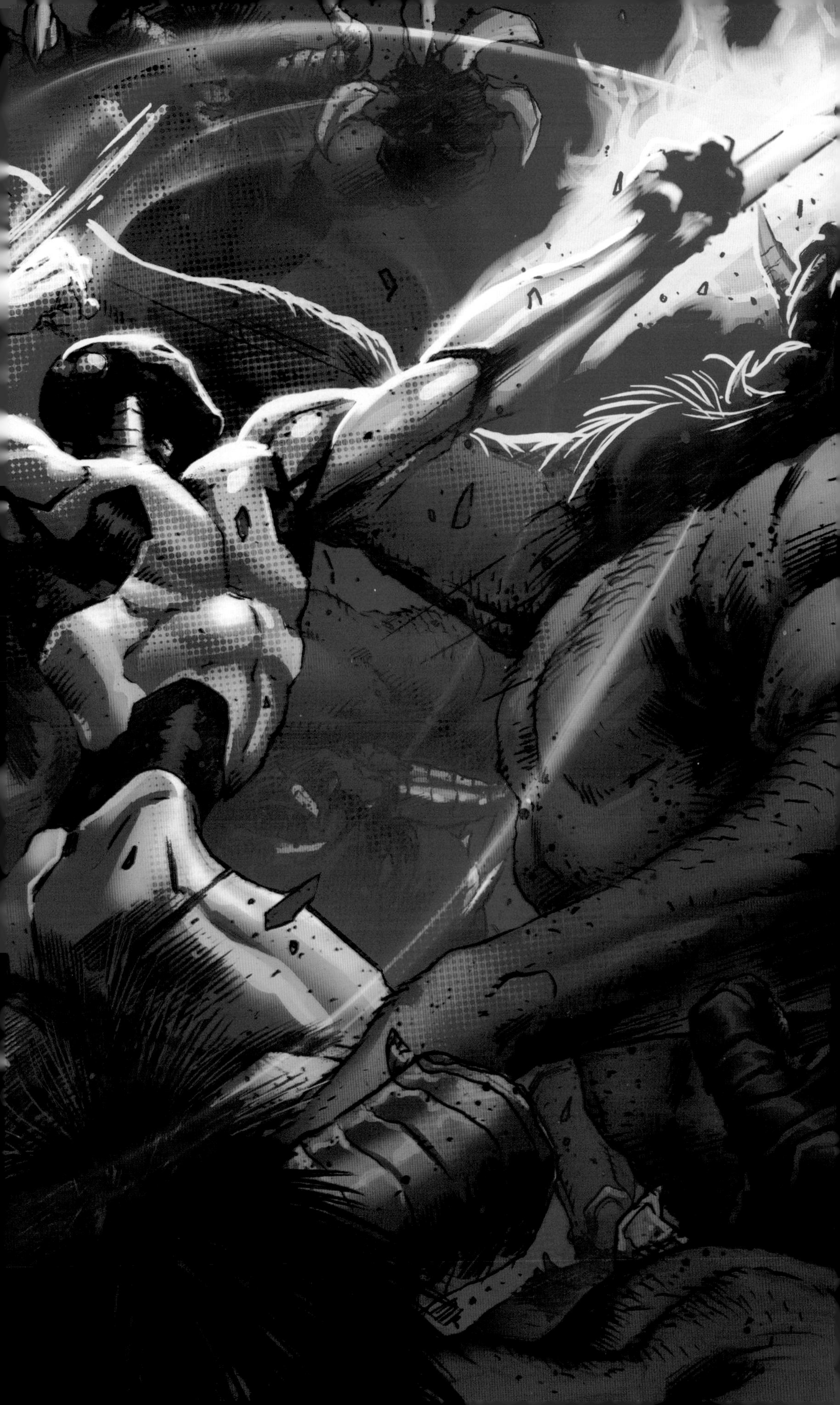

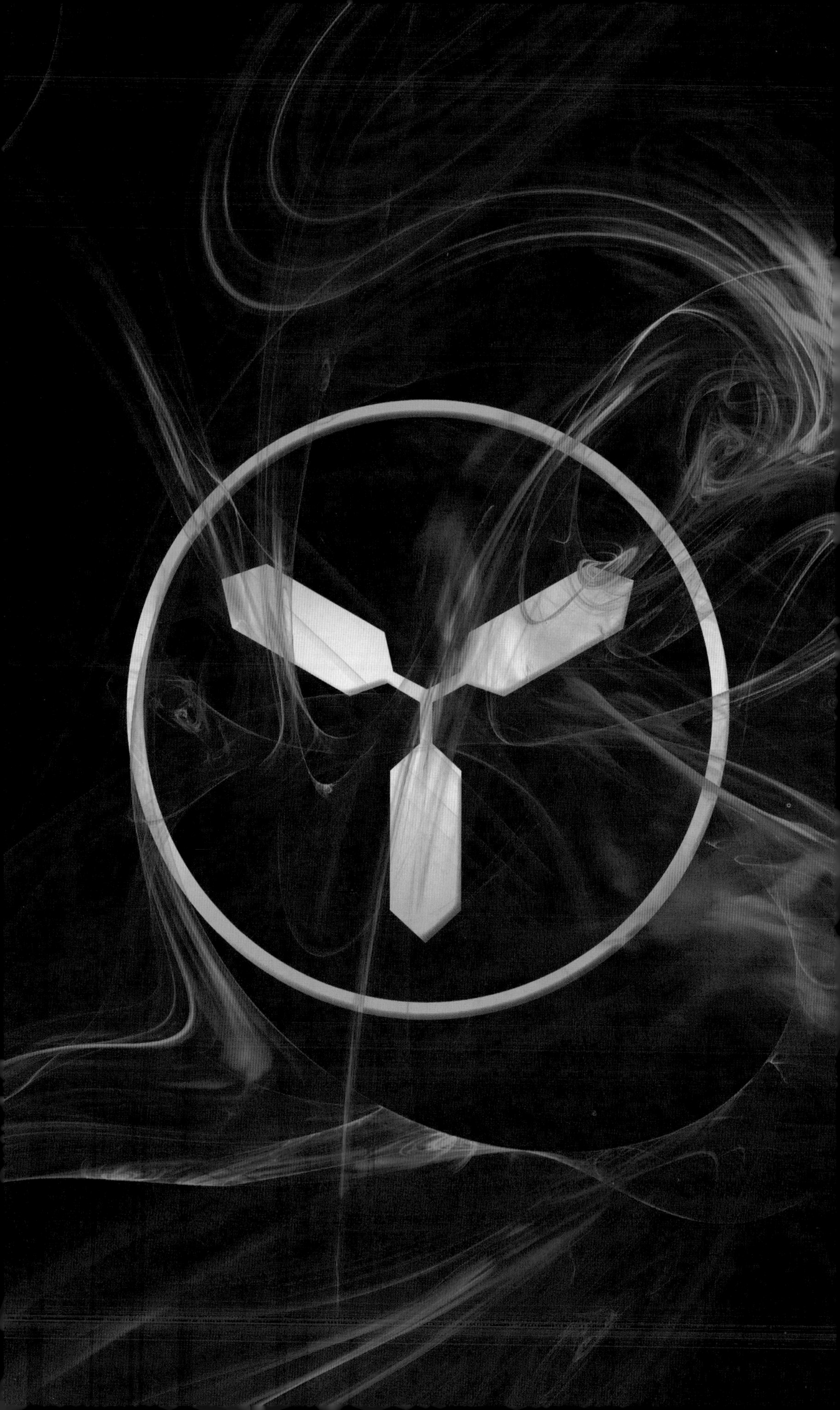

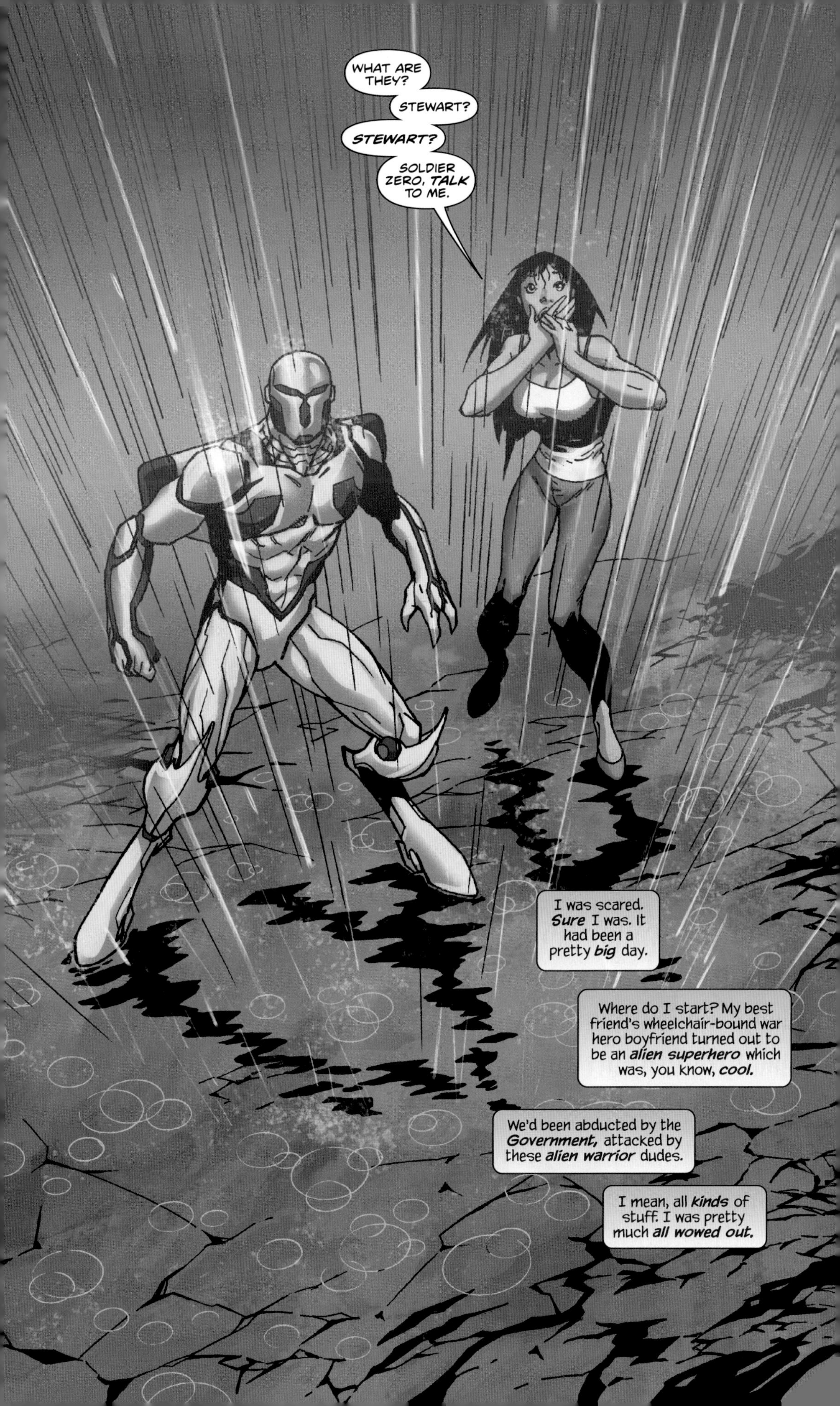
WHAT ARE THEY?
STEWART?
STEWART?
SOLDIER ZERO, TALK TO ME.
I was scared. Sure I was. It had been a pretty big day.
Where do I start? My best friend's wheelchair-bound war hero boyfriend turned out to be an alien superhero which was, you know, cool.
We'd been abducted by the Government, attacked by these alien warrior dudes.
I mean, all kinds of stuff. I was pretty much all wowed out.

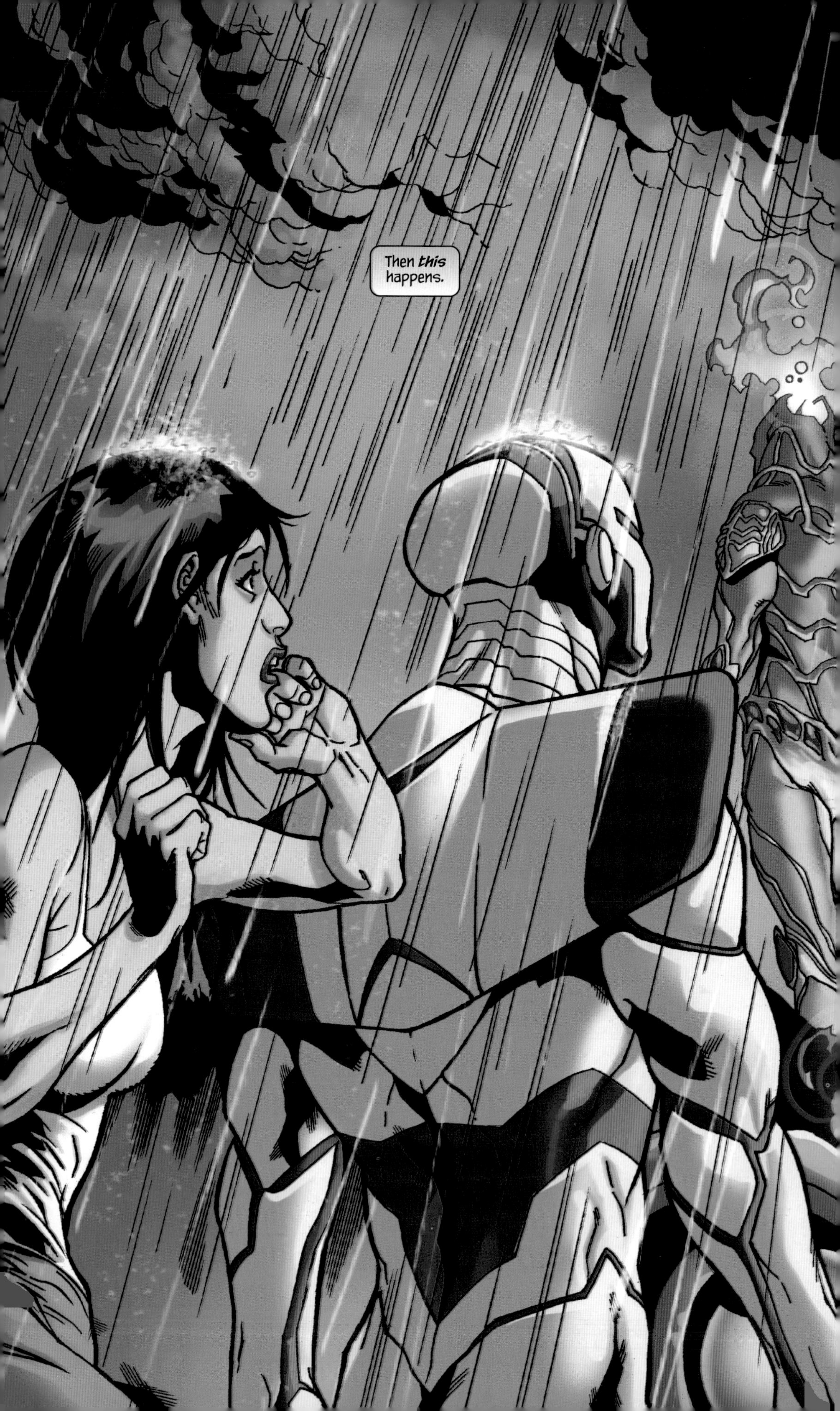
Then *this* happens.

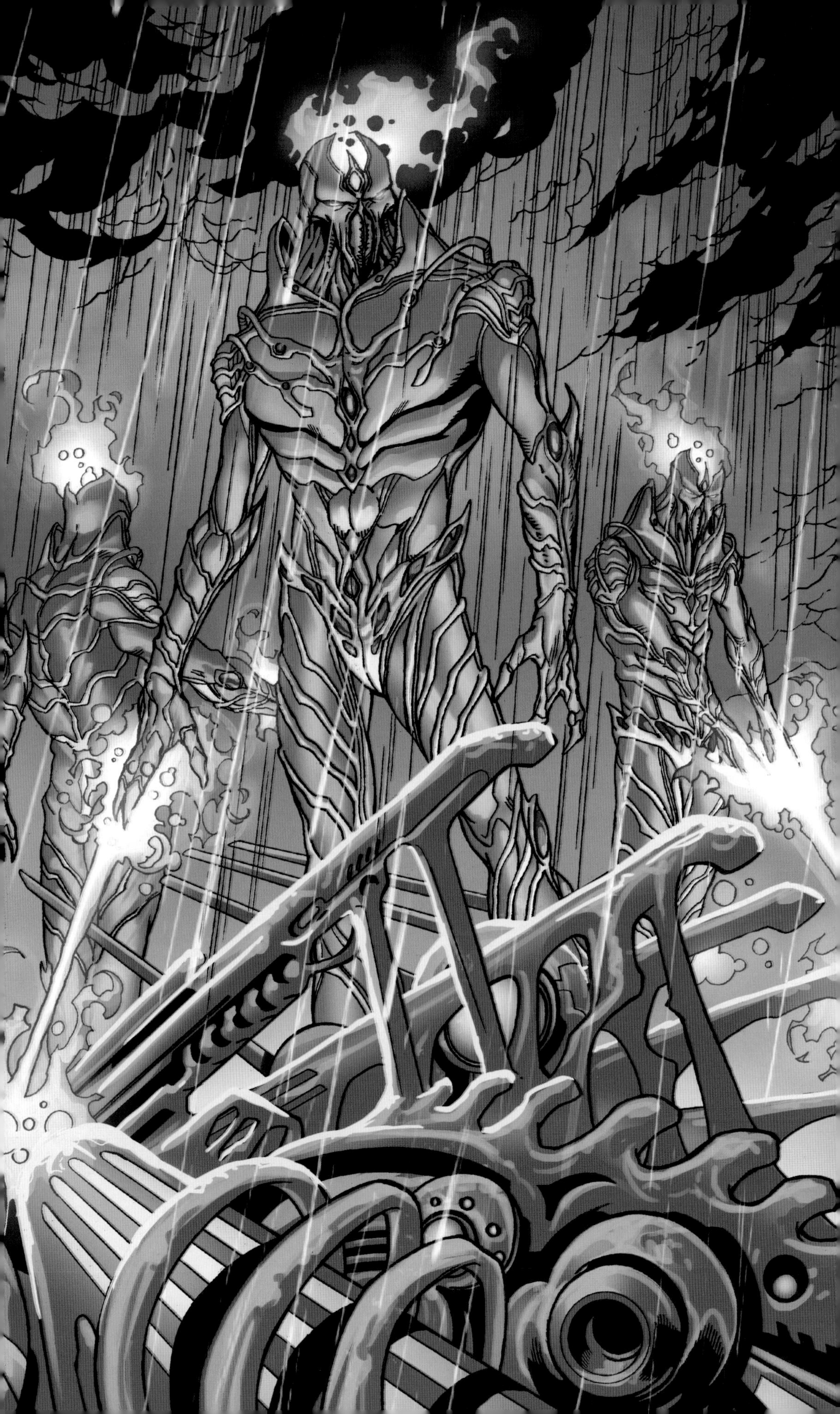

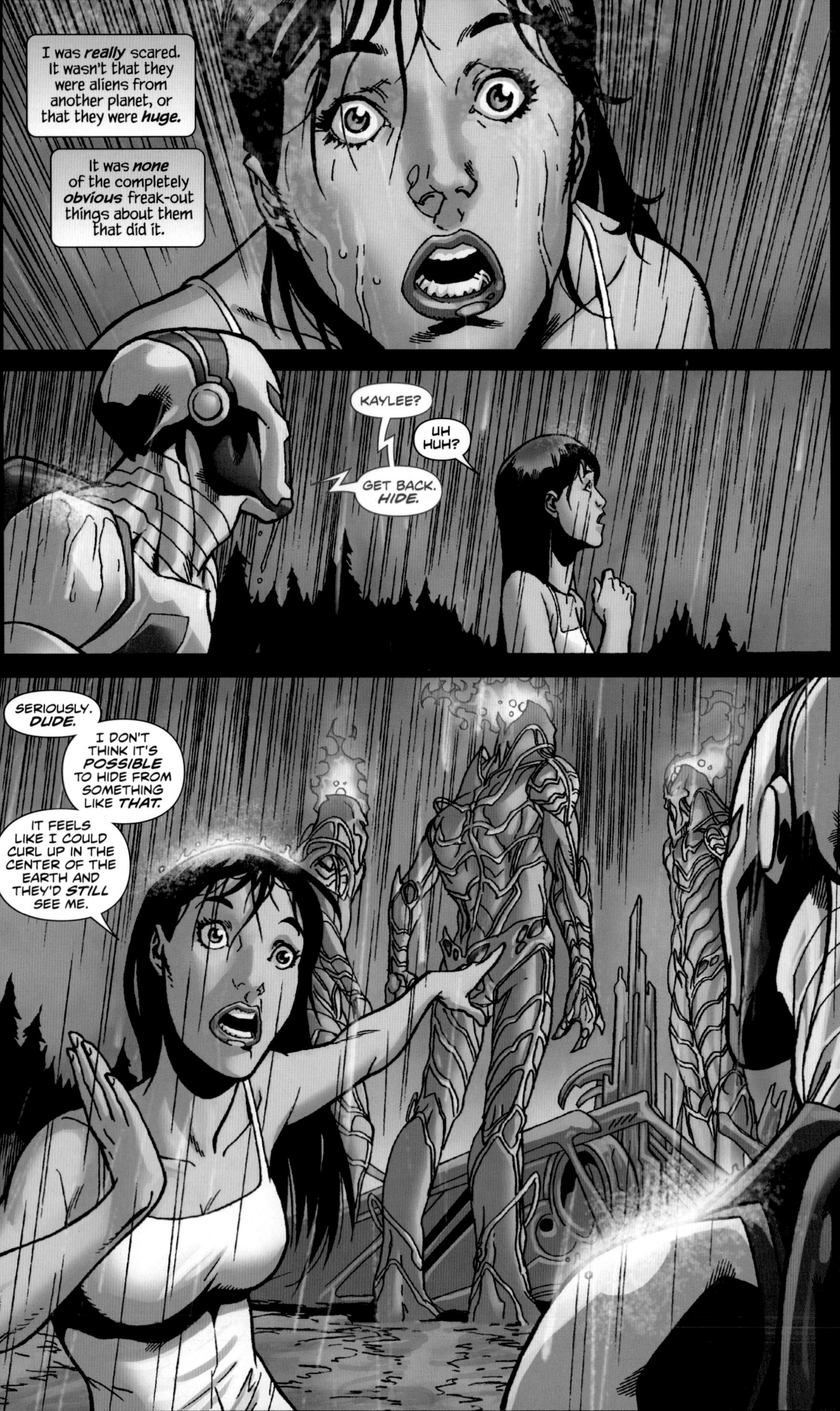
I was *really* scared. It wasn't that they were aliens from another planet, or that they were *huge.*
It was *none* of the completely *obvious* freak-out things about them that did it.
KAYLEE?
GET BACK. *HIDE.*
UH HUH?
SERIOUSLY. *DUDE.*
I DON'T THINK IT'S *POSSIBLE* TO HIDE FROM SOMETHING LIKE *THAT.*
IT FEELS LIKE I COULD CURL UP IN THE CENTER OF THE EARTH AND THEY'D *STILL* SEE ME.

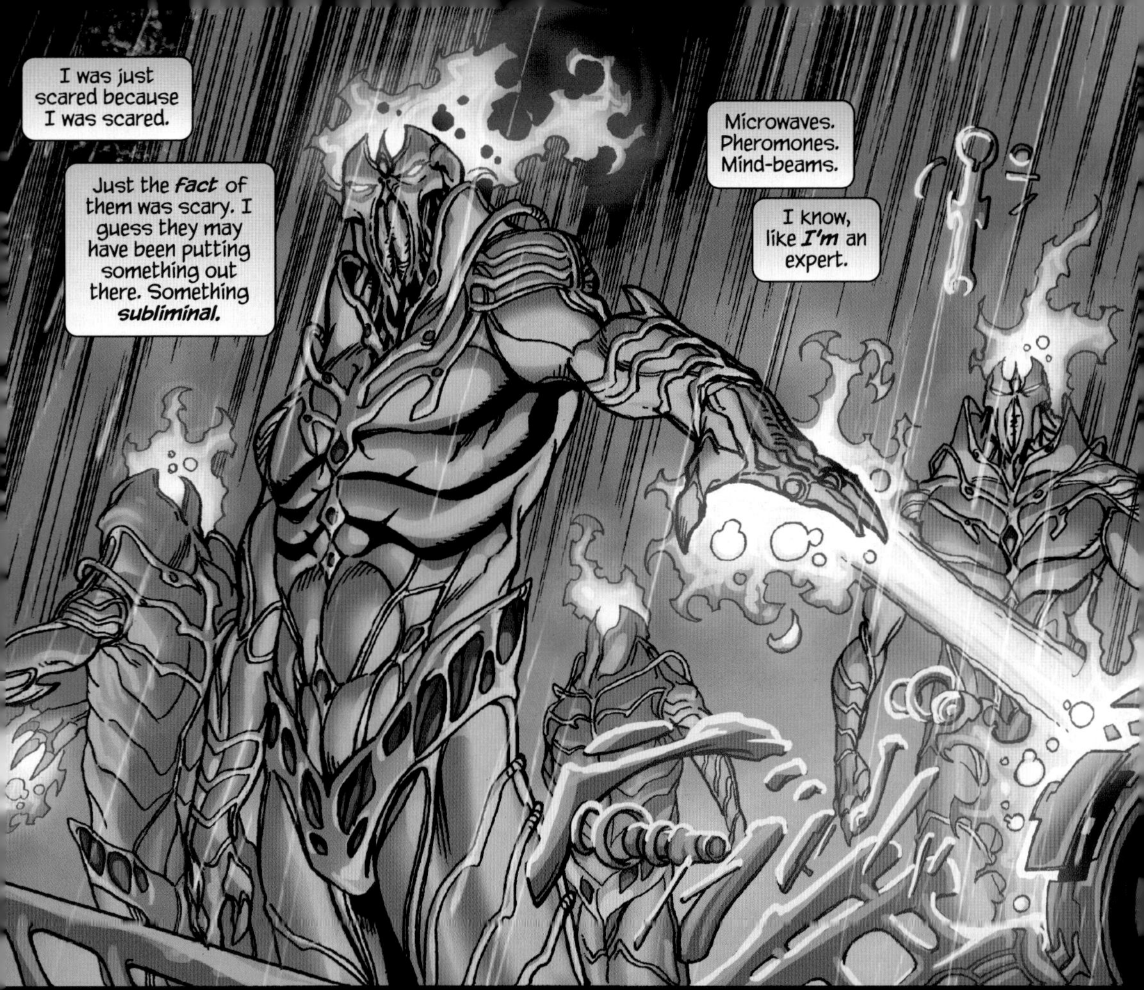
I was just scared because I was scared.
Just the *fact* of them was scary. I guess they may have been putting something out there. Something ***subliminal.***
Microwaves. Pheromones. Mind-beams.
I know, like ***I'm*** an expert.

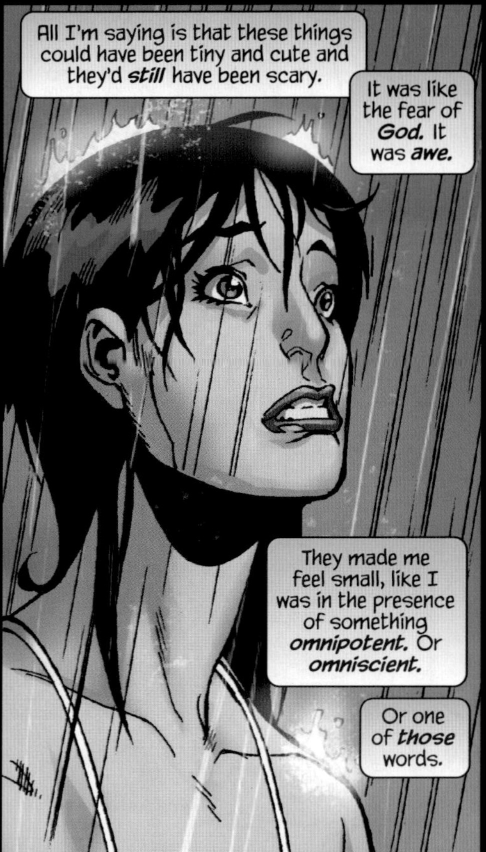
All I'm saying is that these things could have been tiny and cute and they'd ***still*** have been scary.
It was like the fear of ***God.*** It was ***awe.***
They made me feel small, like I was in the presence of something ***omnipotent.*** Or ***omniscient.***
Or one of ***those*** words.

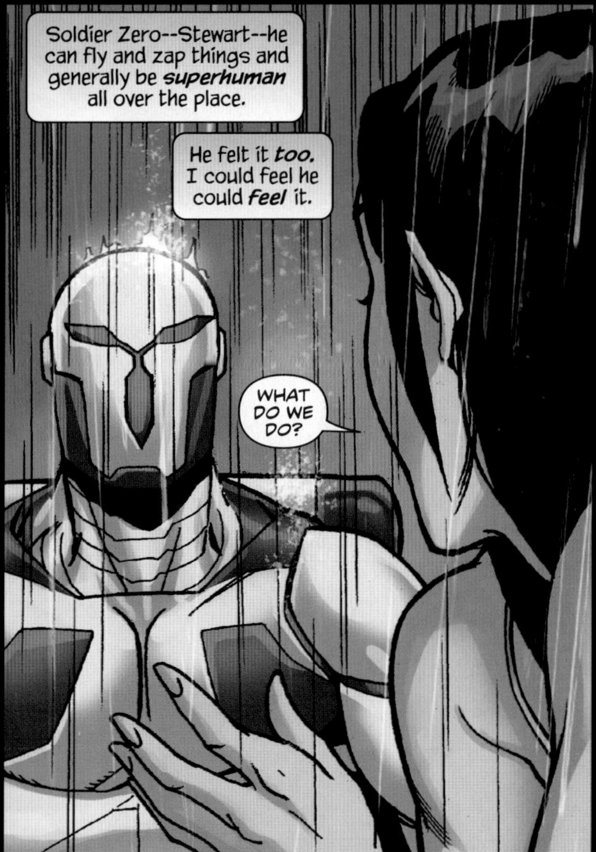
Soldier Zero--Stewart--he can fly and zap things and generally be ***superhuman*** all over the place.
He felt it ***too.*** I could feel he could ***feel*** it.
WHAT DO WE DO?

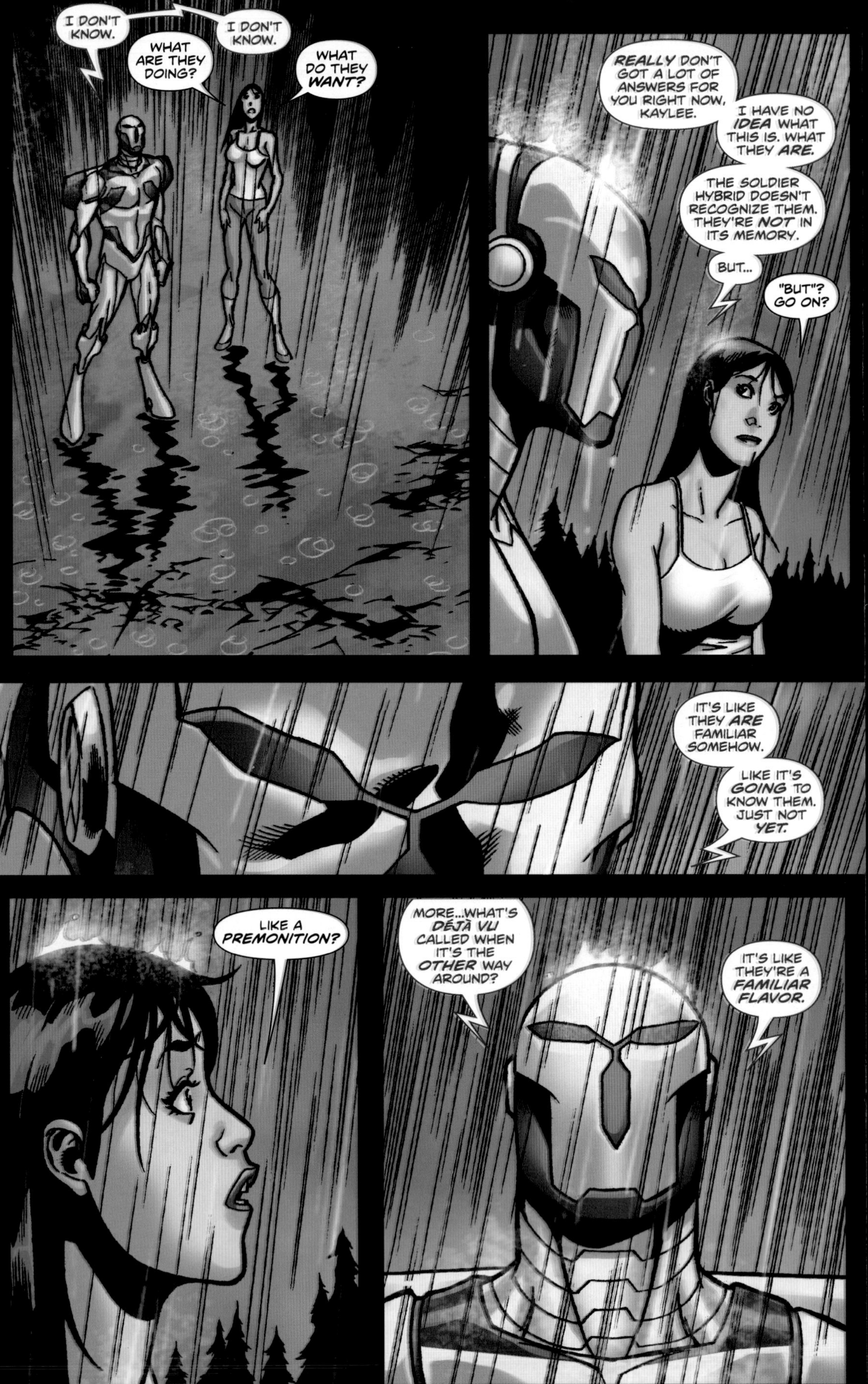
I DON'T KNOW.
WHAT ARE THEY DOING?
I DON'T KNOW.
WHAT DO THEY WANT?
REALLY DON'T GOT A LOT OF ANSWERS FOR YOU RIGHT NOW, KAYLEE.
I HAVE NO IDEA WHAT THIS IS. WHAT THEY ARE.
THE SOLDIER HYBRID DOESN'T RECOGNIZE THEM. THEY'RE NOT IN ITS MEMORY.
BUT...
"BUT"? GO ON?
IT'S LIKE THEY ARE FAMILIAR SOMEHOW.
LIKE IT'S GOING TO KNOW THEM. JUST NOT YET.
LIKE A PREMONITION?
MORE...WHAT'S DÉJÀ VU CALLED WHEN IT'S THE OTHER WAY AROUND?
IT'S LIKE THEY'RE A FAMILIAR FLAVOR.

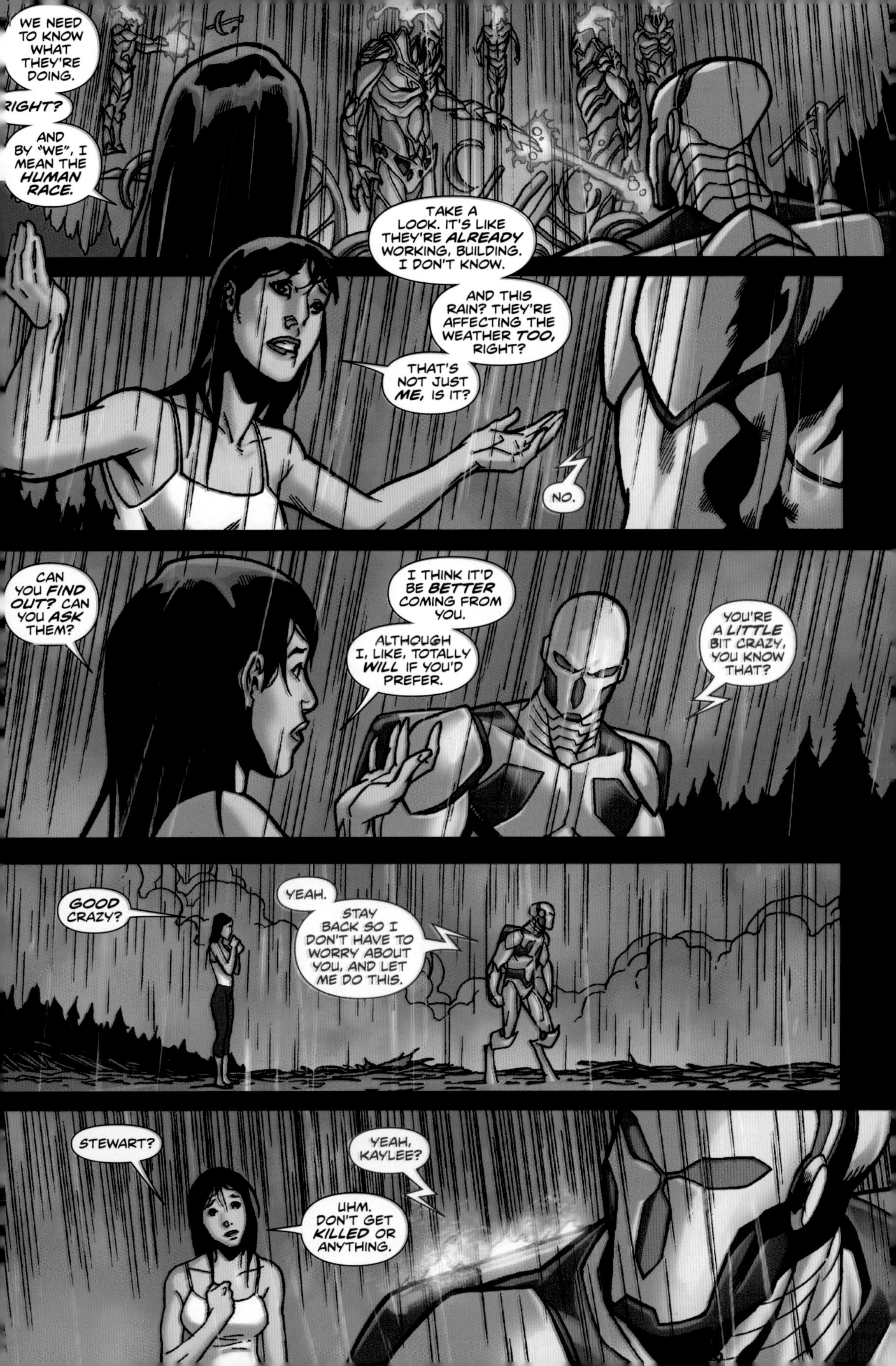
WE NEED TO KNOW WHAT THEY'RE DOING.
RIGHT?
AND BY "WE", I MEAN THE HUMAN RACE.
TAKE A LOOK. IT'S LIKE THEY'RE ALREADY WORKING, BUILDING. I DON'T KNOW.
AND THIS RAIN? THEY'RE AFFECTING THE WEATHER TOO, RIGHT?
THAT'S NOT JUST ME, IS IT?
NO.
CAN YOU FIND OUT? CAN YOU ASK THEM?
I THINK IT'D BE BETTER COMING FROM YOU.
ALTHOUGH I, LIKE, TOTALLY WILL IF YOU'D PREFER.
YOU'RE A LITTLE BIT CRAZY, YOU KNOW THAT?
GOOD CRAZY?
YEAH.
STAY BACK SO I DON'T HAVE TO WORRY ABOUT YOU, AND LET ME DO THIS.
STEWART?
YEAH, KAYLEE?
UHM. DON'T GET KILLED OR ANYTHING.

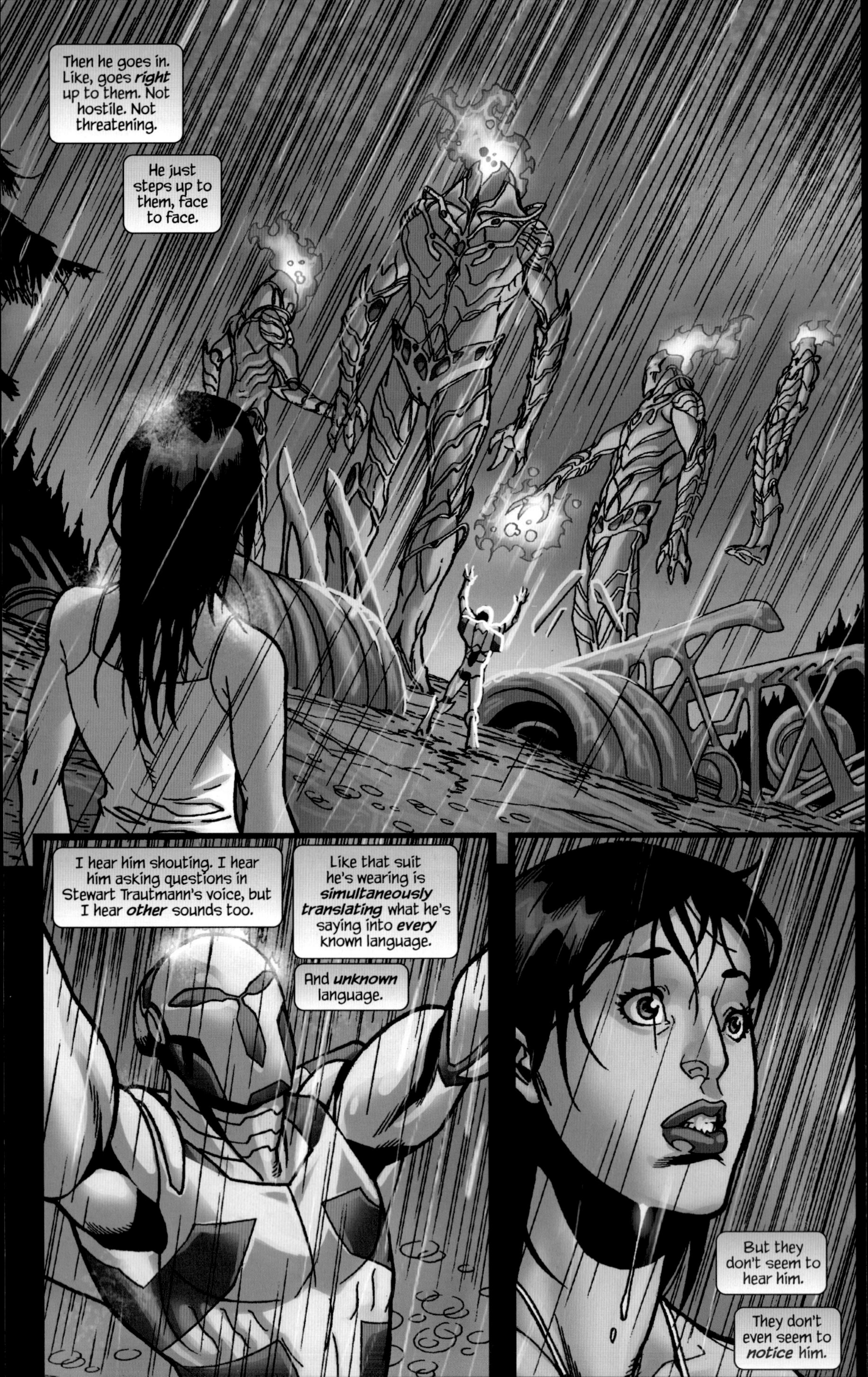
Then he goes in. Like, goes *right* up to them. Not hostile. Not threatening.
He just steps up to them, face to face.
I hear him shouting. I hear him asking questions in Stewart Trautmann's voice, but I hear *other* sounds too.
Like that suit he's wearing is *simultaneously translating* what he's saying into *every* known language.
And *unknown* language.
But they don't seem to hear him.
They don't even seem to *notice* him.

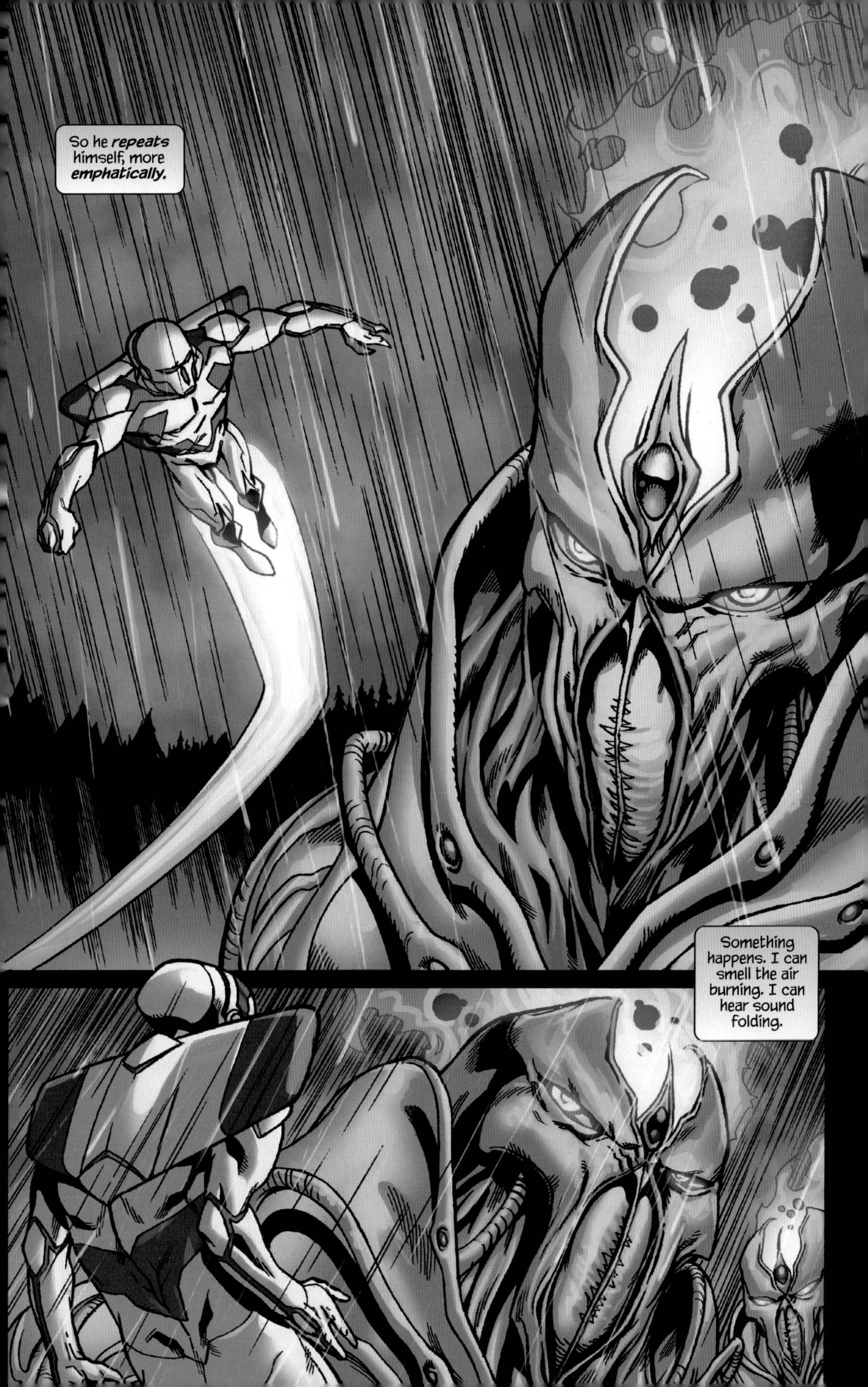
So he *repeats* himself, more ***emphatically.***
Something happens. I can smell the air burning. I can hear sound folding.

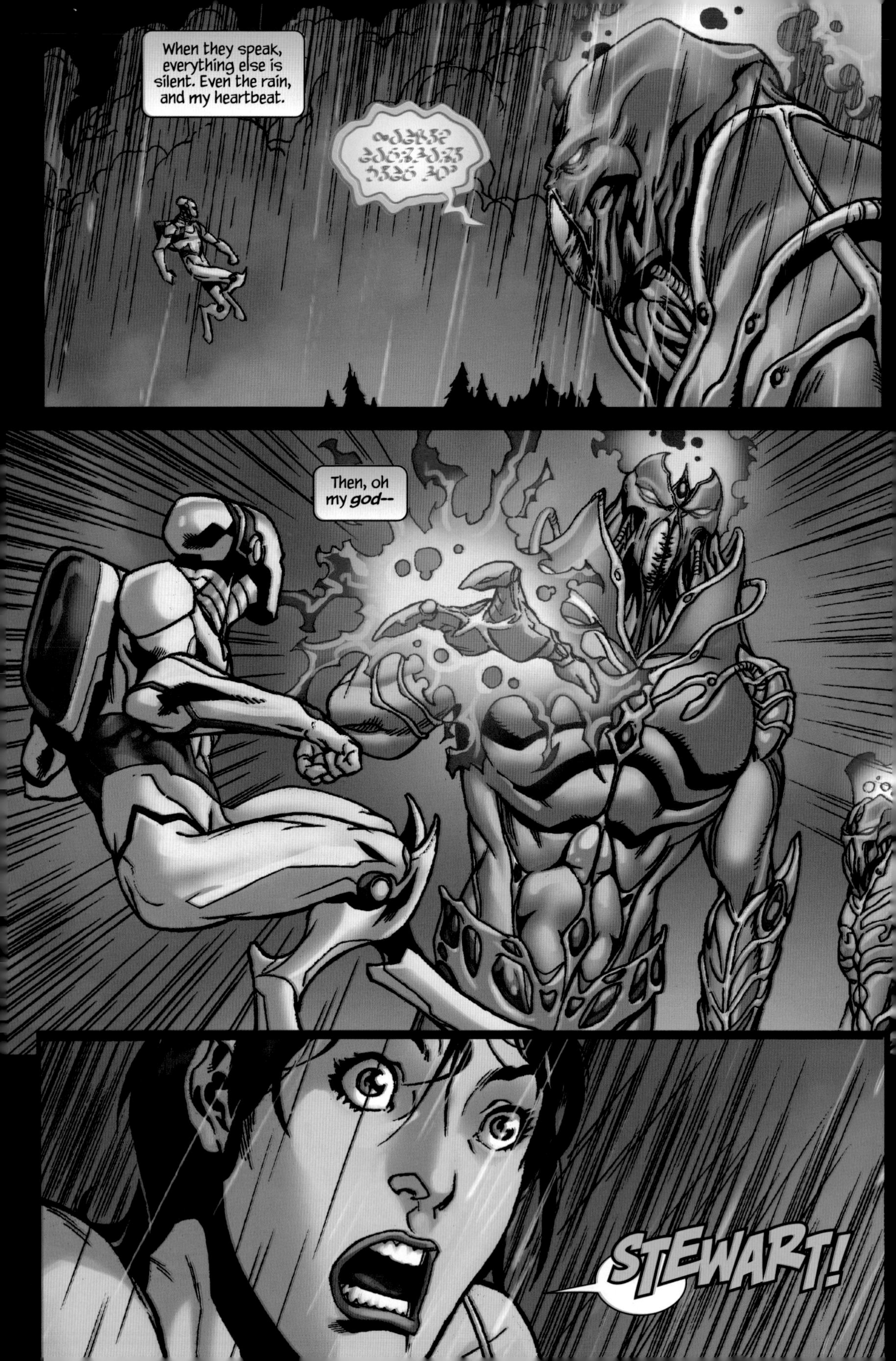
When they speak, everything else is silent. Even the rain, and my heartbeat.
Then, oh my *god*--
STEWART!

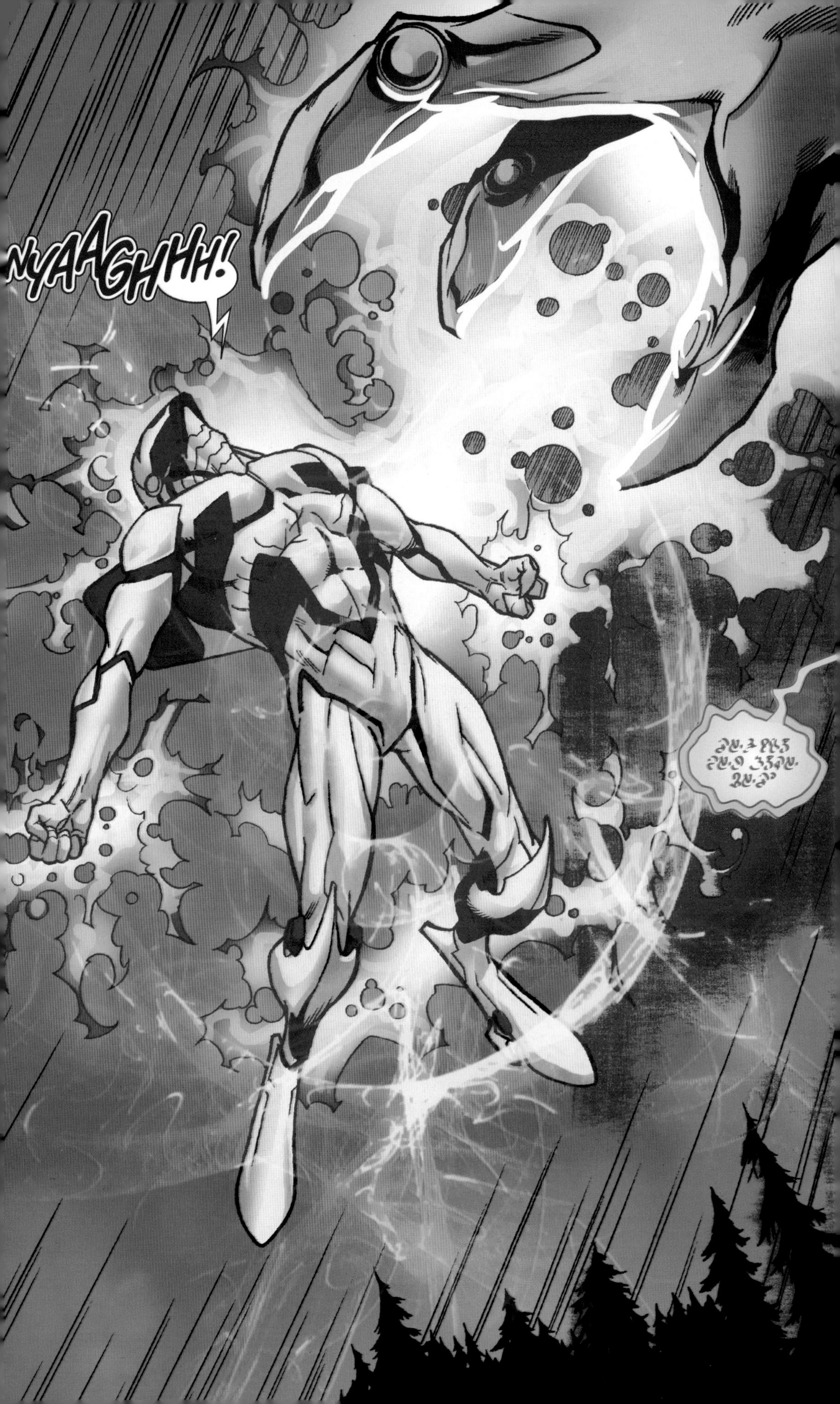
NYAAGHHH!

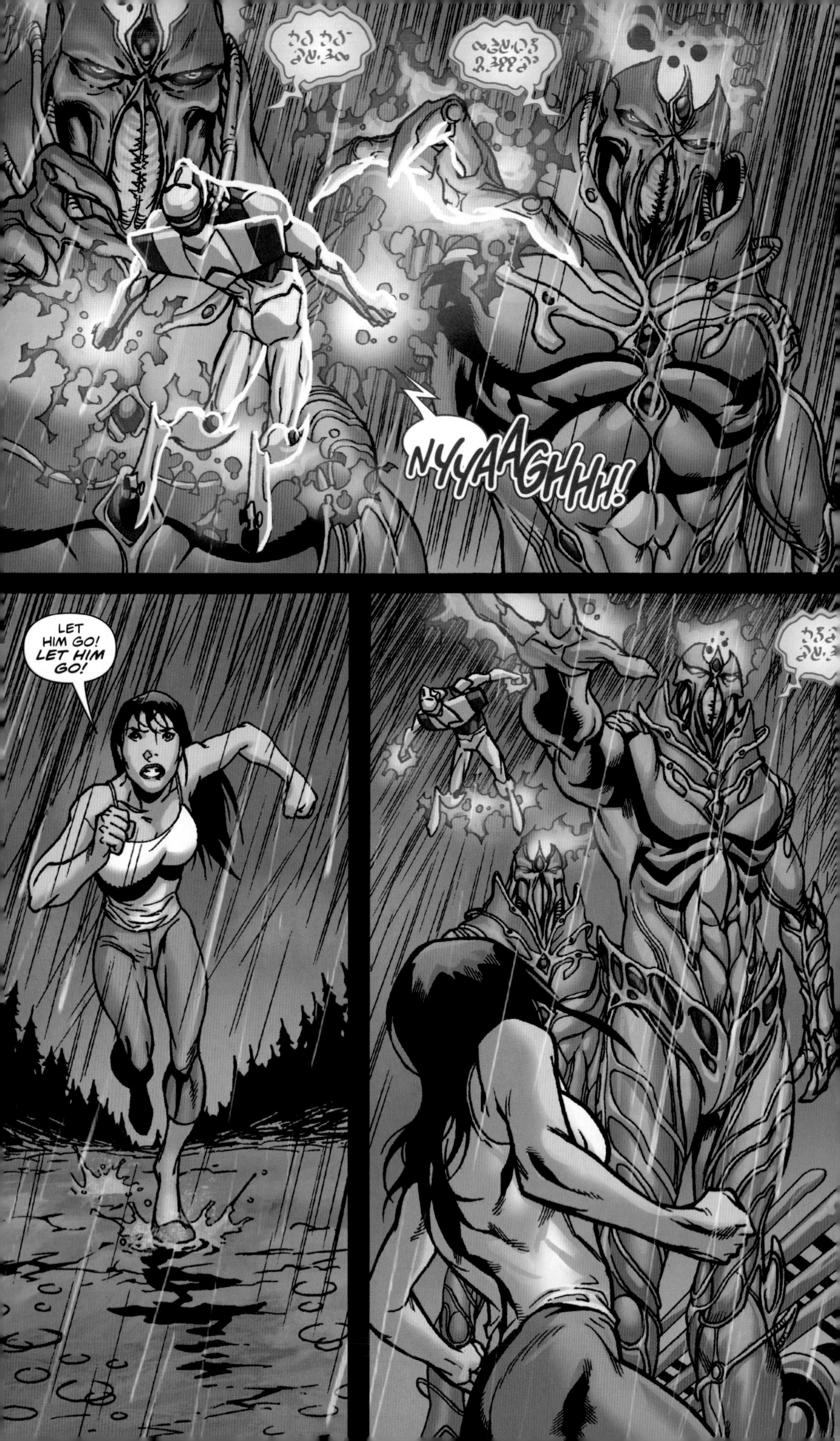
NYYAAGHHH!
LET HIM GO! LET HIM GO!

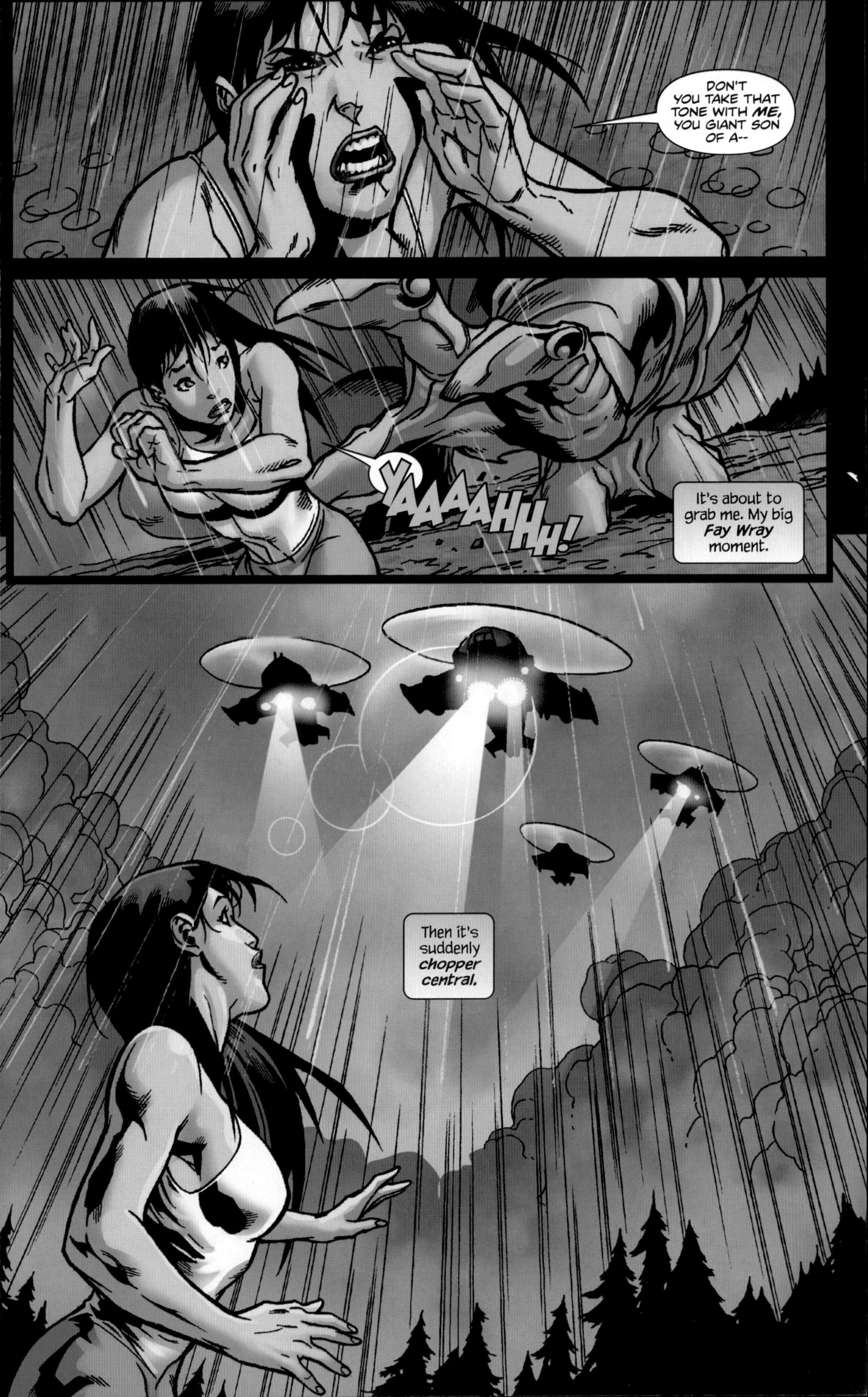
DON'T YOU TAKE THAT TONE WITH ME, YOU GIANT SON OF A--
YAAAAAHHHH!
It's about to grab me. My big Fay Wray moment.
Then it's suddenly chopper central.

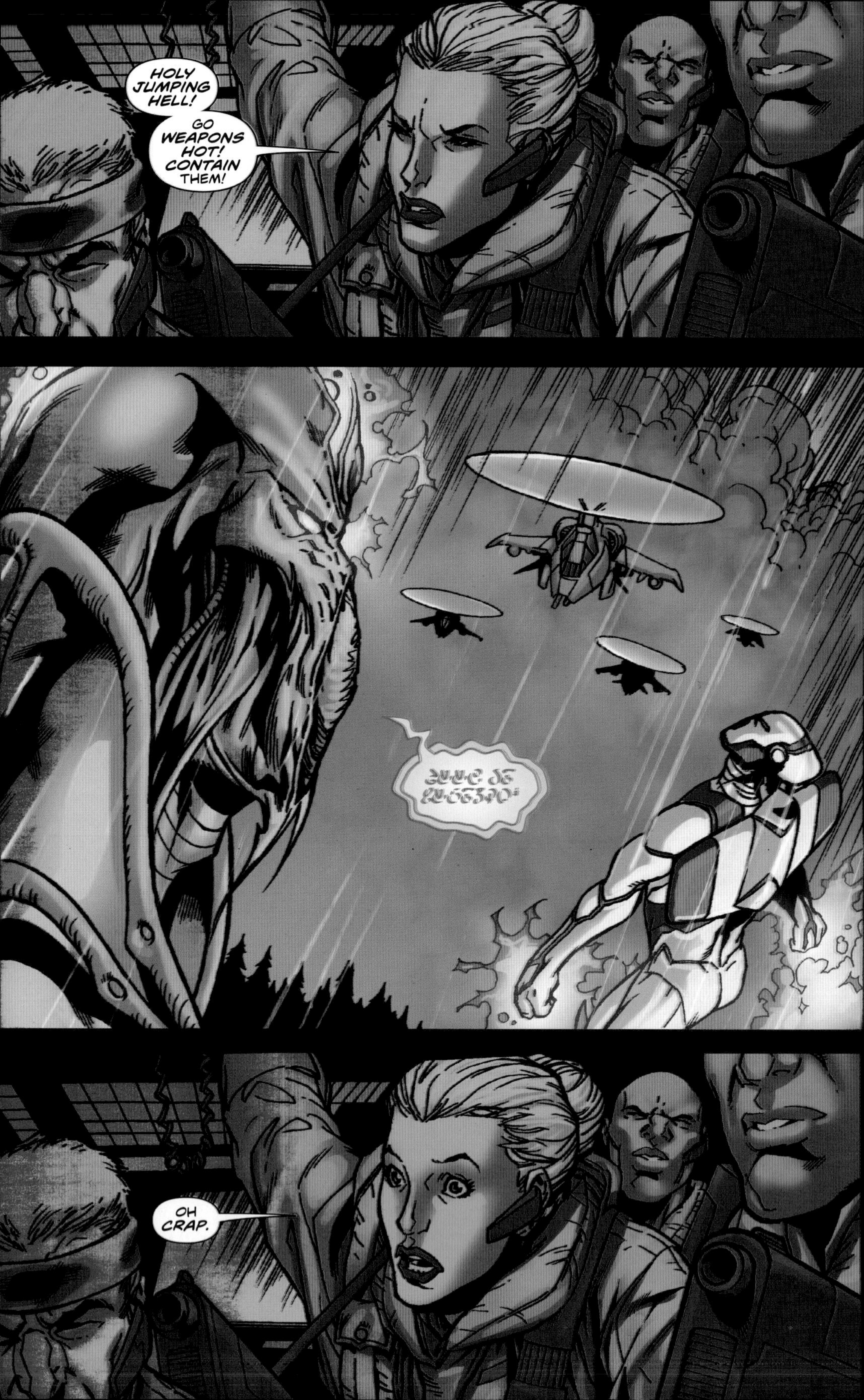
HOLY JUMPING HELL!
GO WEAPONS HOT! CONTAIN THEM!
OH CRAP.

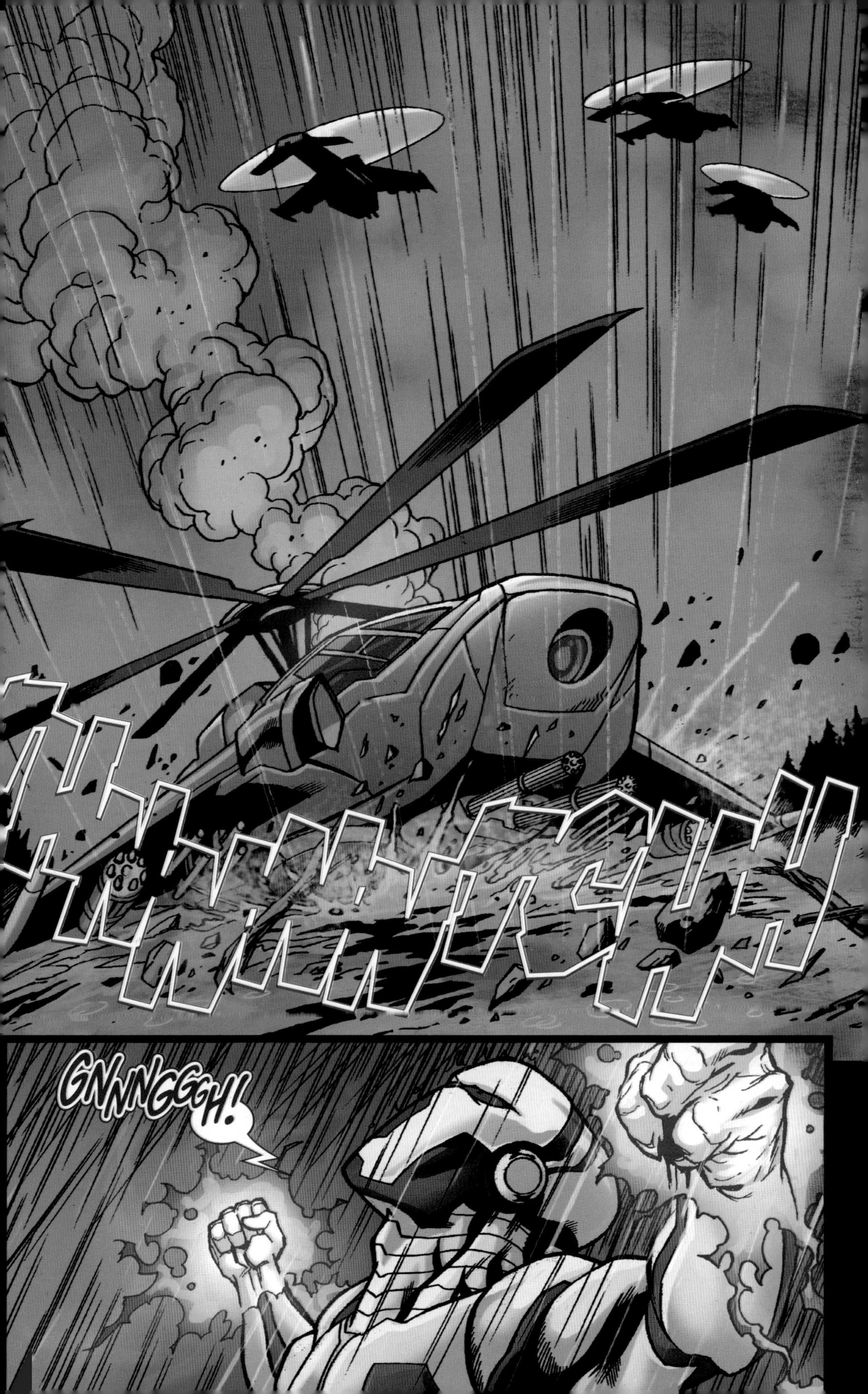
GNNNGGGH!

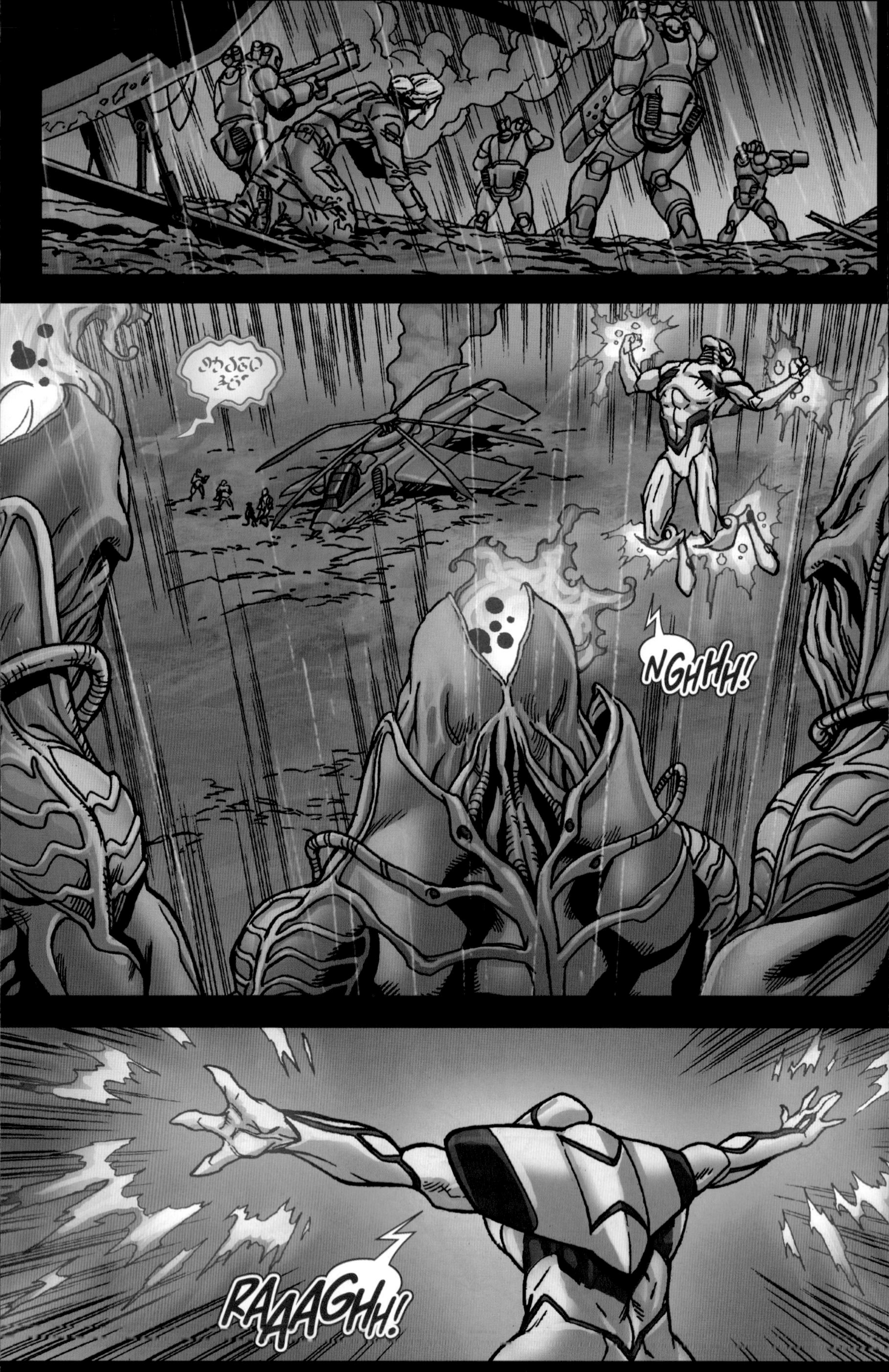
NGHHH!
RAAAGHH!

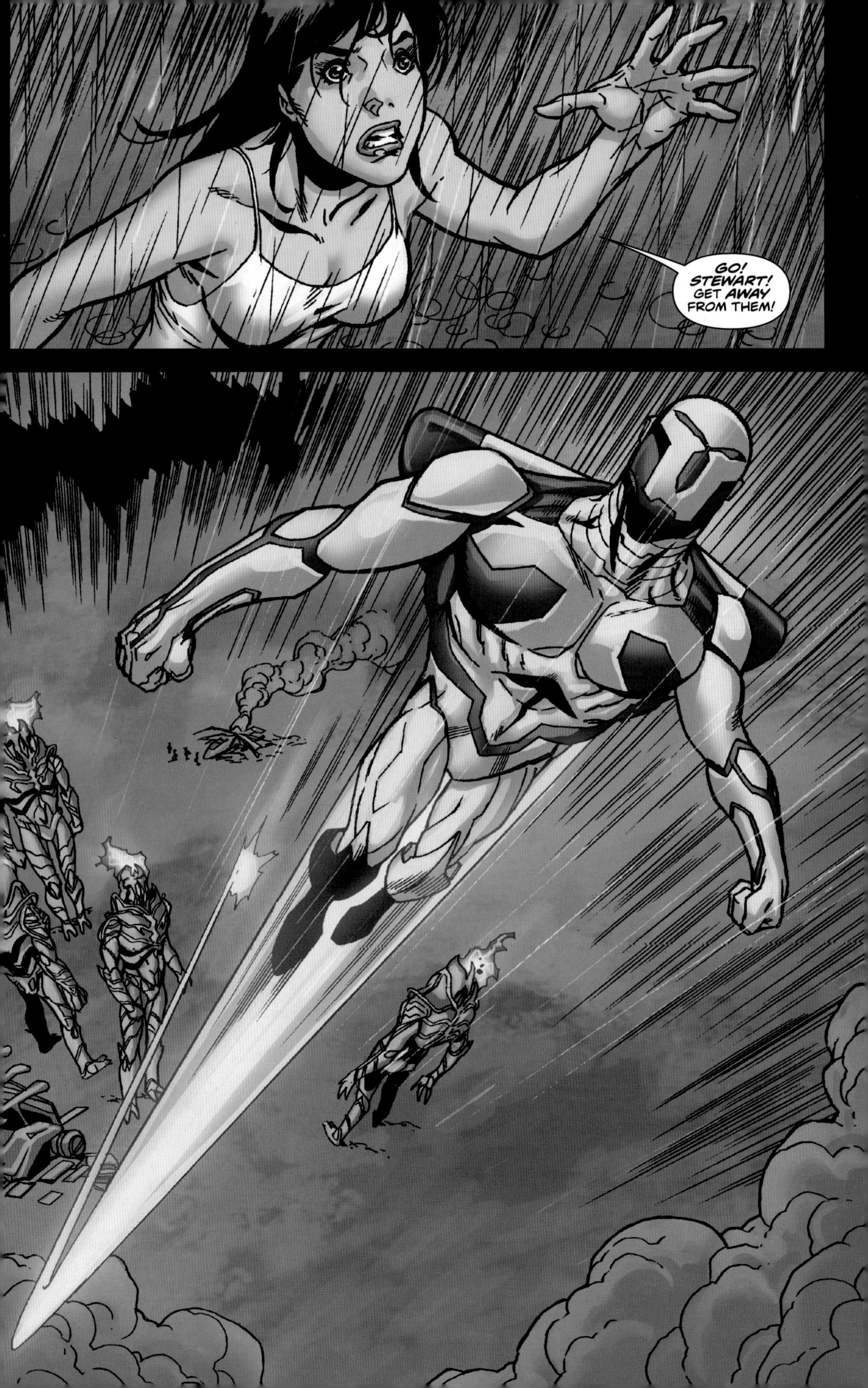
GO! STEWART! GET AWAY FROM THEM!

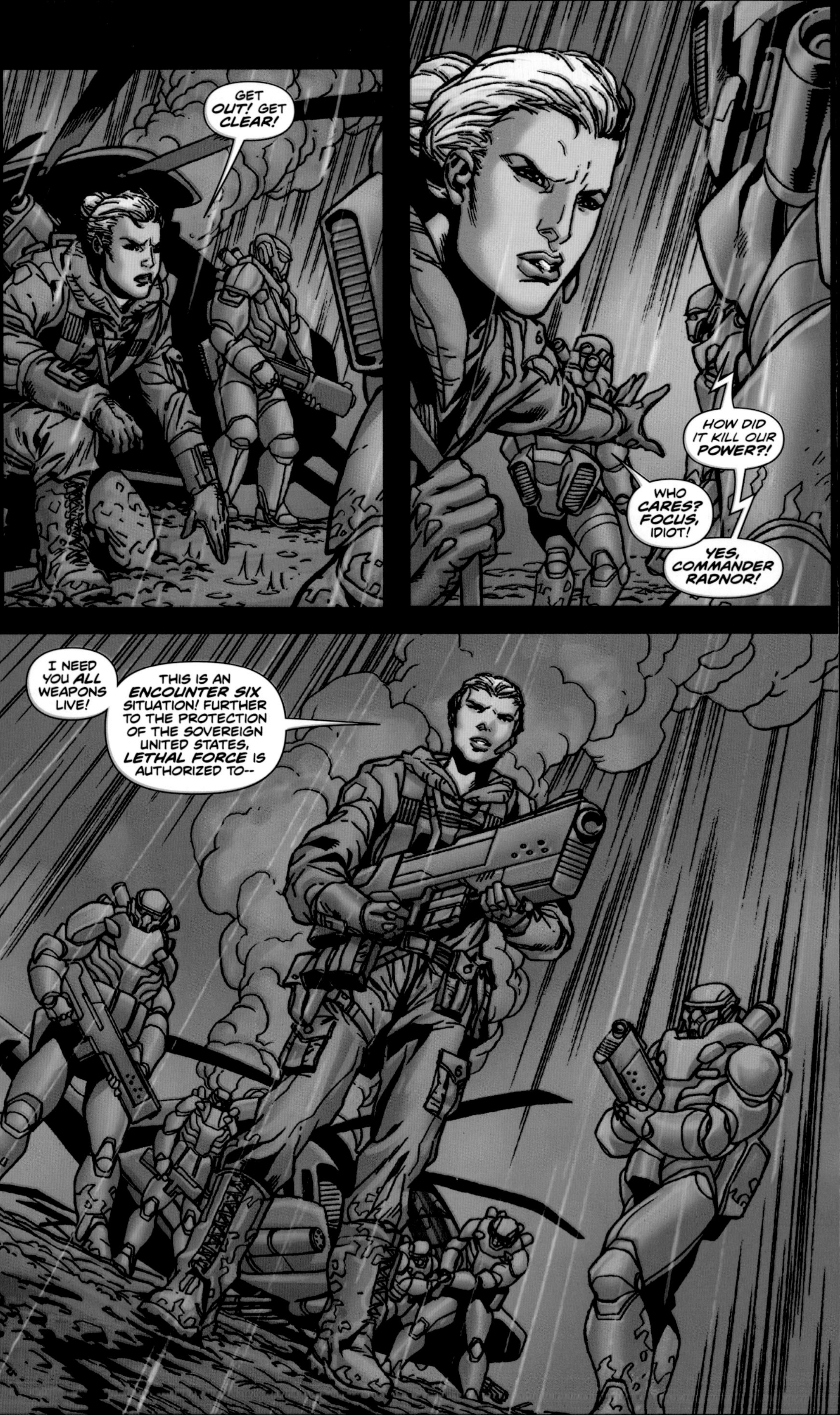
GET OUT! GET CLEAR!
HOW DID IT KILL OUR POWER?!
WHO CARES? FOCUS, IDIOT!
YES, COMMANDER RADNOR!
I NEED YOU ALL WEAPONS LIVE!
THIS IS AN ENCOUNTER SIX SITUATION! FURTHER TO THE PROTECTION OF THE SOVEREIGN UNITED STATES, LETHAL FORCE IS AUTHORIZED TO--

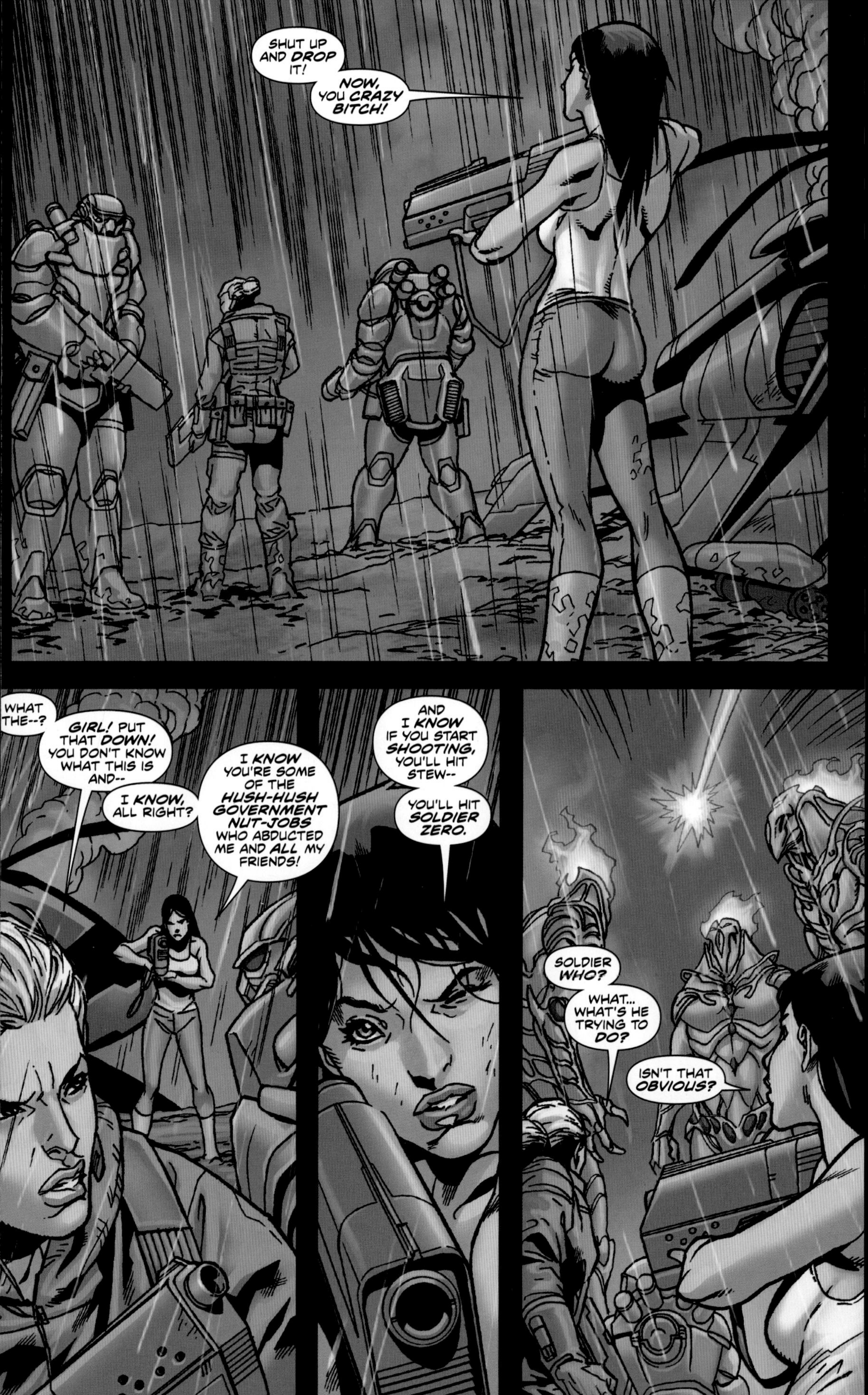
SHUT UP AND DROP IT!
NOW, YOU CRAZY BITCH!
WHAT THE--?
GIRL! PUT THAT DOWN! YOU DON'T KNOW WHAT THIS IS AND--
I KNOW, ALL RIGHT?
I KNOW YOU'RE SOME OF THE HUSH-HUSH GOVERNMENT NUT-JOBS WHO ABDUCTED ME AND ALL MY FRIENDS!
AND I KNOW IF YOU START SHOOTING, YOU'LL HIT STEW--
YOU'LL HIT SOLDIER ZERO.
SOLDIER WHO?
WHAT... WHAT'S HE TRYING TO DO?
ISN'T THAT OBVIOUS?

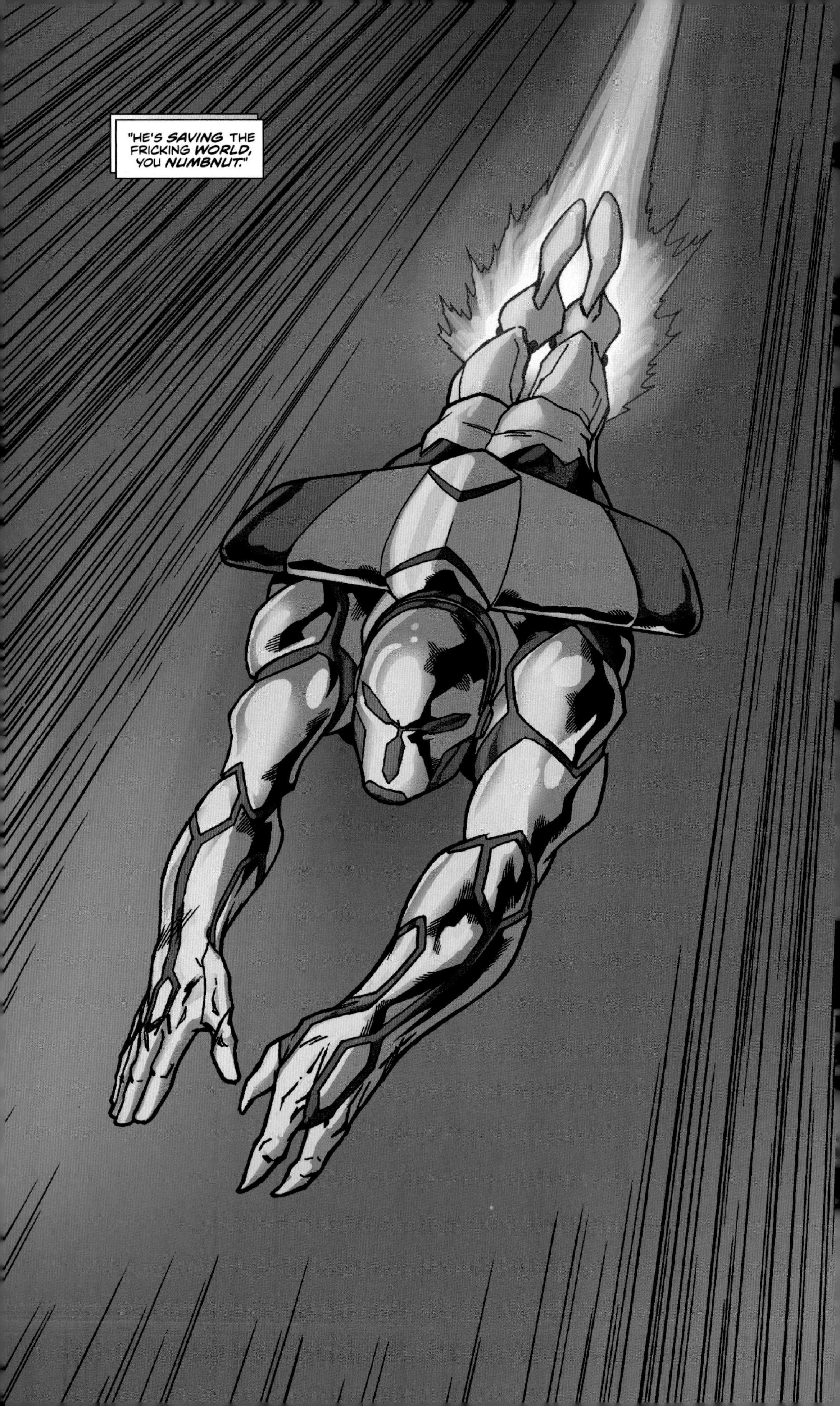
"HE'S SAVING THE FRICKING WORLD, YOU NUMBNUT."

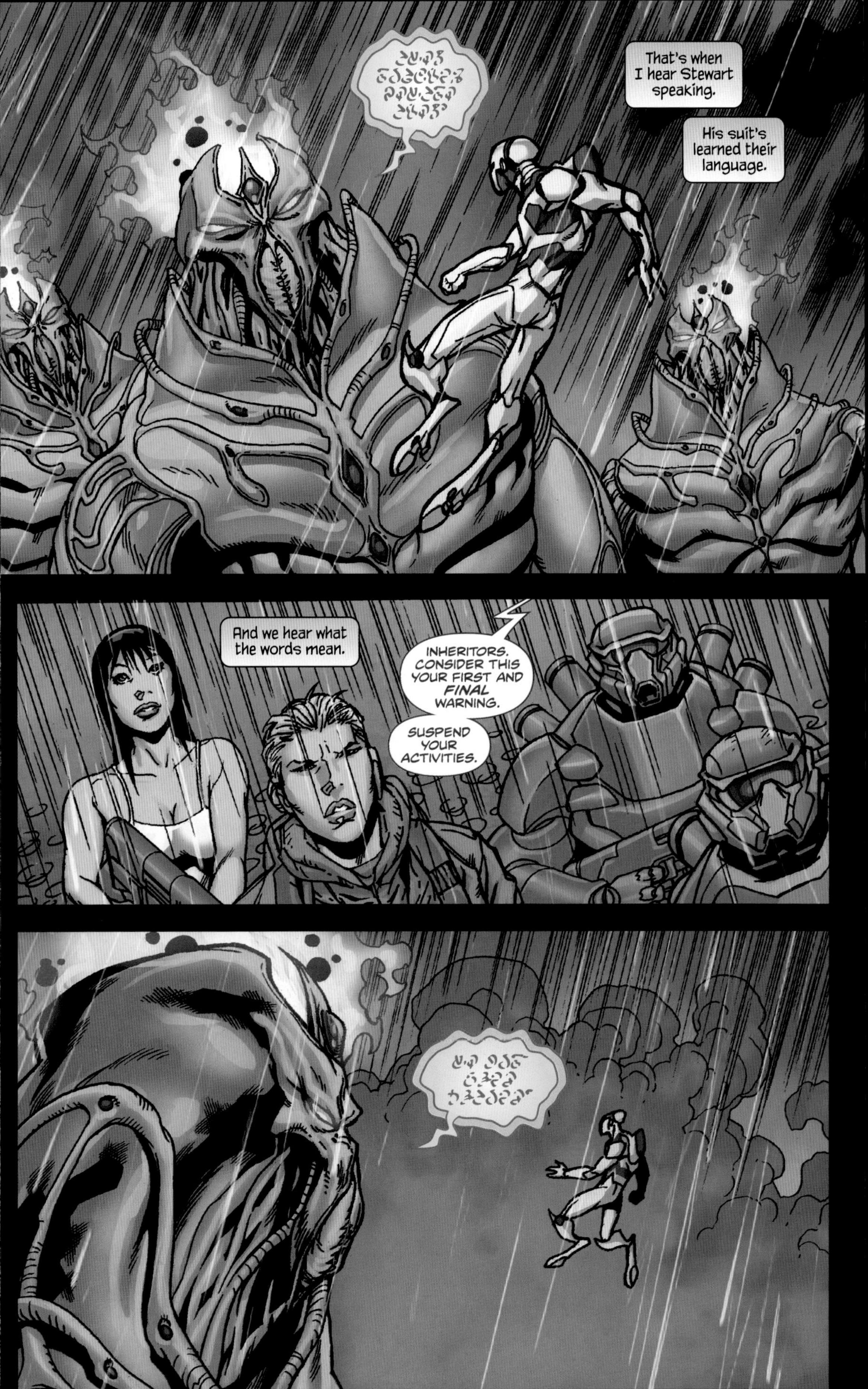
That's when I hear Stewart speaking.
His suit's learned their language.
And we hear what the words mean.
INHERITORS. CONSIDER THIS YOUR FIRST AND *FINAL* WARNING.
SUSPEND YOUR ACTIVITIES.

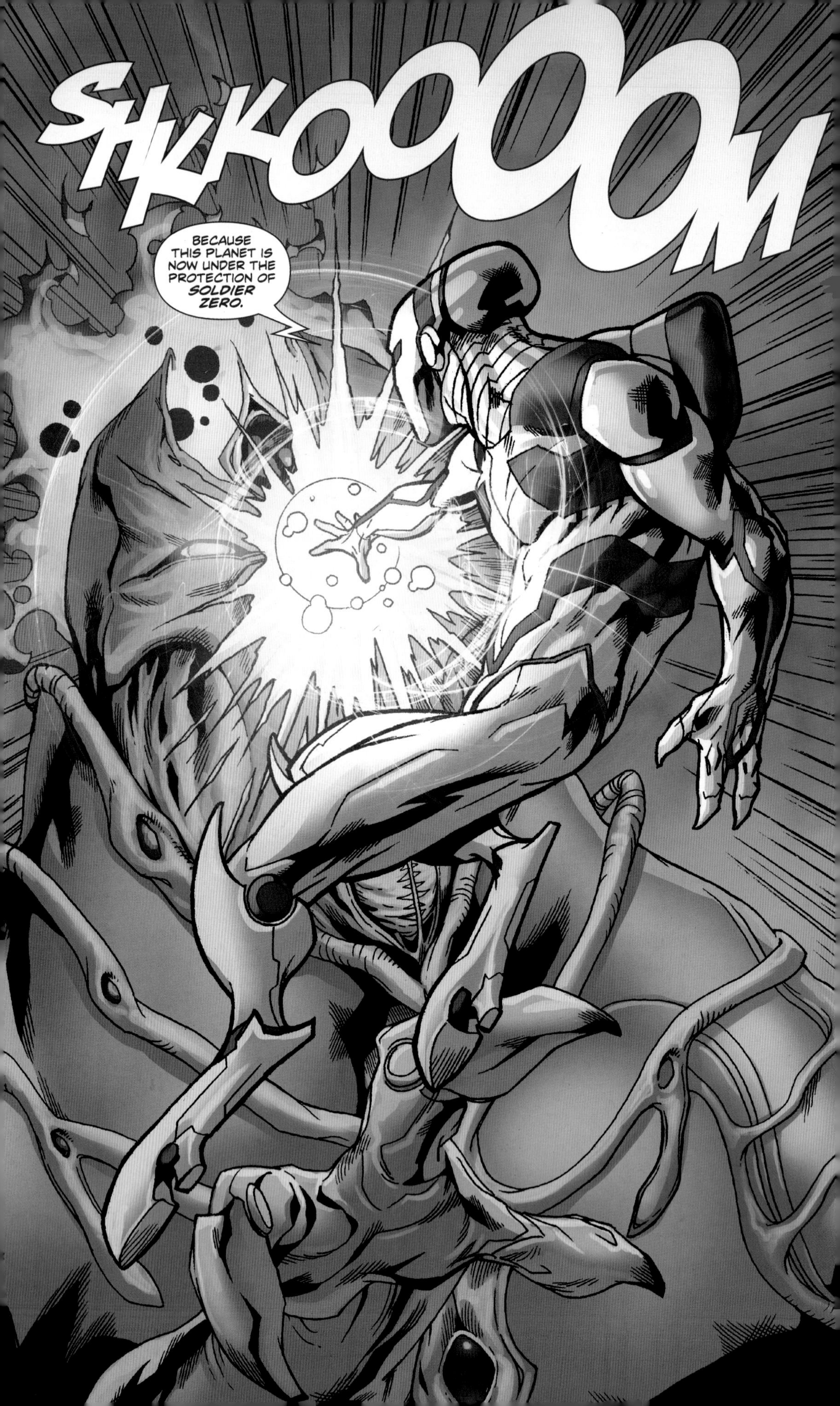
SHKOOOOM
BECAUSE THIS PLANET IS NOW UNDER THE PROTECTION OF *SOLDIER ZERO.*

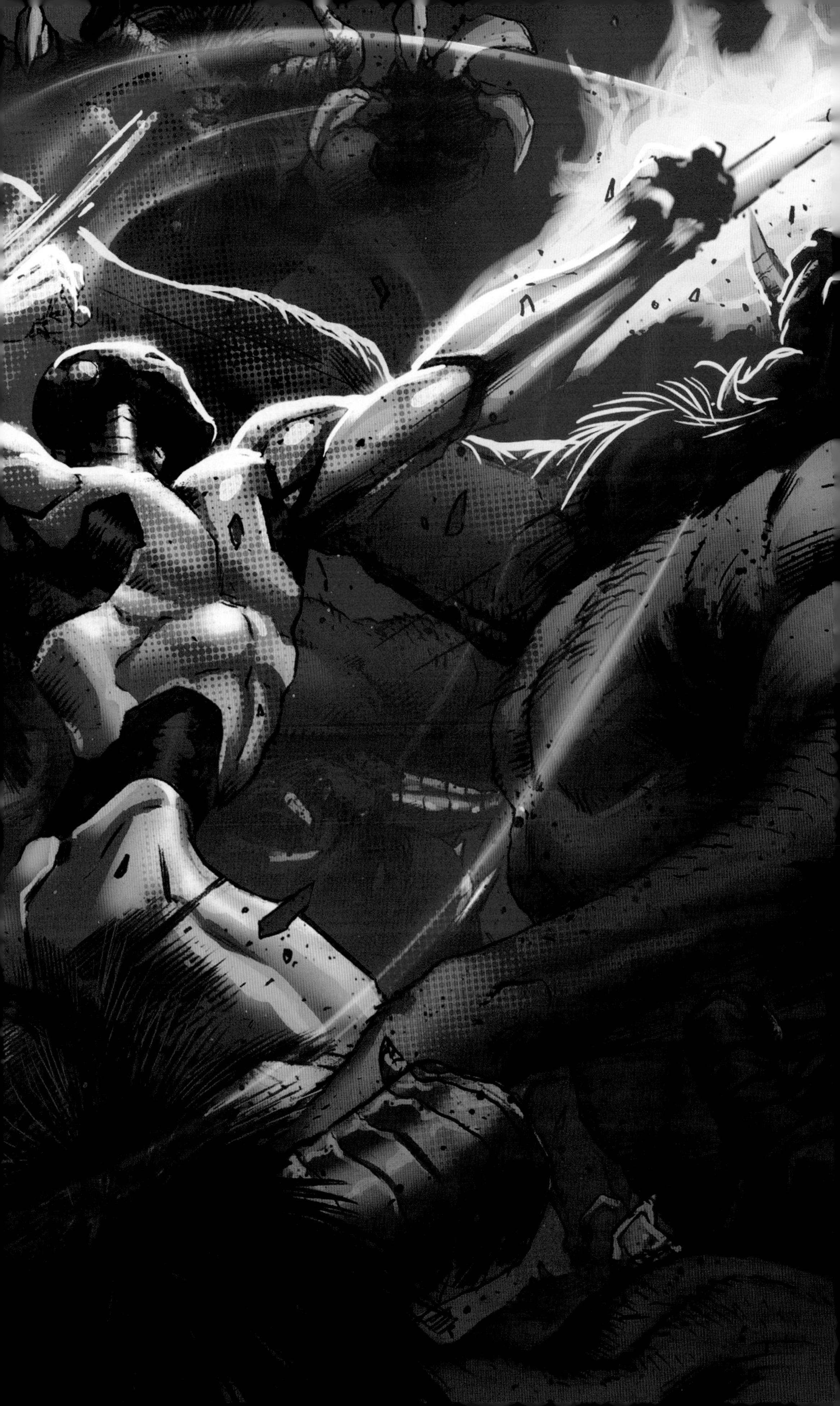

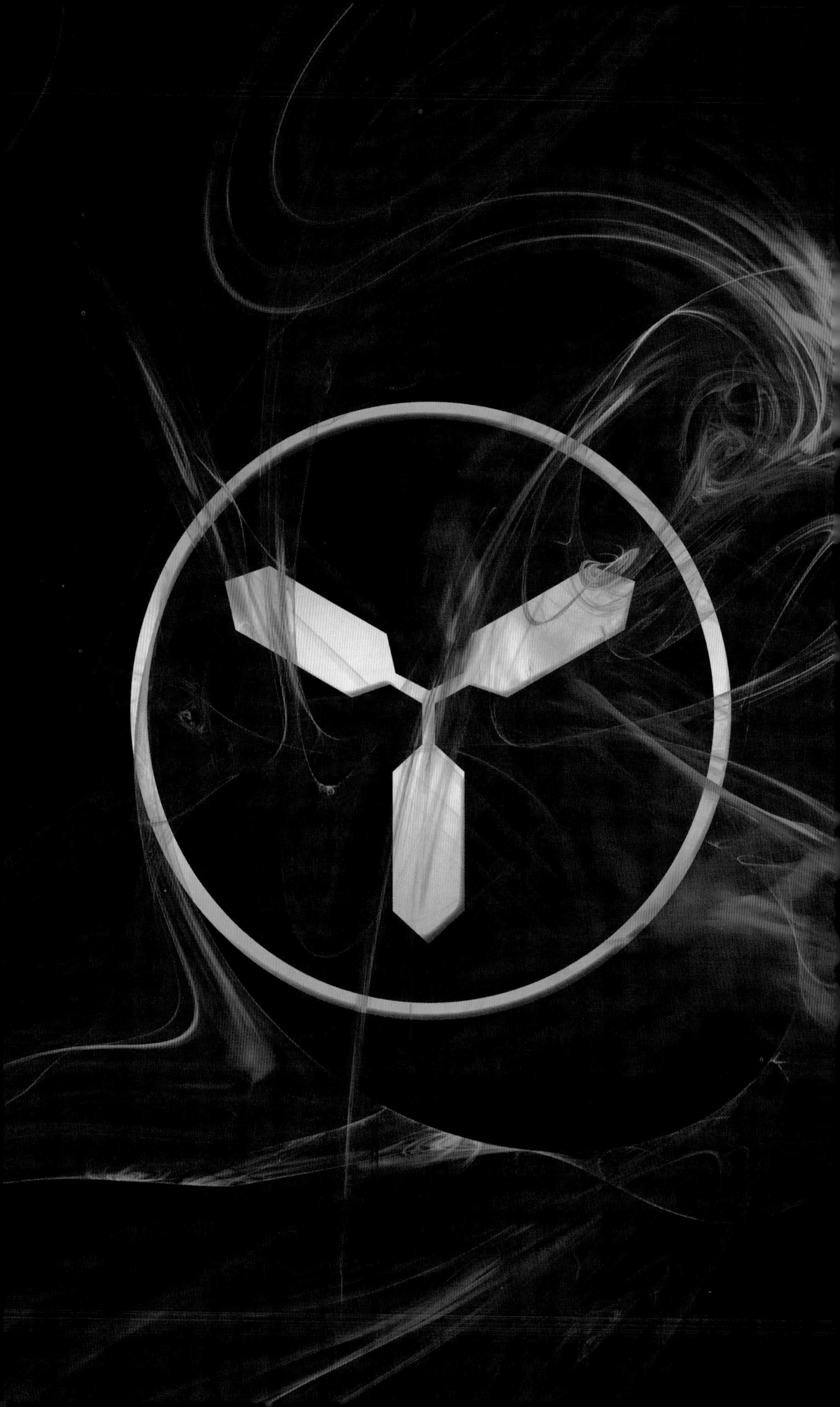

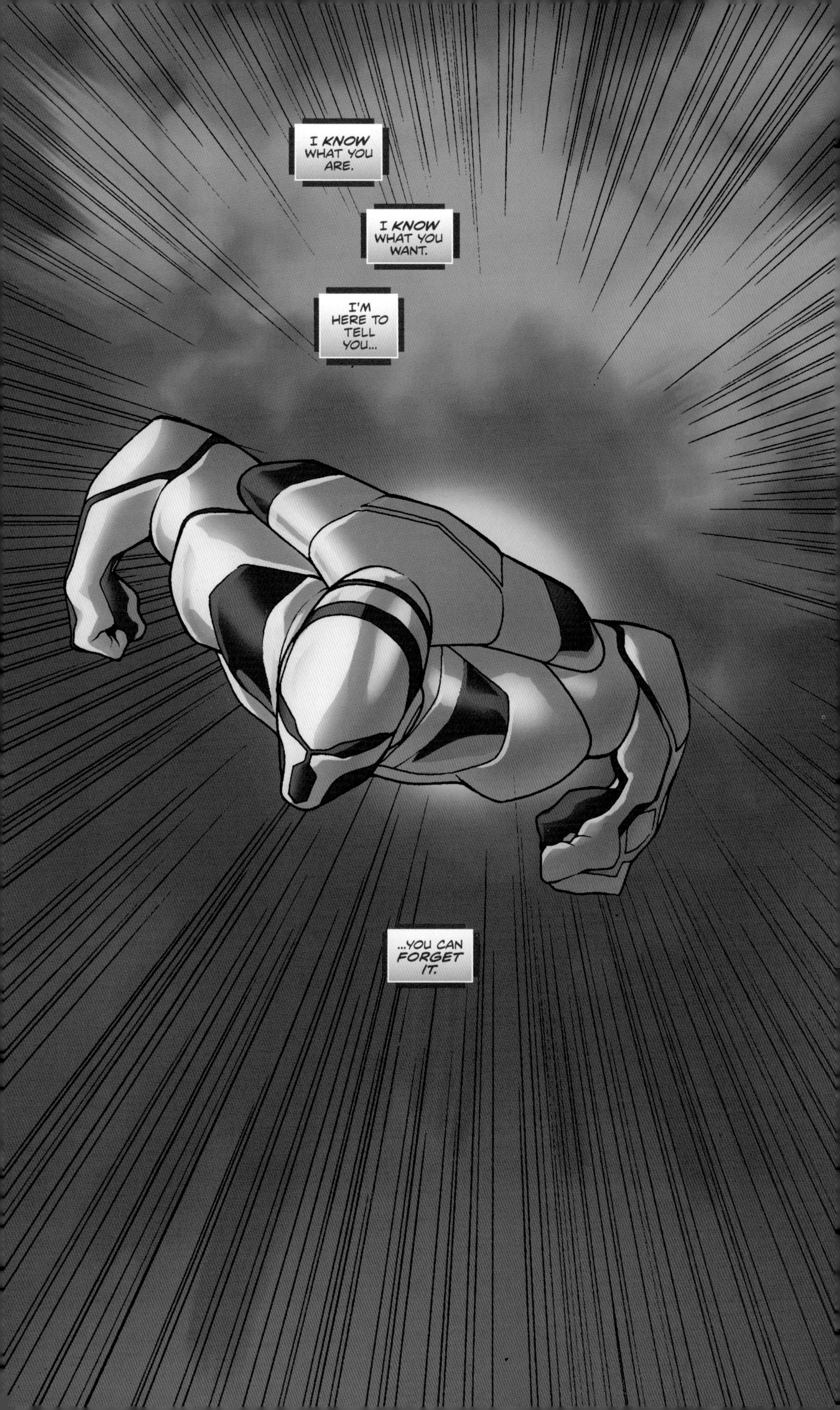
I KNOW WHAT YOU ARE.
I KNOW WHAT YOU WANT.
I'M HERE TO TELL YOU...
...YOU CAN FORGET IT.

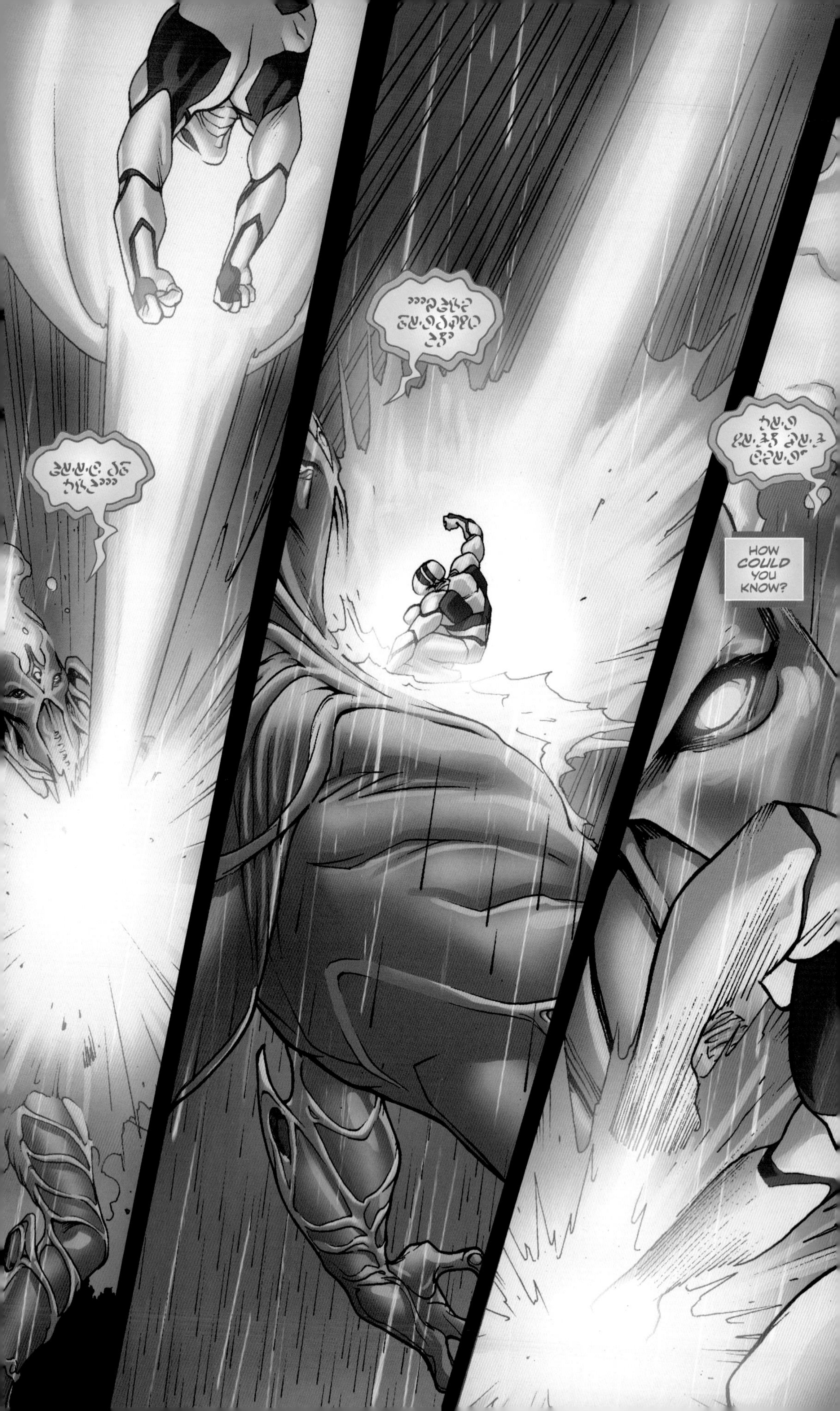
HOW COULD YOU KNOW?

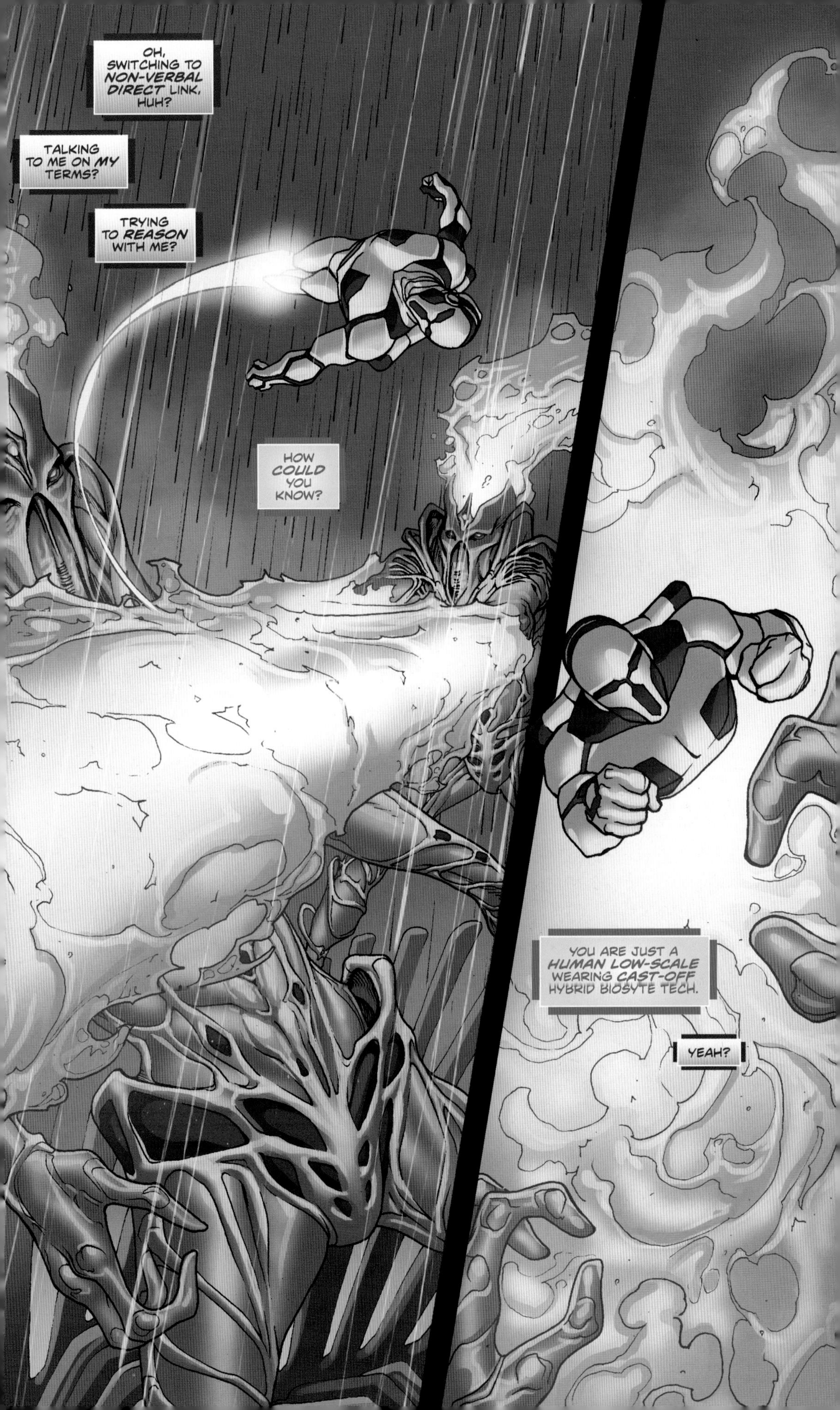
OH, SWITCHING TO NON-VERBAL DIRECT LINK, HUH?
TALKING TO ME ON MY TERMS?
TRYING TO REASON WITH ME?
HOW COULD YOU KNOW?
YOU ARE JUST A HUMAN LOW-SCALE WEARING CAST-OFF HYBRID BIOSYTE TECH.
YEAH?

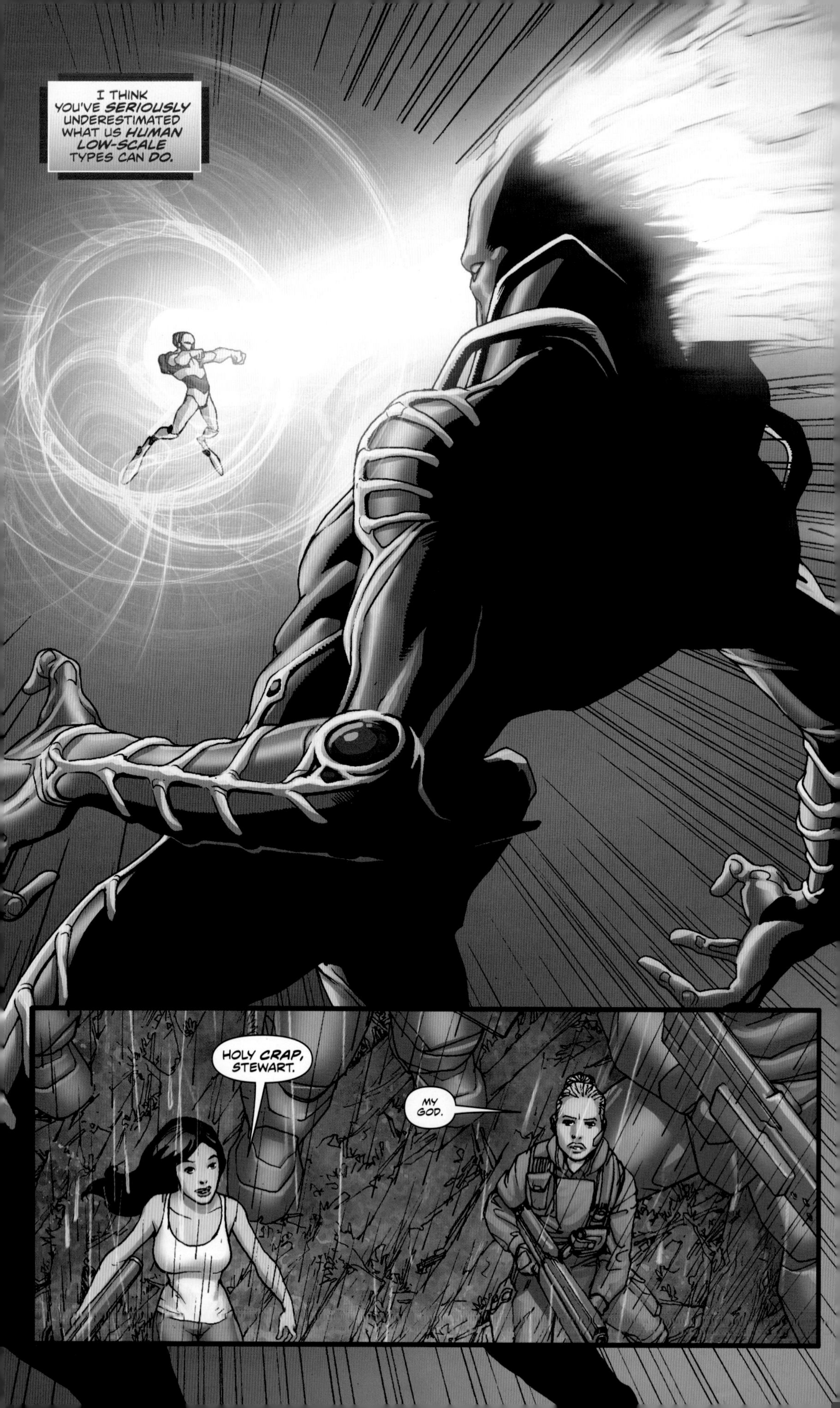
I THINK YOU'VE SERIOUSLY UNDERESTIMATED WHAT US HUMAN LOW-SCALE TYPES CAN DO.
HOLY CRAP, STEWART.
MY GOD.

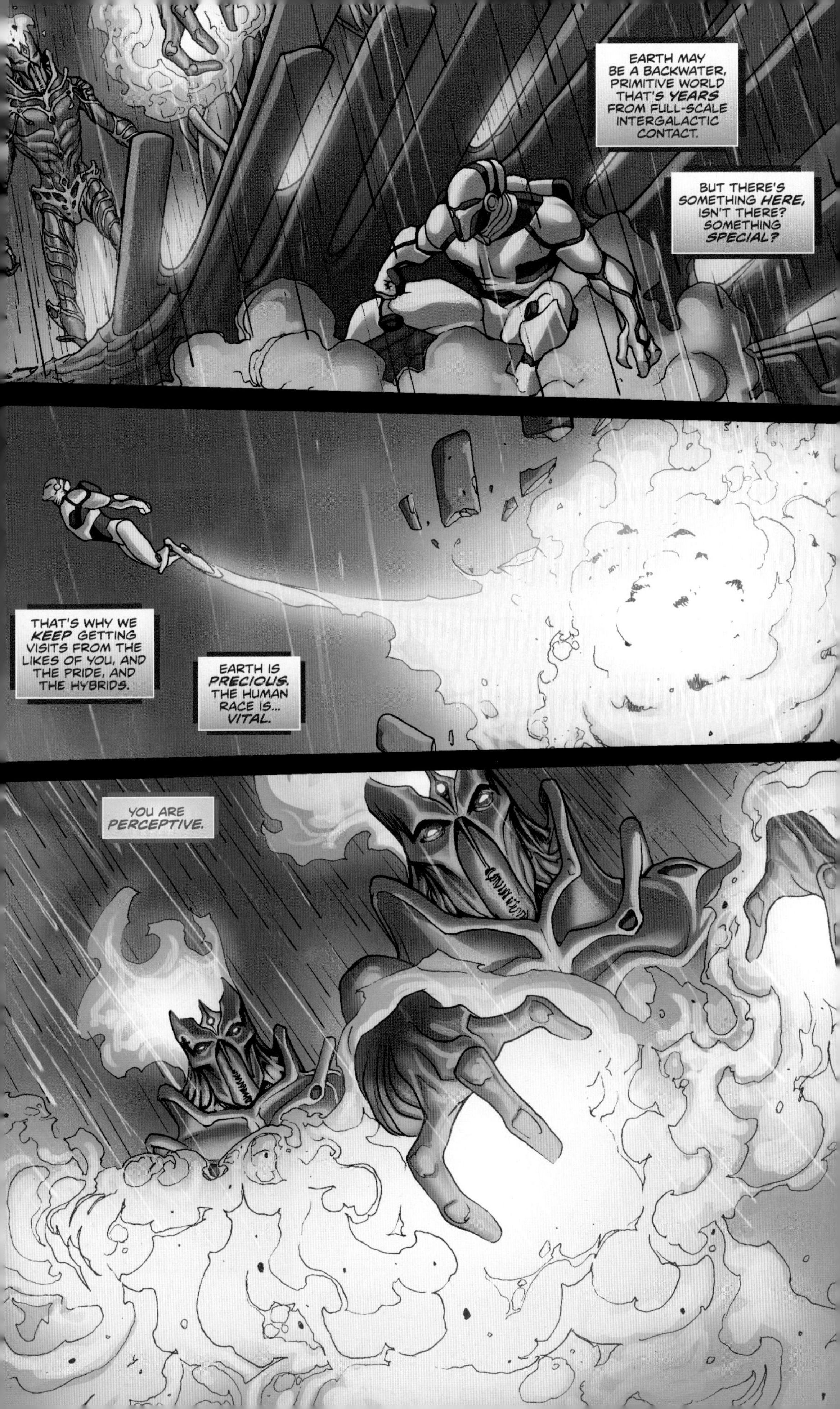
EARTH MAY BE A BACKWATER, PRIMITIVE WORLD THAT'S *YEARS* FROM FULL-SCALE INTERGALACTIC CONTACT.
BUT THERE'S SOMETHING *HERE*, ISN'T THERE? SOMETHING *SPECIAL*?
THAT'S WHY WE *KEEP* GETTING VISITS FROM THE LIKES OF YOU, AND THE PRIDE, AND THE HYBRIDS.
EARTH IS *PRECIOUS*. THE HUMAN RACE IS... *VITAL*.
YOU ARE *PERCEPTIVE*.

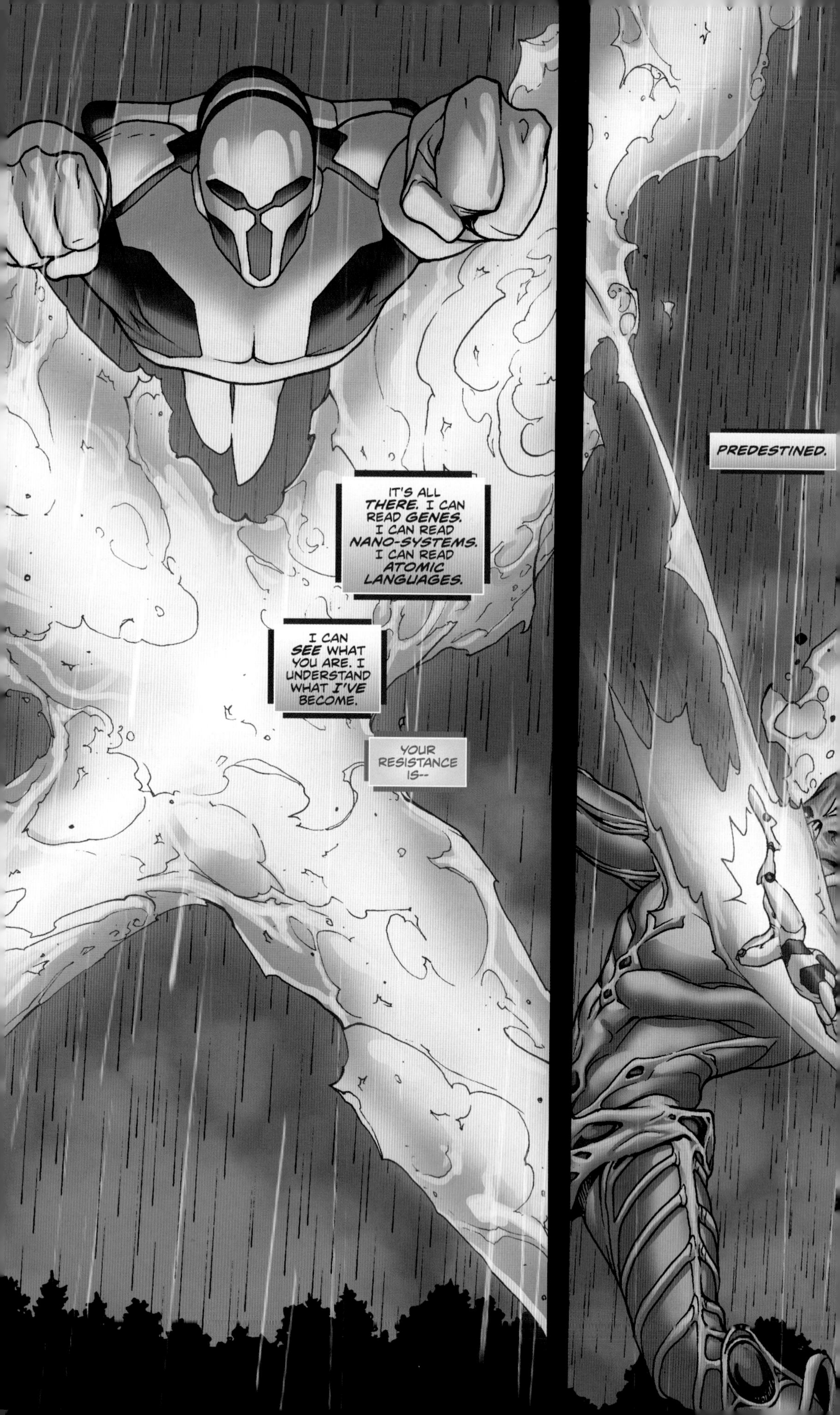

IT'S ALL THERE. I CAN READ GENES. I CAN READ NANO-SYSTEMS. I CAN READ ATOMIC LANGUAGES.
I CAN SEE WHAT YOU ARE. I UNDERSTAND WHAT I'VE BECOME.
YOUR RESISTANCE IS--
PREDESTINED.

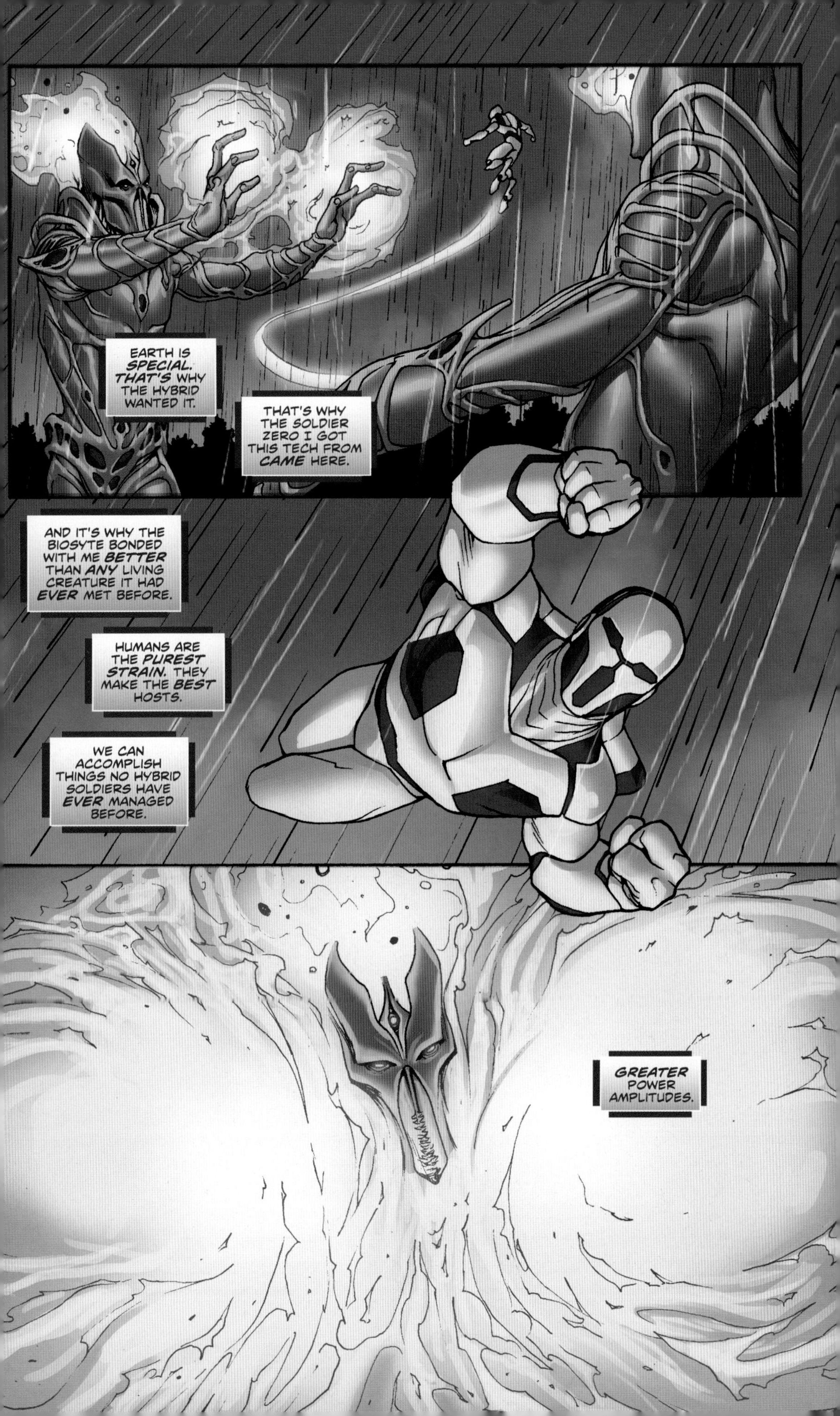
EARTH IS SPECIAL. THAT'S WHY THE HYBRID WANTED IT.
THAT'S WHY THE SOLDIER ZERO I GOT THIS TECH FROM CAME HERE.
AND IT'S WHY THE BIOSYTE BONDED WITH ME BETTER THAN ANY LIVING CREATURE IT HAD EVER MET BEFORE.
HUMANS ARE THE PUREST STRAIN. THEY MAKE THE BEST HOSTS.
WE CAN ACCOMPLISH THINGS NO HYBRID SOLDIERS HAVE EVER MANAGED BEFORE.
GREATER POWER AMPLITUDES.

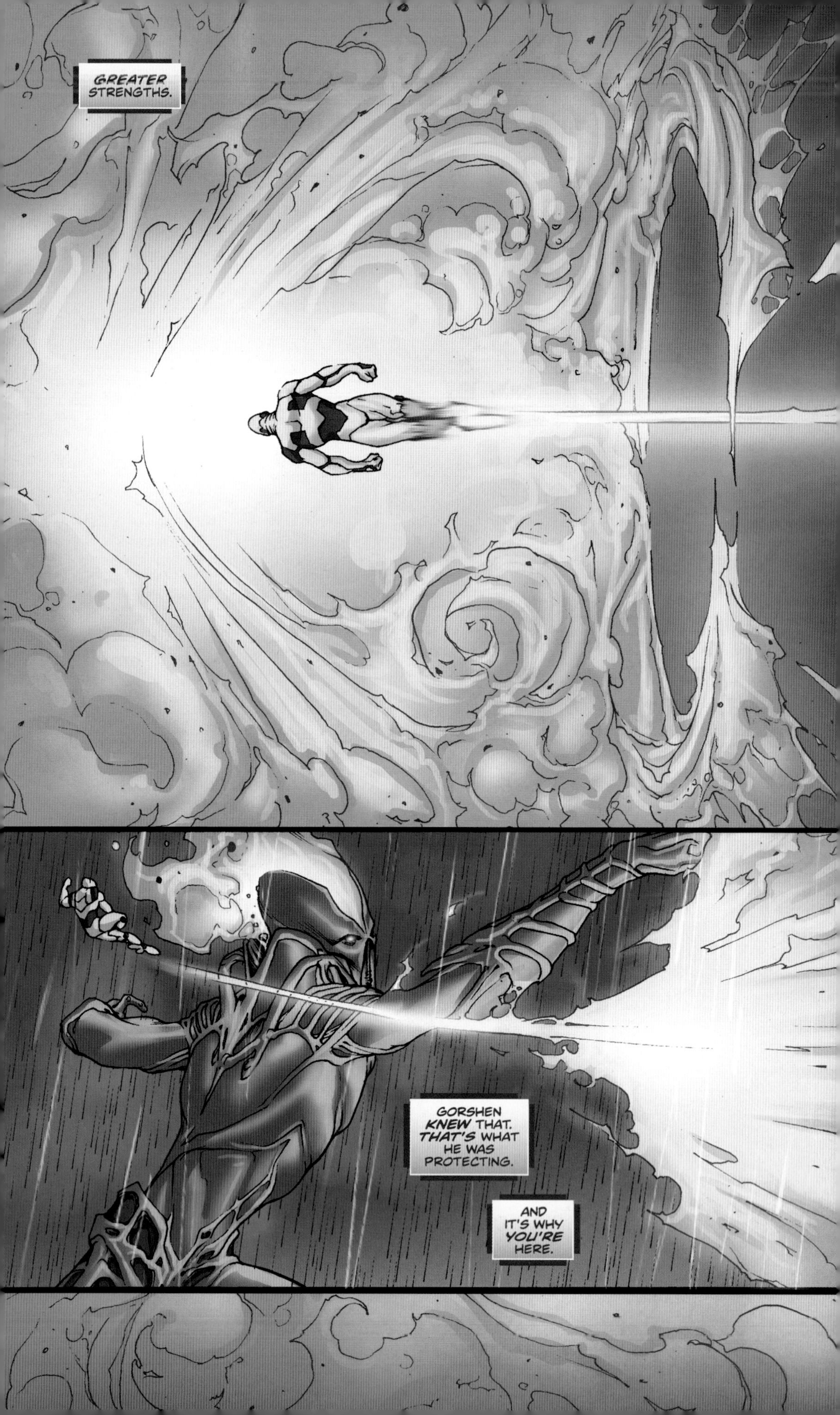
GREATER STRENGTHS.
GORSHEN KNEW THAT. THAT'S WHAT HE WAS PROTECTING.
AND IT'S WHY YOU'RE HERE.

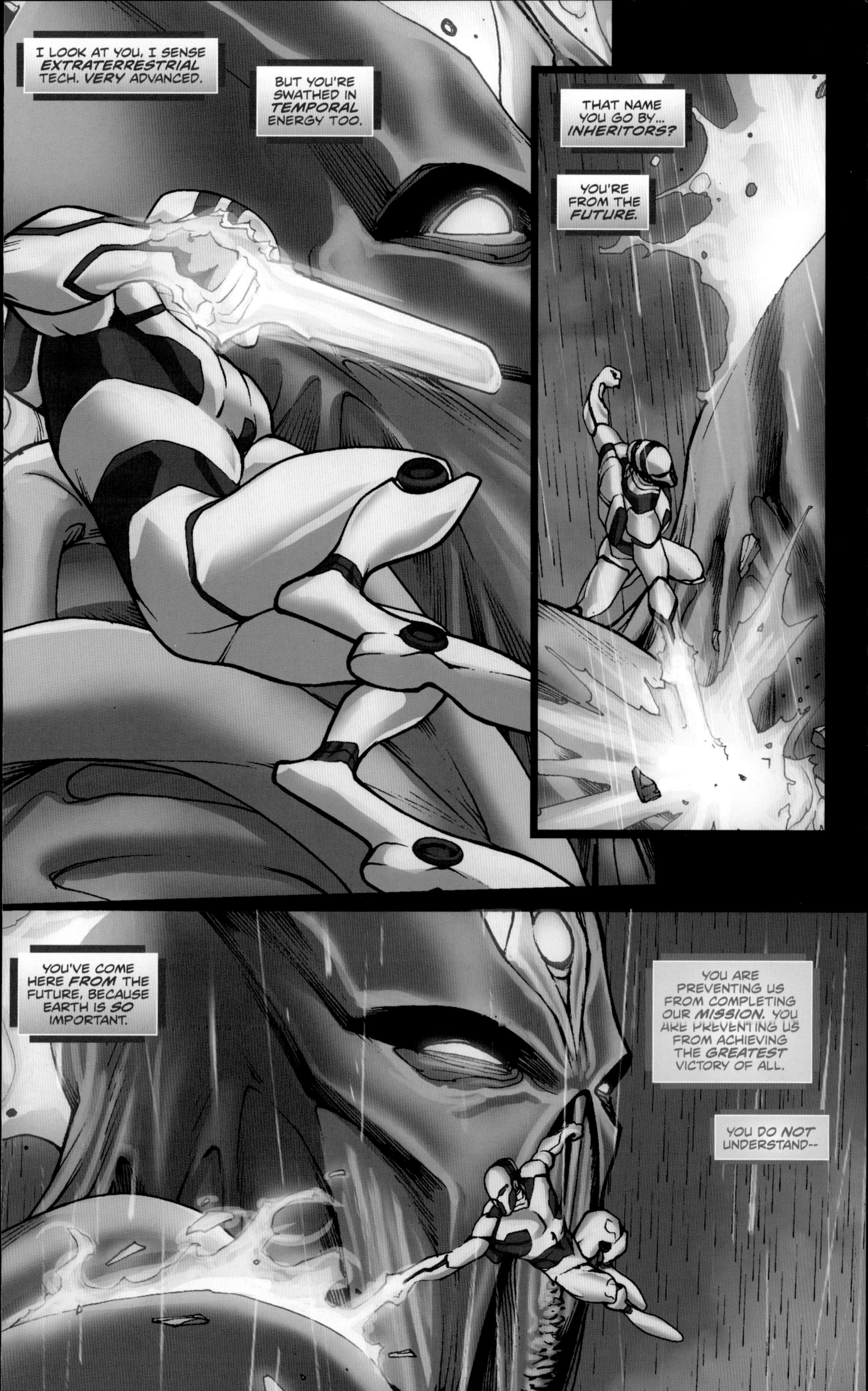
I LOOK AT YOU, I SENSE EXTRATERRESTRIAL TECH. VERY ADVANCED.
BUT YOU'RE SWATHED IN TEMPORAL ENERGY TOO.
THAT NAME YOU GO BY... INHERITORS?
YOU'RE FROM THE FUTURE.
YOU'VE COME HERE FROM THE FUTURE, BECAUSE EARTH IS SO IMPORTANT.
YOU ARE PREVENTING US FROM COMPLETING OUR MISSION. YOU ARE PREVENTING US FROM ACHIEVING THE GREATEST VICTORY OF ALL.
YOU DO NOT UNDERSTAND--

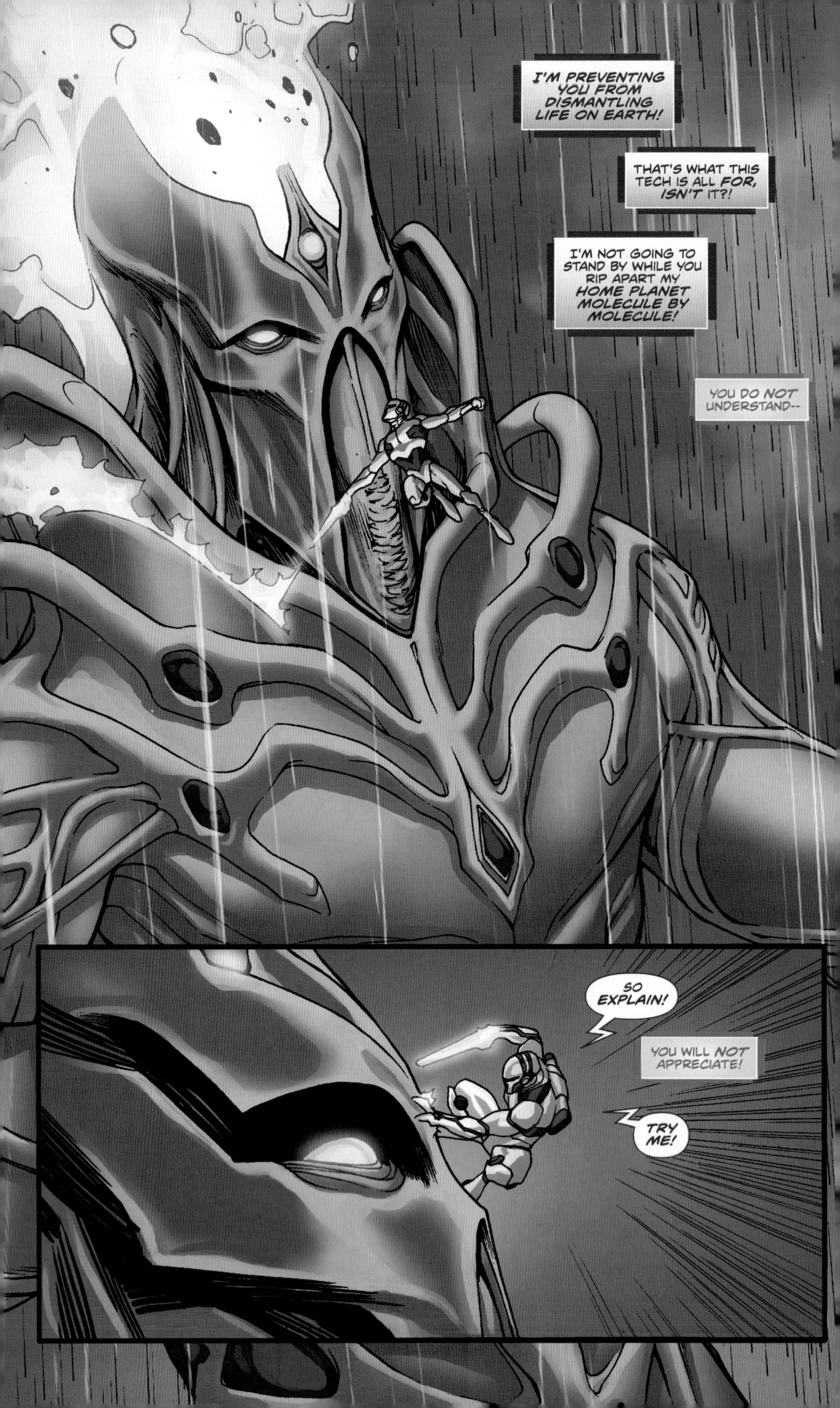
I'M PREVENTING YOU FROM DISMANTLING LIFE ON EARTH!
THAT'S WHAT THIS TECH IS ALL FOR, ISN'T IT?!
I'M NOT GOING TO STAND BY WHILE YOU RIP APART MY HOME PLANET MOLECULE BY MOLECULE!
YOU DO NOT UNDERSTAND--
SO EXPLAIN!
YOU WILL NOT APPRECIATE!
TRY ME!

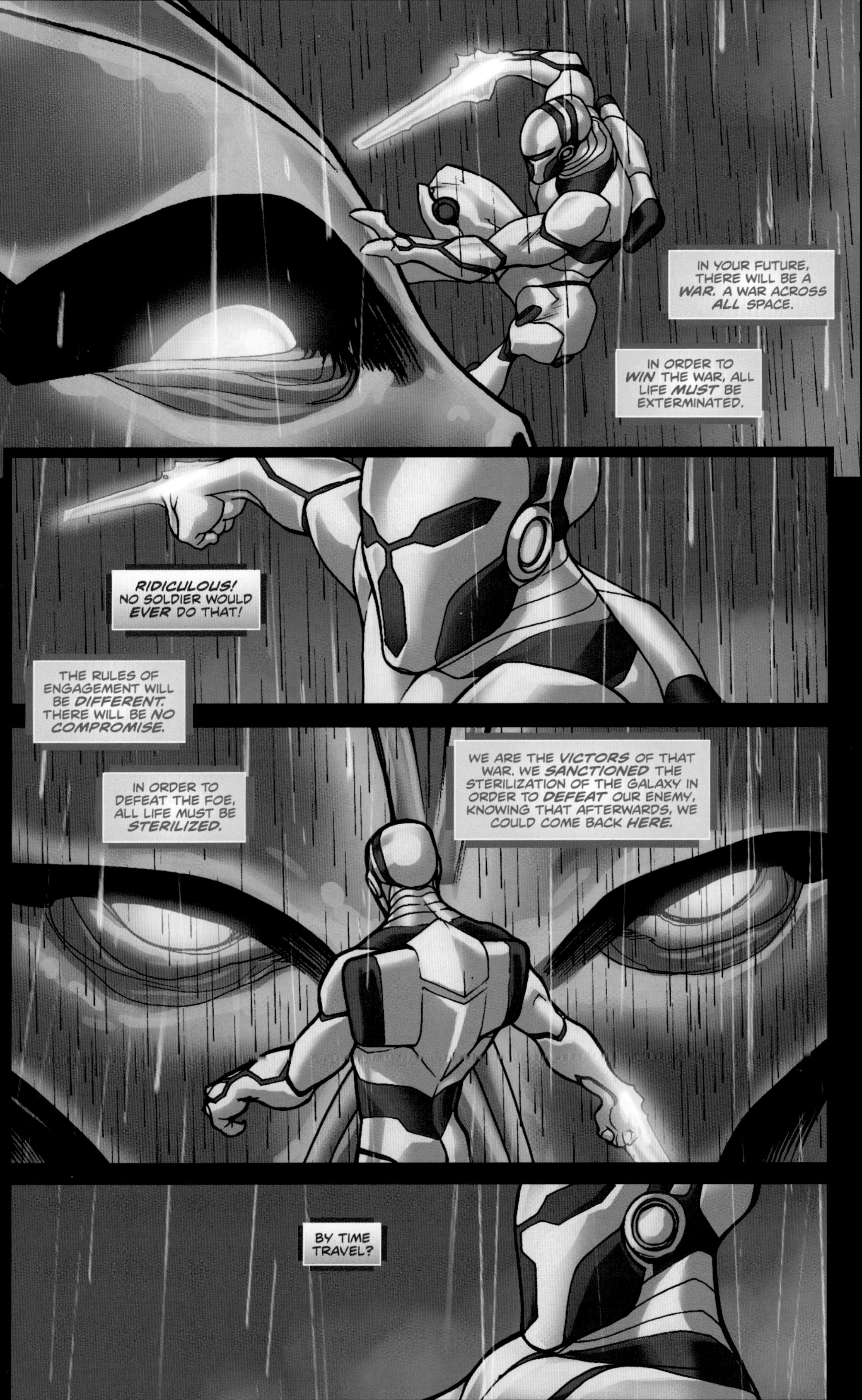

IN YOUR FUTURE, THERE WILL BE A WAR. A WAR ACROSS ALL SPACE.
IN ORDER TO WIN THE WAR, ALL LIFE MUST BE EXTERMINATED.
RIDICULOUS! NO SOLDIER WOULD EVER DO THAT!
THE RULES OF ENGAGEMENT WILL BE DIFFERENT. THERE WILL BE NO COMPROMISE.
IN ORDER TO DEFEAT THE FOE, ALL LIFE MUST BE STERILIZED.
WE ARE THE VICTORS OF THAT WAR. WE SANCTIONED THE STERILIZATION OF THE GALAXY IN ORDER TO DEFEAT OUR ENEMY, KNOWING THAT AFTERWARDS, WE COULD COME BACK HERE.
BY TIME TRAVEL?

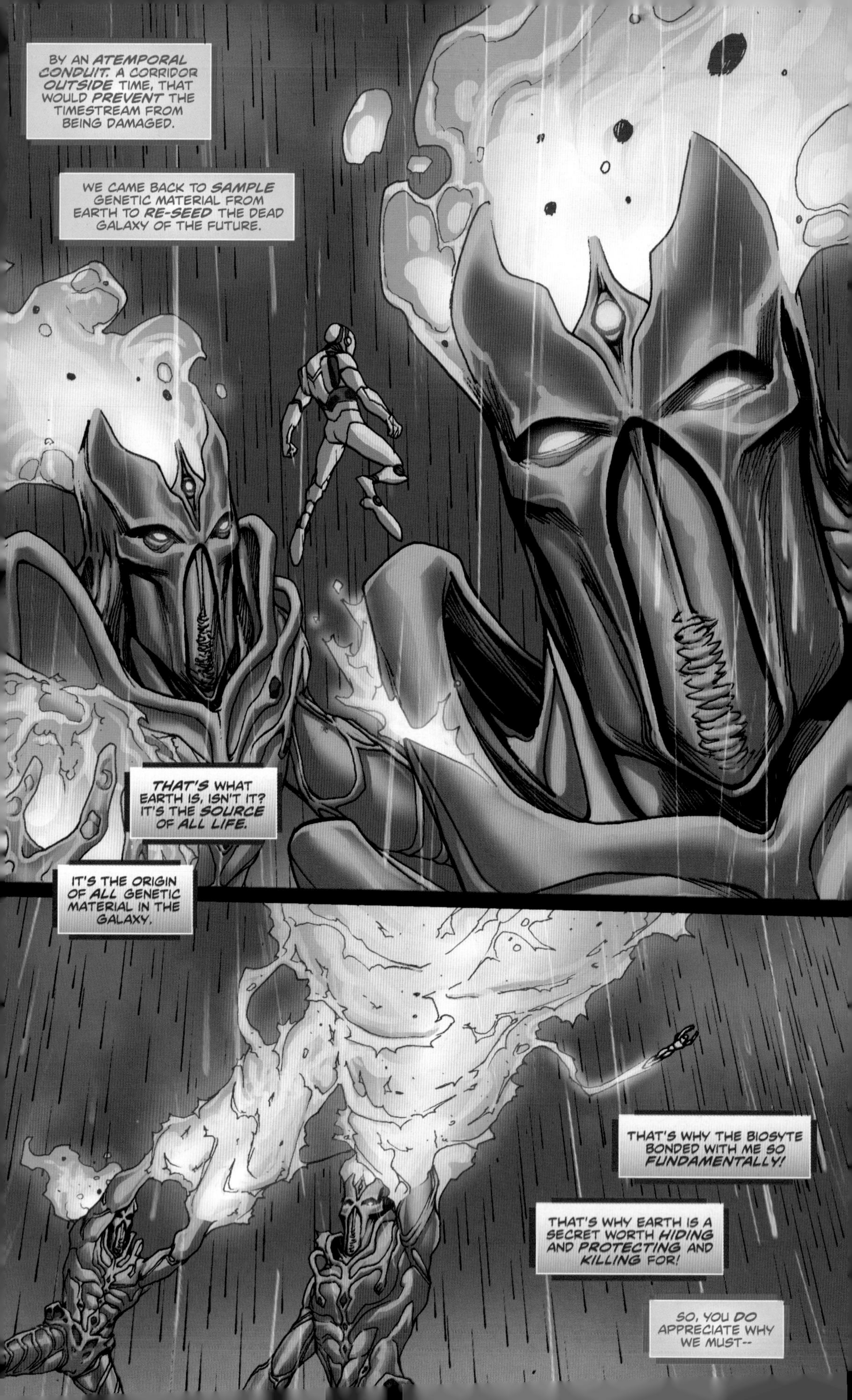

BY AN ATEMPORAL CONDUIT. A CORRIDOR OUTSIDE TIME, THAT WOULD PREVENT THE TIMESTREAM FROM BEING DAMAGED.
WE CAME BACK TO SAMPLE GENETIC MATERIAL FROM EARTH TO RE-SEED THE DEAD GALAXY OF THE FUTURE.
THAT'S WHAT EARTH IS, ISN'T IT? IT'S THE SOURCE OF ALL LIFE.
IT'S THE ORIGIN OF ALL GENETIC MATERIAL IN THE GALAXY.
THAT'S WHY THE BIOSYTE BONDED WITH ME SO FUNDAMENTALLY!
THAT'S WHY EARTH IS A SECRET WORTH HIDING AND PROTECTING AND KILLING FOR!
SO, YOU DO APPRECIATE WHY WE MUST--

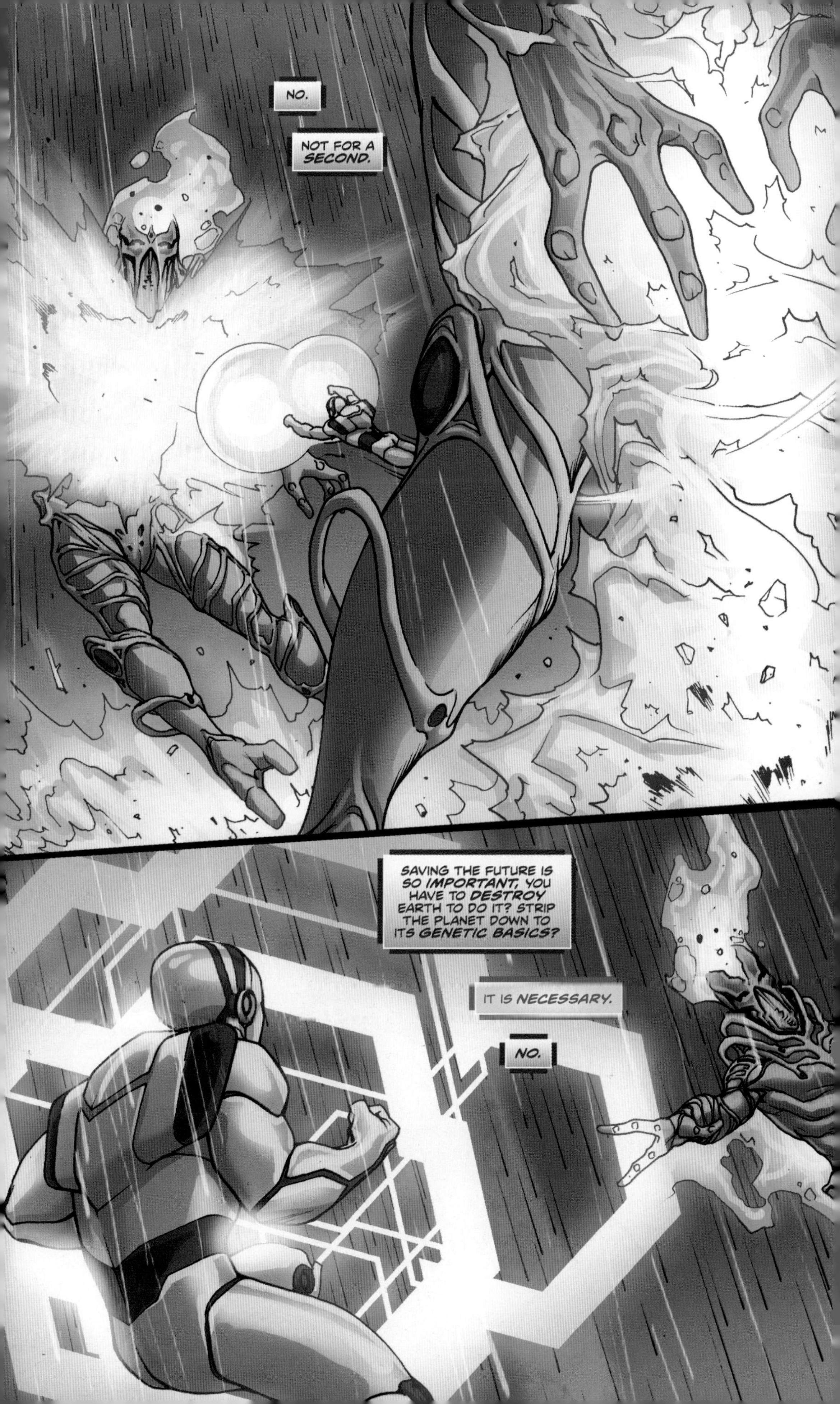
NO.
NOT FOR A SECOND.
SAVING THE FUTURE IS SO IMPORTANT, YOU HAVE TO DESTROY EARTH TO DO IT? STRIP THE PLANET DOWN TO ITS GENETIC BASICS?
IT IS NECESSARY.
NO.

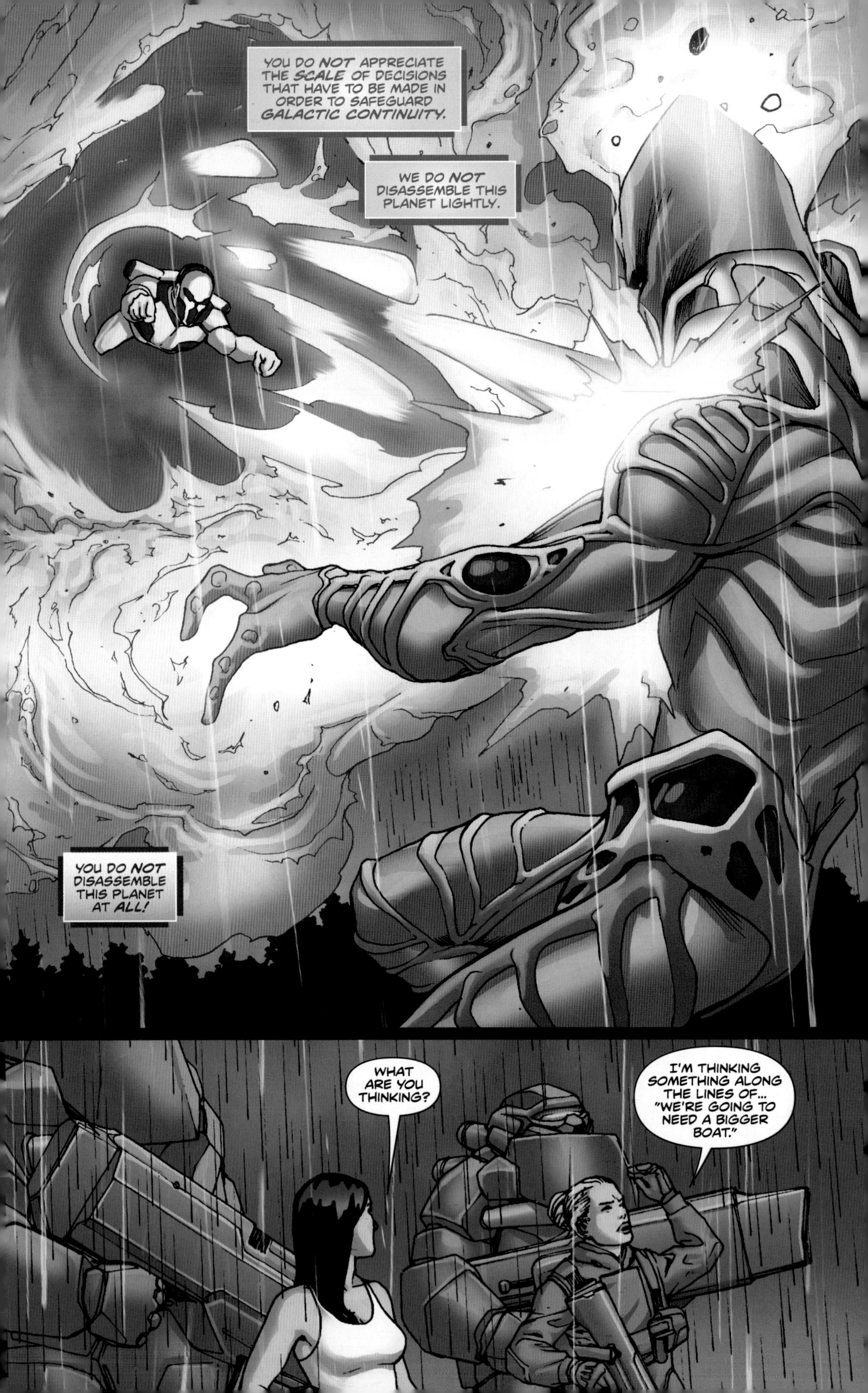
YOU DO NOT APPRECIATE THE SCALE OF DECISIONS THAT HAVE TO BE MADE IN ORDER TO SAFEGUARD GALACTIC CONTINUITY.
WE DO NOT DISASSEMBLE THIS PLANET LIGHTLY.
YOU DO NOT DISASSEMBLE THIS PLANET AT ALL!
WHAT ARE YOU THINKING?
I'M THINKING SOMETHING ALONG THE LINES OF... "WE'RE GOING TO NEED A BIGGER BOAT."

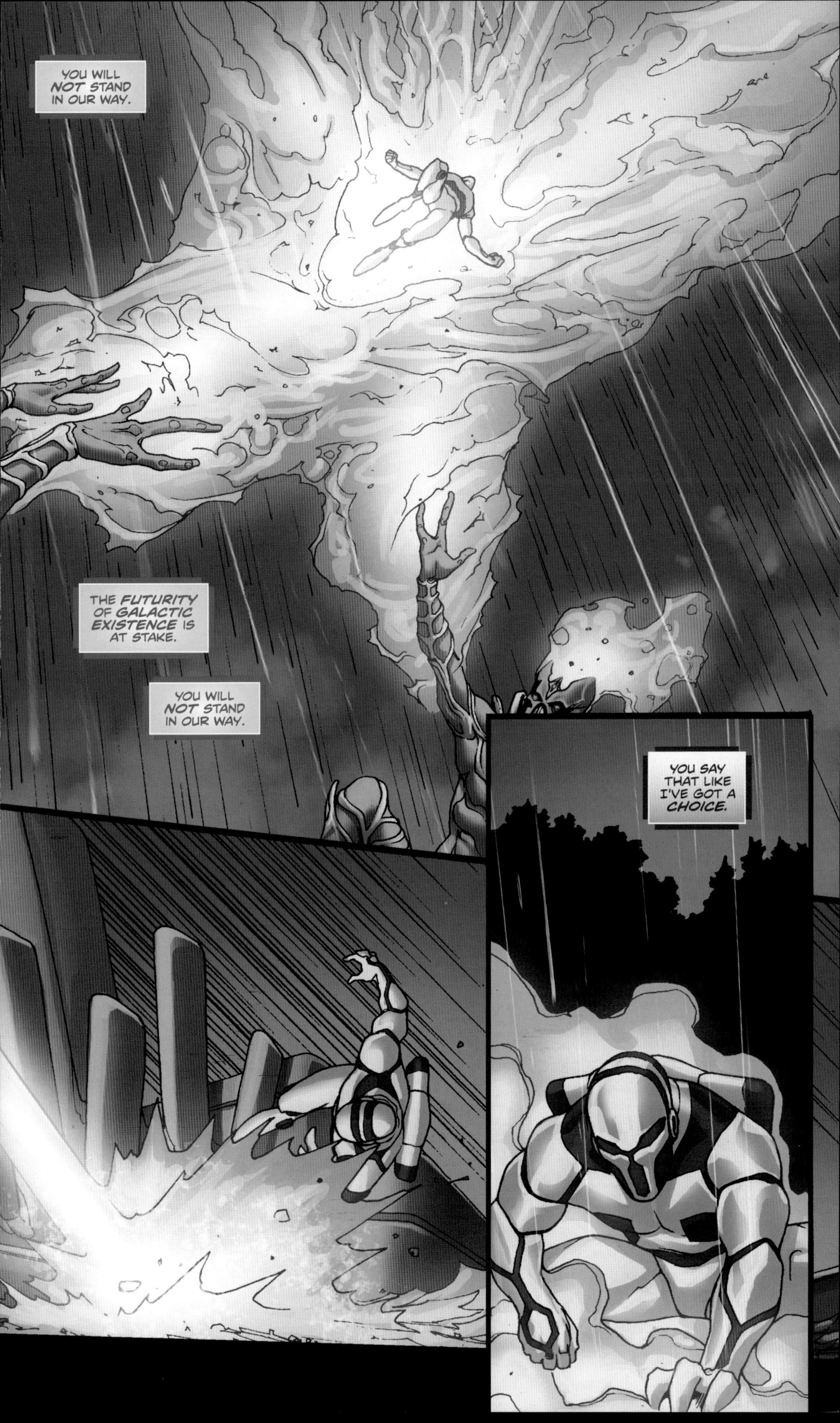
YOU WILL NOT STAND IN OUR WAY.
THE FUTURITY OF GALACTIC EXISTENCE IS AT STAKE.
YOU WILL NOT STAND IN OUR WAY.
YOU SAY THAT LIKE I'VE GOT A CHOICE.

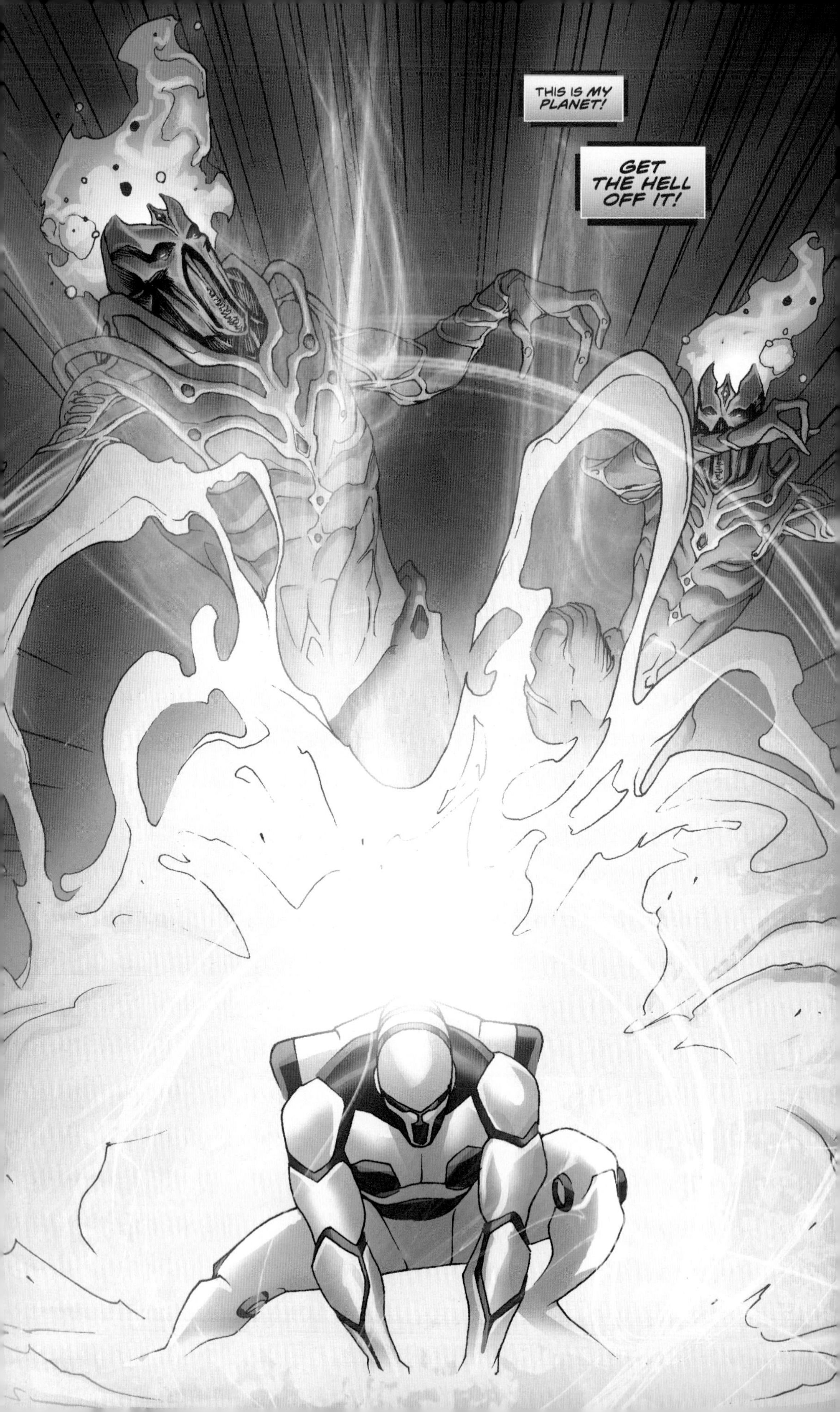
THIS IS MY PLANET!
GET THE HELL OFF IT!

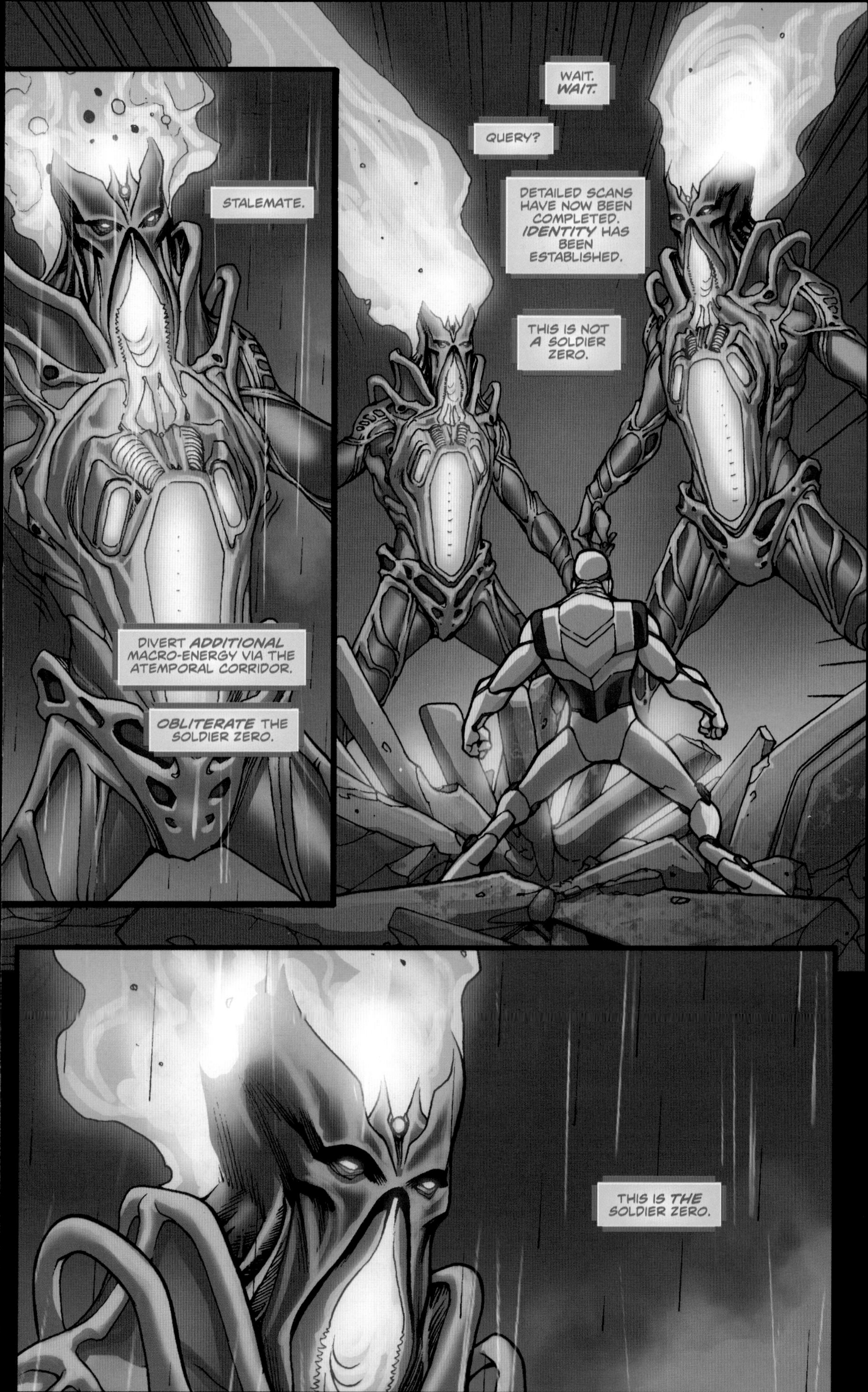
STALEMATE.
DIVERT *ADDITIONAL* MACRO-ENERGY VIA THE ATEMPORAL CORRIDOR.
OBLITERATE THE SOLDIER ZERO.
WAIT. *WAIT.*
QUERY?
DETAILED SCANS HAVE NOW BEEN COMPLETED. *IDENTITY* HAS BEEN ESTABLISHED.
THIS IS NOT *A* SOLDIER ZERO.
THIS IS *THE* SOLDIER ZERO.

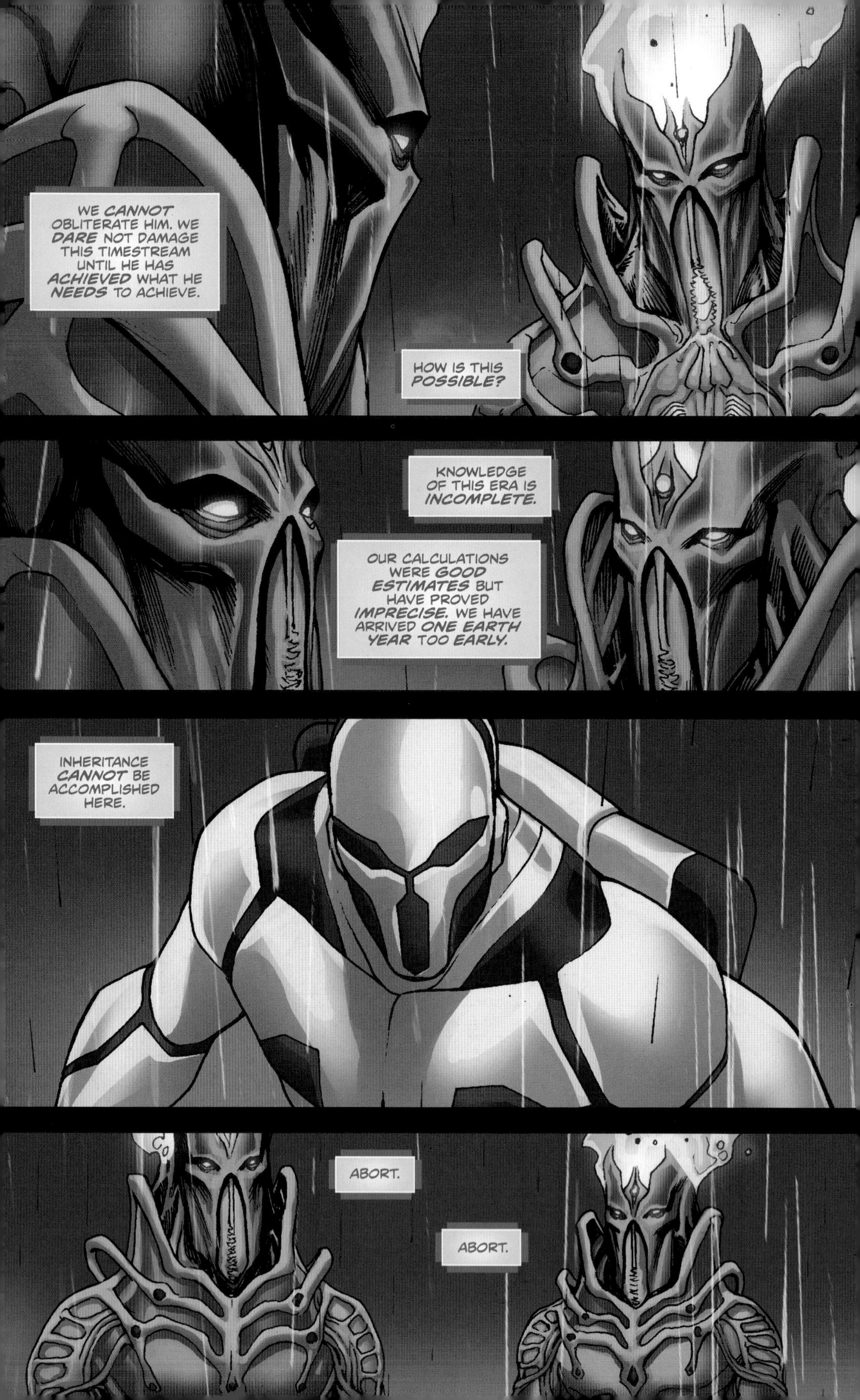
WE CANNOT OBLITERATE HIM. WE DARE NOT DAMAGE THIS TIMESTREAM UNTIL HE HAS ACHIEVED WHAT HE NEEDS TO ACHIEVE.
HOW IS THIS POSSIBLE?
KNOWLEDGE OF THIS ERA IS INCOMPLETE.
OUR CALCULATIONS WERE GOOD ESTIMATES BUT HAVE PROVED IMPRECISE. WE HAVE ARRIVED ONE EARTH YEAR TOO EARLY.
INHERITANCE CANNOT BE ACCOMPLISHED HERE.
ABORT.
ABORT.

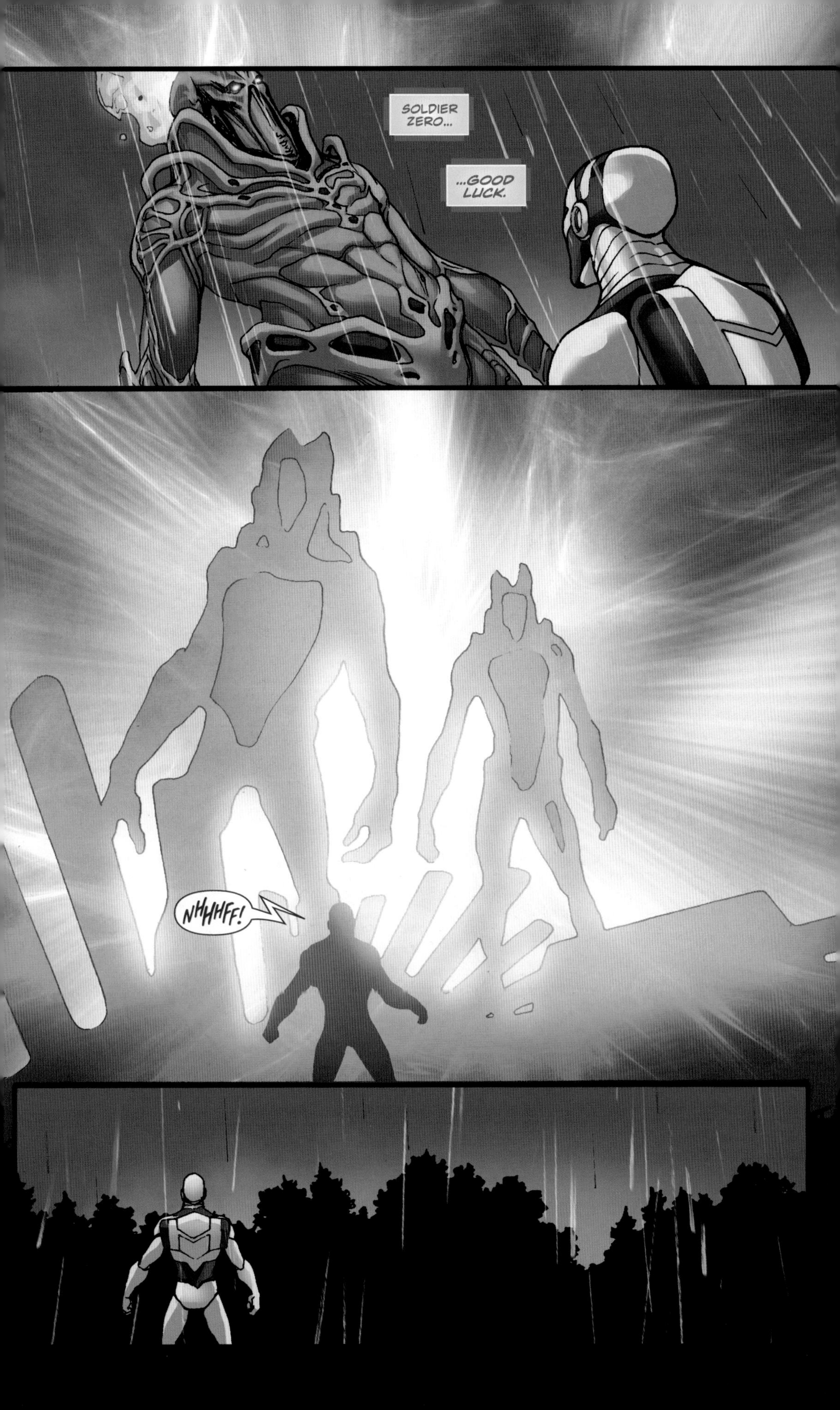
SOLDIER ZERO...
...GOOD LUCK.
NHHHFF!

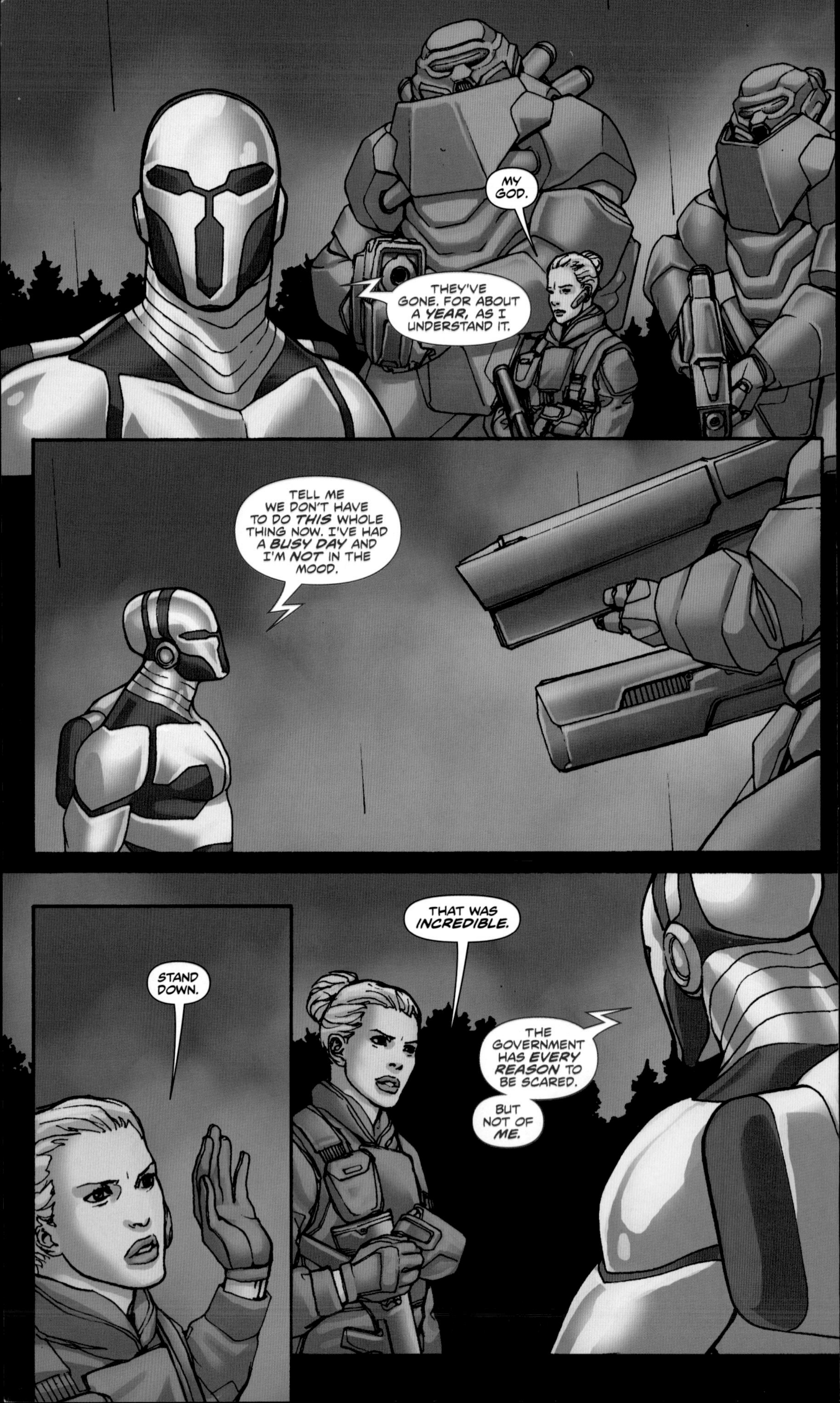
MY GOD.
THEY'VE GONE. FOR ABOUT A YEAR, AS I UNDERSTAND IT.
TELL ME WE DON'T HAVE TO DO THIS WHOLE THING NOW. I'VE HAD A BUSY DAY AND I'M NOT IN THE MOOD.
STAND DOWN.
THAT WAS INCREDIBLE.
THE GOVERNMENT HAS EVERY REASON TO BE SCARED.
BUT NOT OF ME.

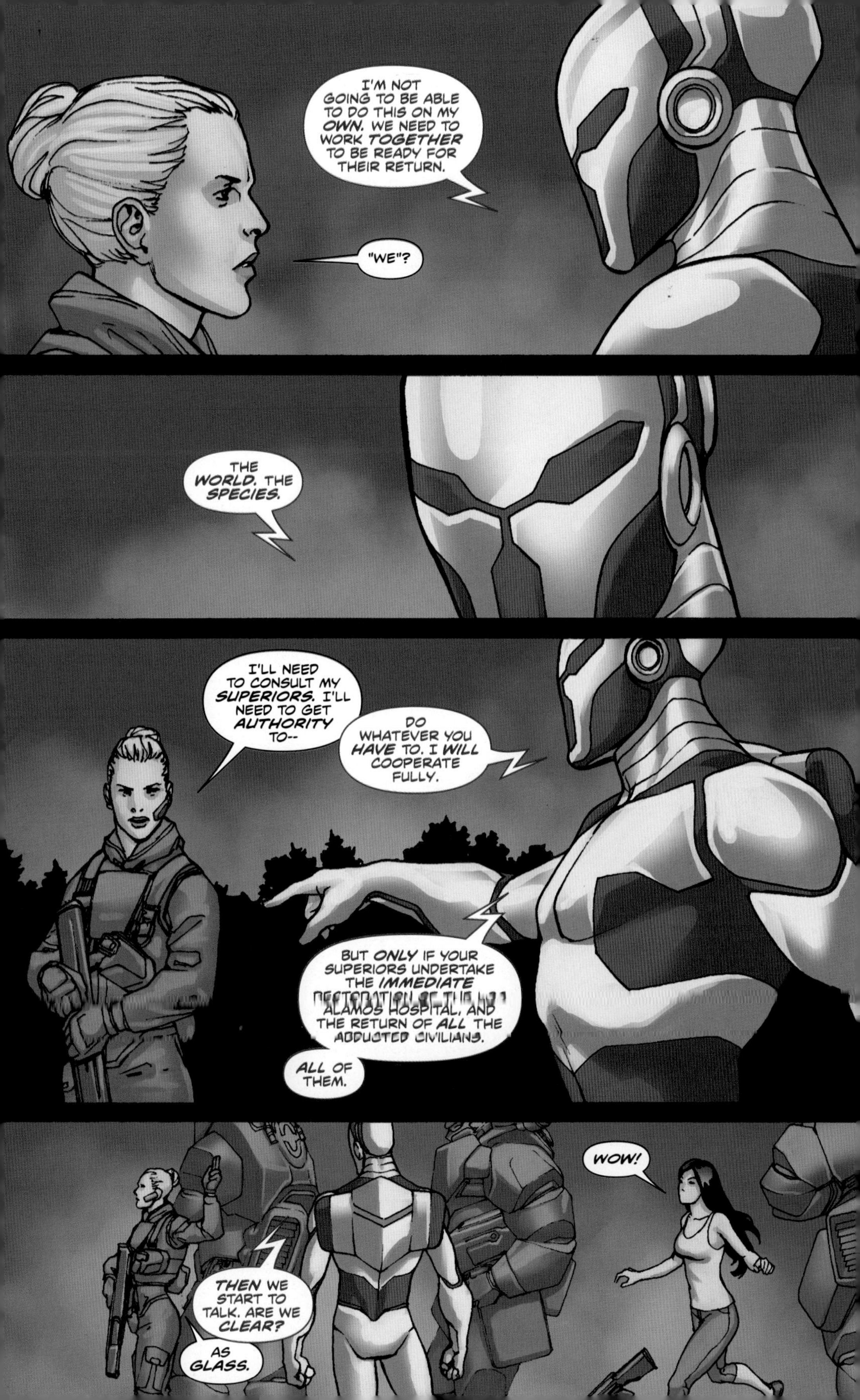
I'M NOT GOING TO BE ABLE TO DO THIS ON MY OWN. WE NEED TO WORK TOGETHER TO BE READY FOR THEIR RETURN.
"WE"?
THE WORLD. THE SPECIES.
I'LL NEED TO CONSULT MY SUPERIORS. I'LL NEED TO GET AUTHORITY TO--
DO WHATEVER YOU HAVE TO. I WILL COOPERATE FULLY.
BUT ONLY IF YOUR SUPERIORS UNDERTAKE THE IMMEDIATE
ALAMOS HOSPITAL, AND THE RETURN OF ALL THE ABDUCTED CIVILIANS.
ALL OF THEM.
WOW!
THEN WE START TO TALK. ARE WE CLEAR?
AS GLASS.

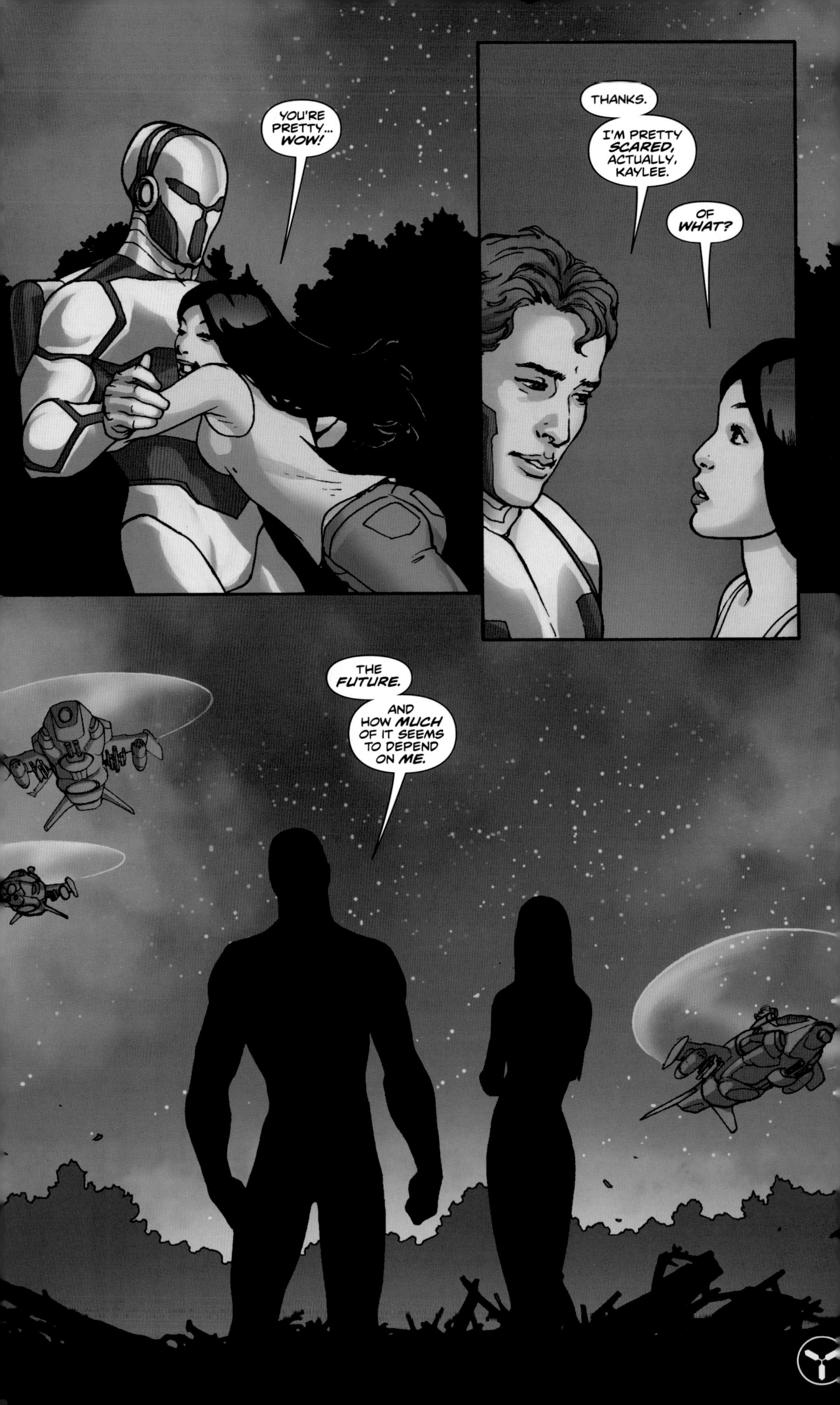
YOU'RE PRETTY... WOW!
THANKS.
I'M PRETTY SCARED, ACTUALLY, KAYLEE.
OF WHAT?
THE FUTURE.
AND HOW MUCH OF IT SEEMS TO DEPEND ON ME.

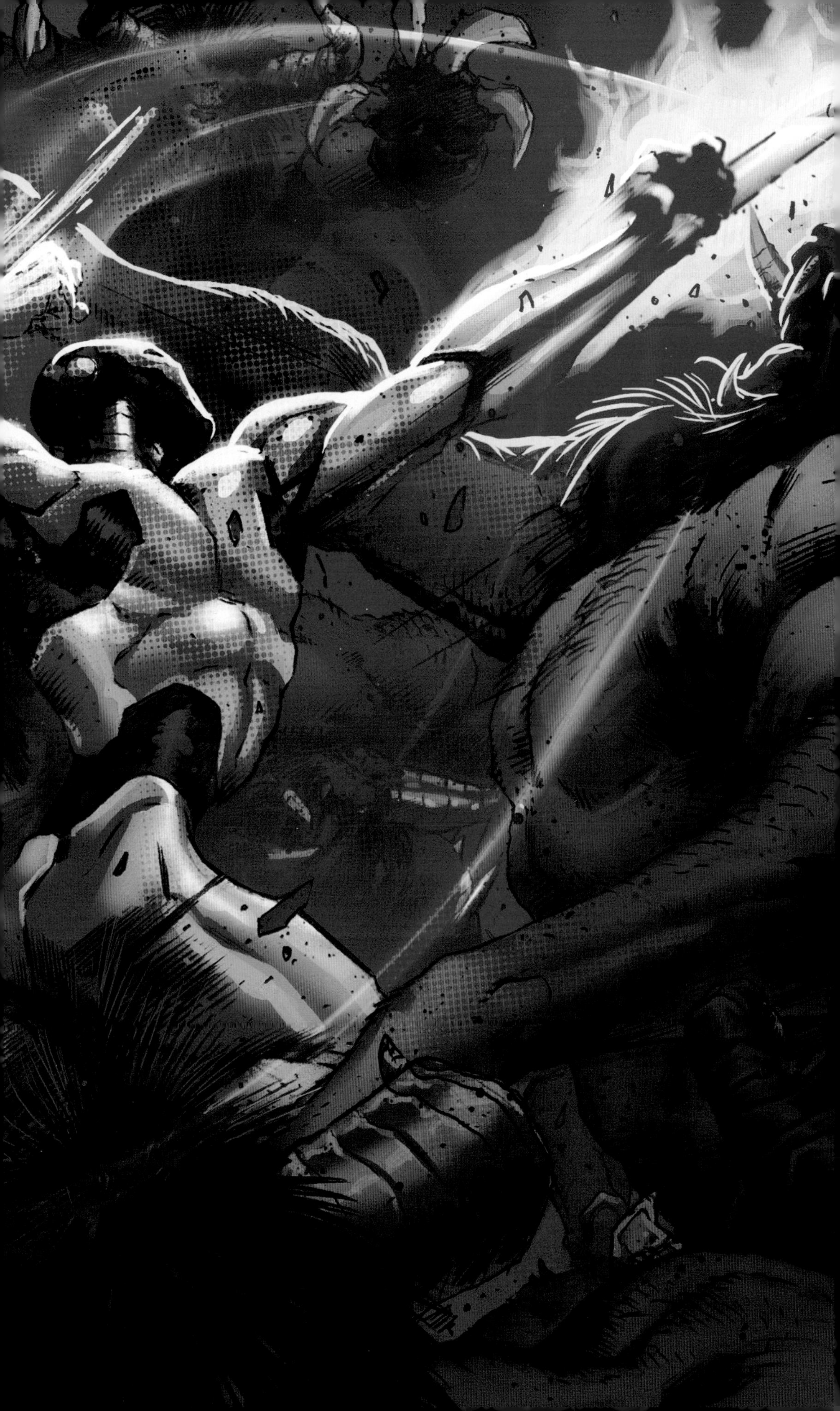

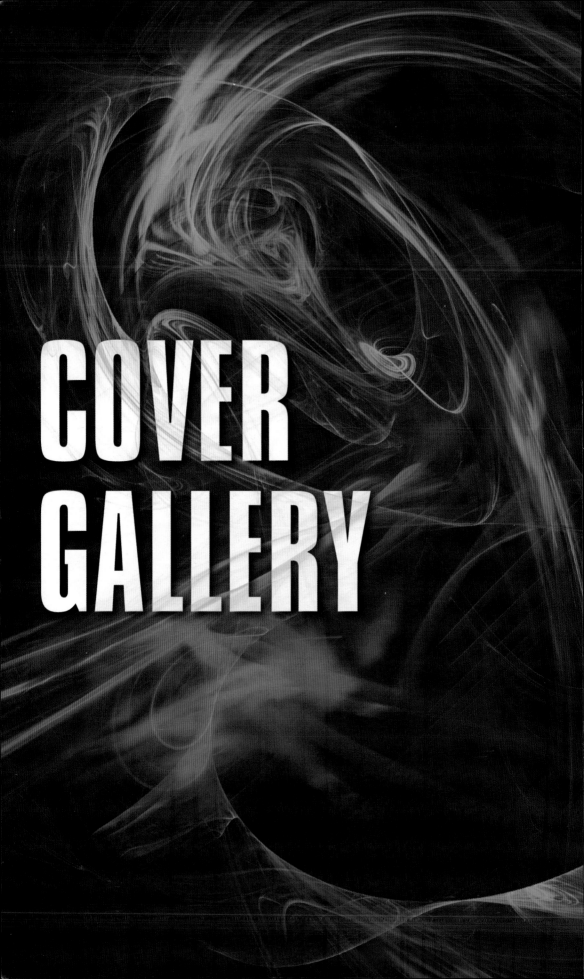

COVER GALLERY

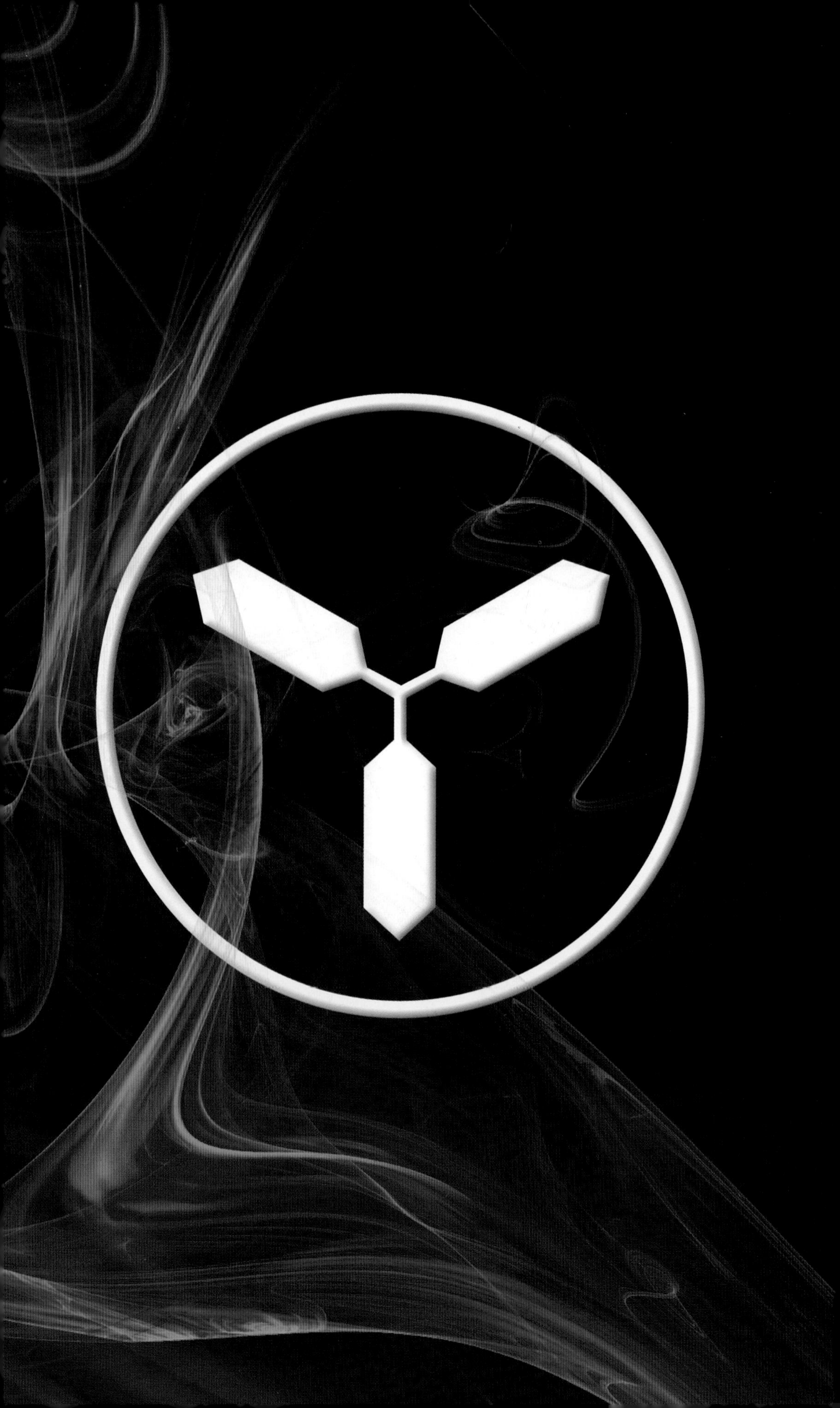

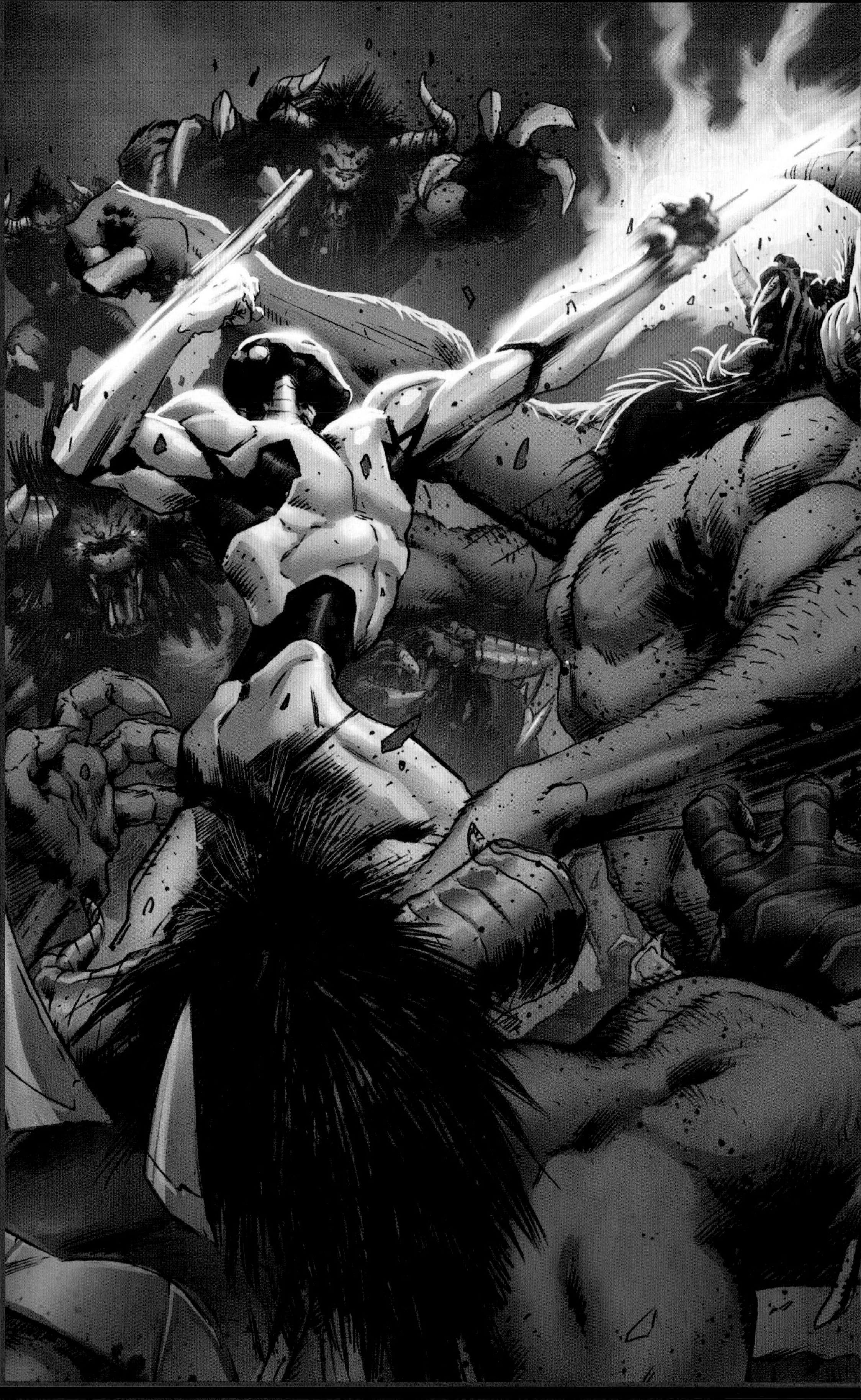

ISSUE NINE: **TREVOR HAIRSINE**
WITH ARCHIE VAN BUREN

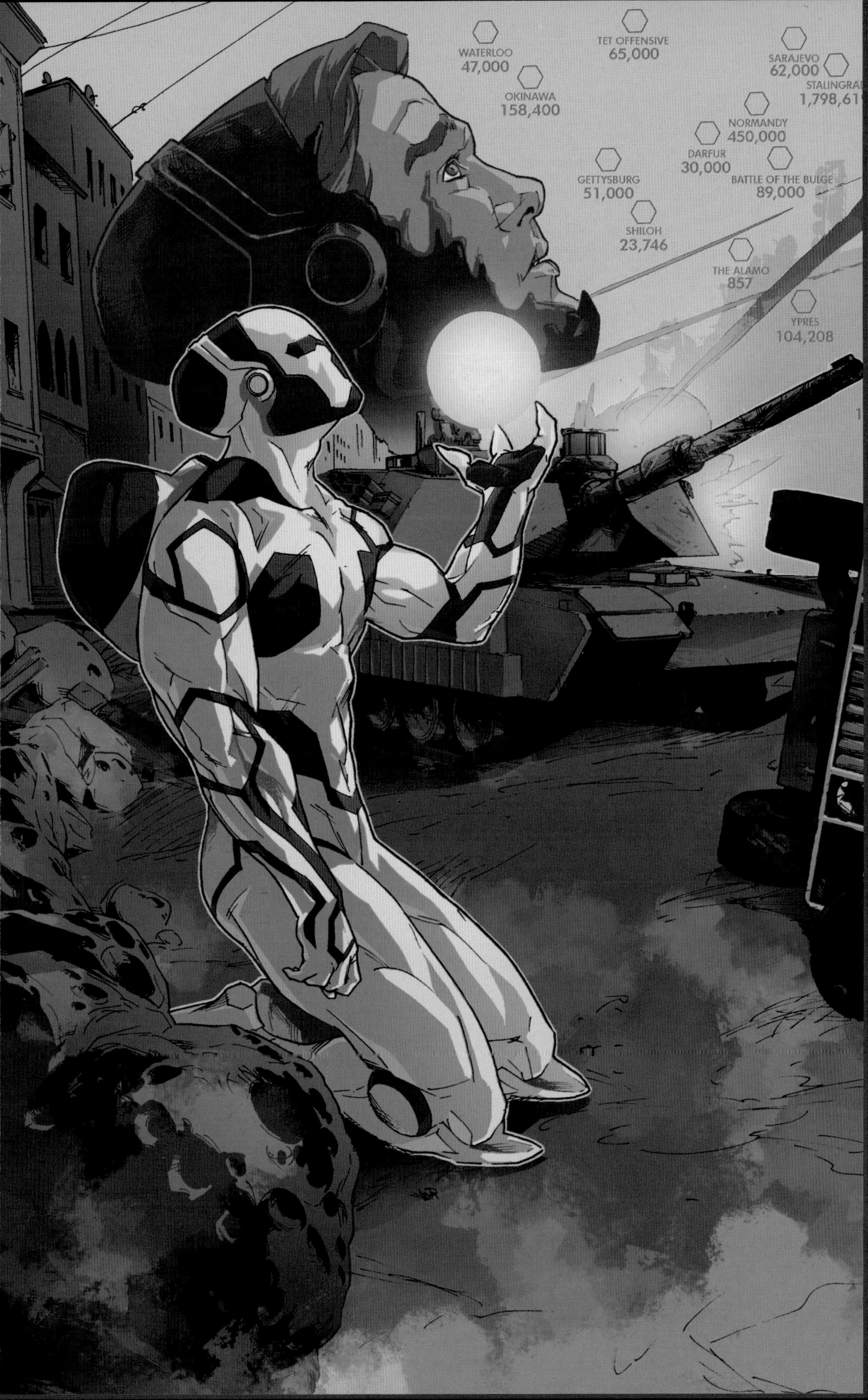
WATERLOO
47,000
TET OFFENSIVE
65,000
SARAJEVO
62,000
OKINAWA
158,400
NORMANDY
450,000
DARFUR
30,000
GETTYSBURG
51,000
BATTLE OF THE BULGE
89,000
SHILOH
23,746
THE ALAMO
857
YPRES
104,208

ISSUE NINE: KALMAN ANDRASOFSZKY

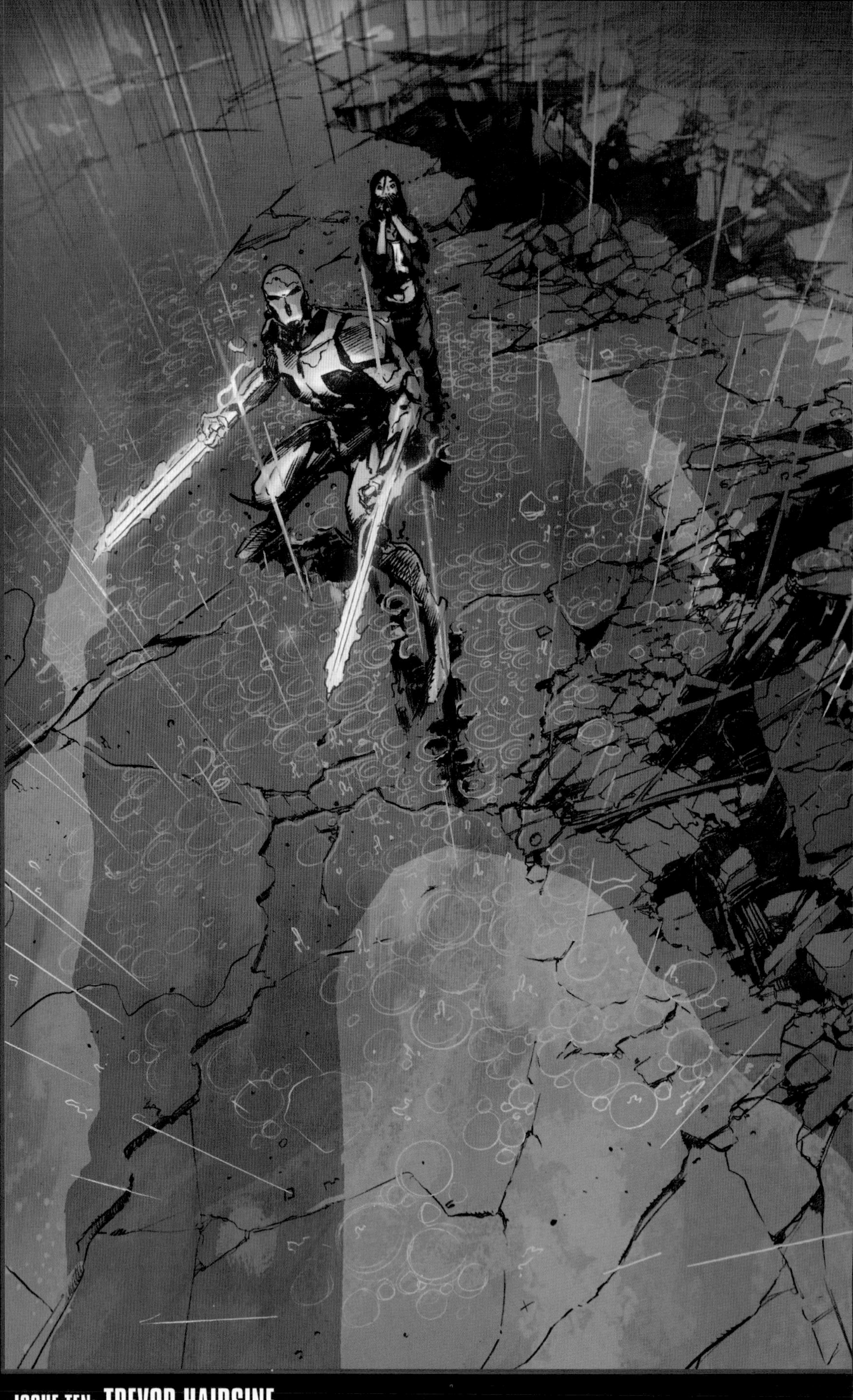

ISSUE TEN: **TREVOR HAIRSINE**
WITH ARCHIE VAN BUREN

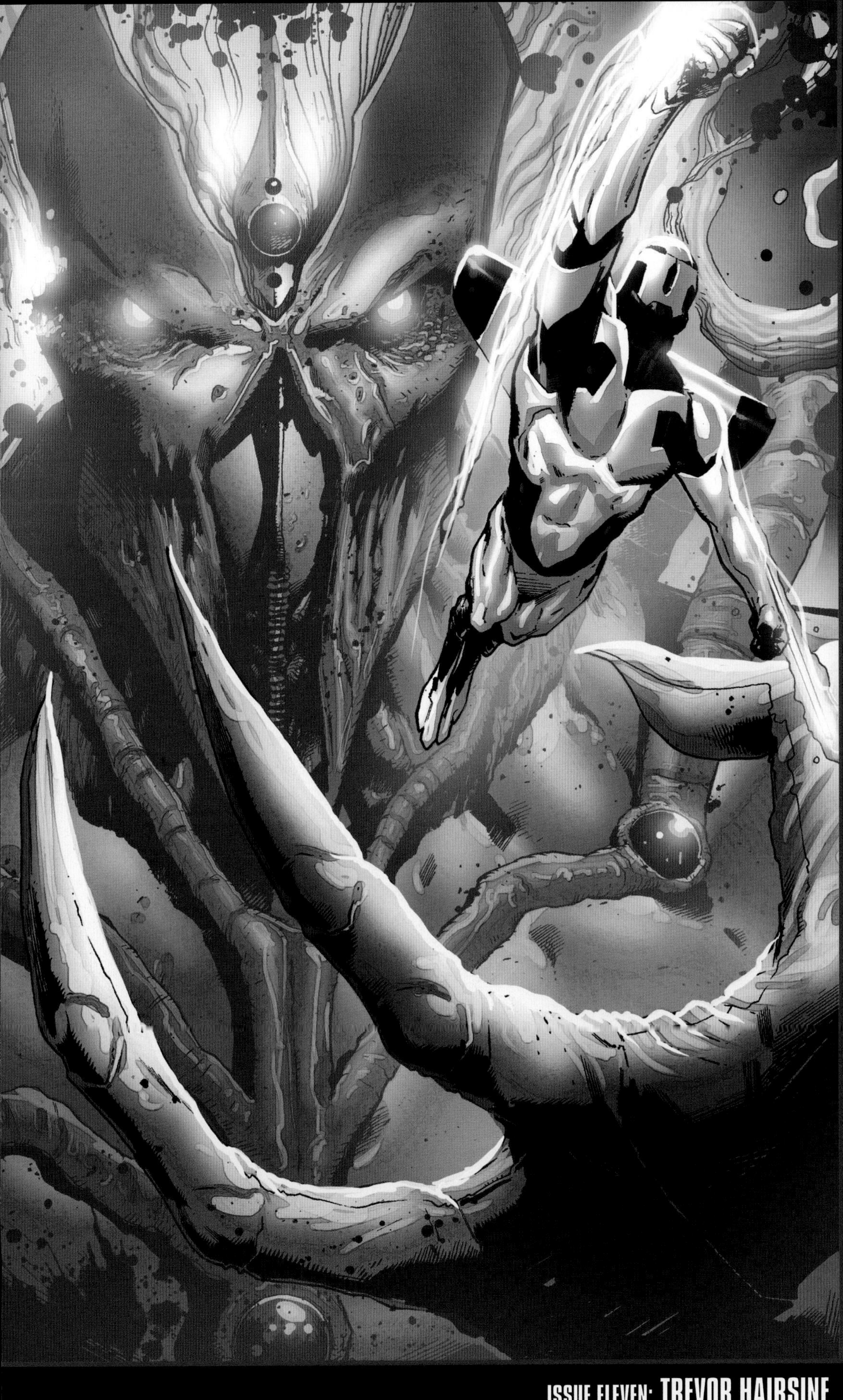

ISSUE ELEVEN: **TREVOR HAIRSINE**
WITH ARCHIE VAN BUREN

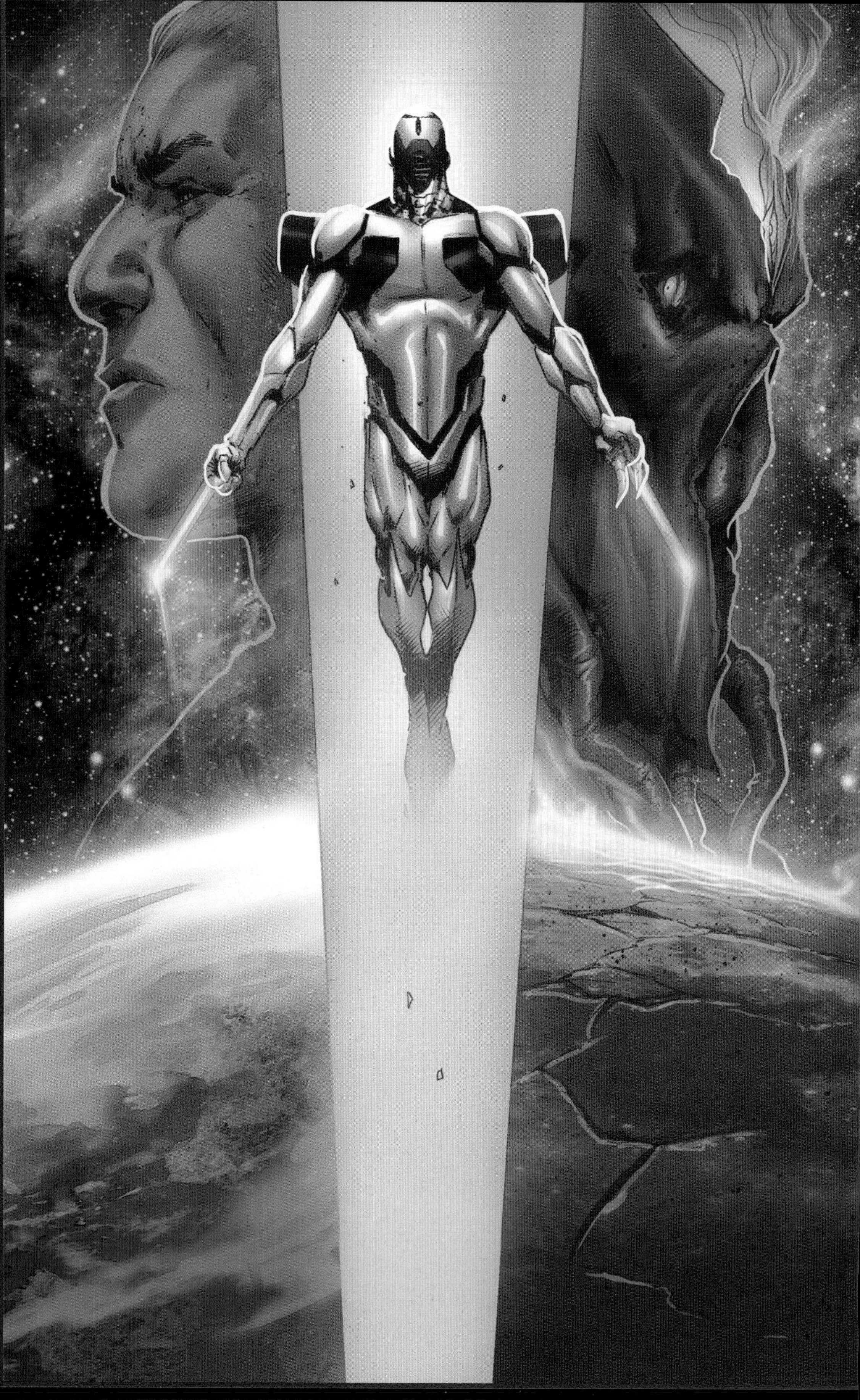

ISSUE TWELVE: **TREVOR HAIRSINE**
WITH ARCHIE VAN BUREN

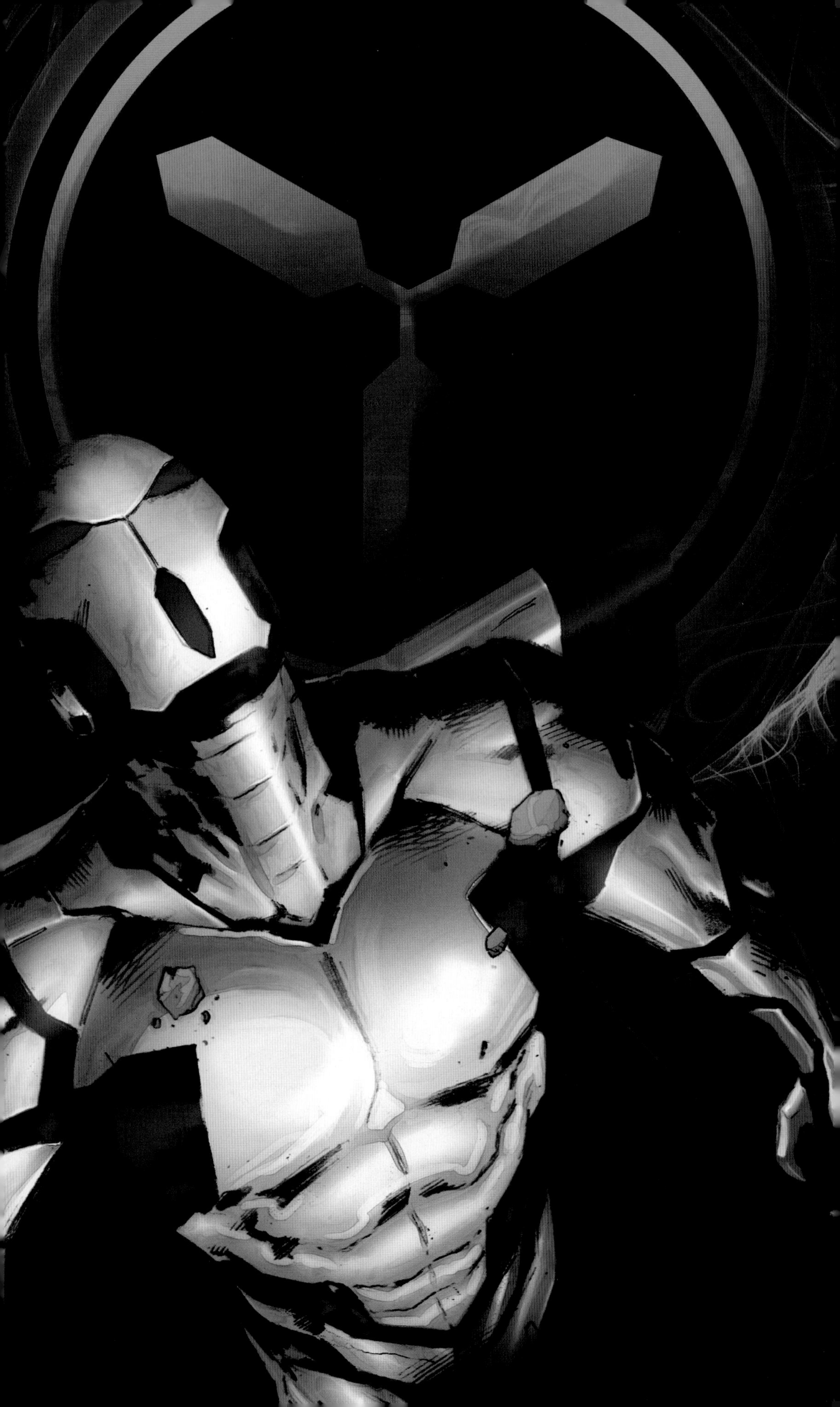

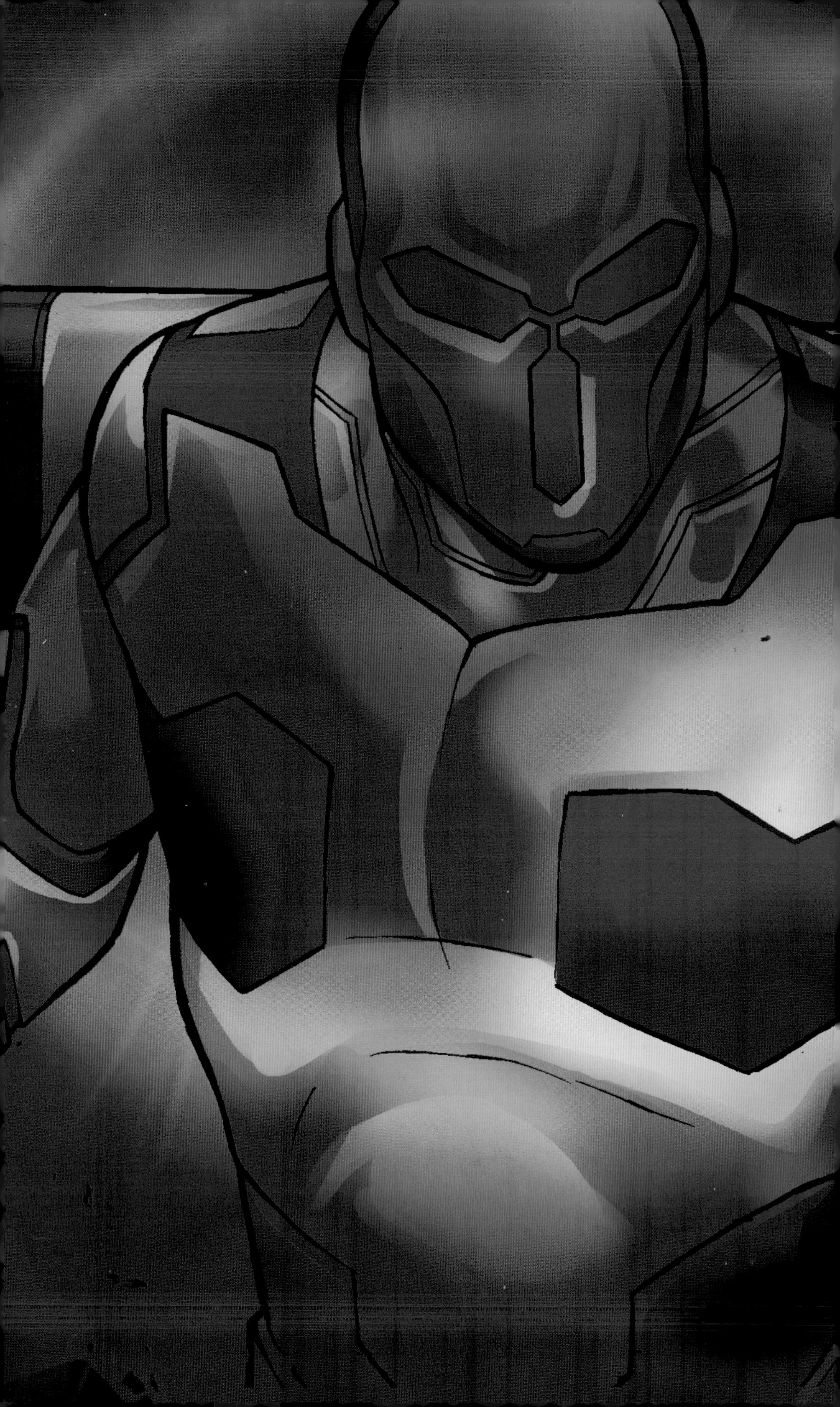

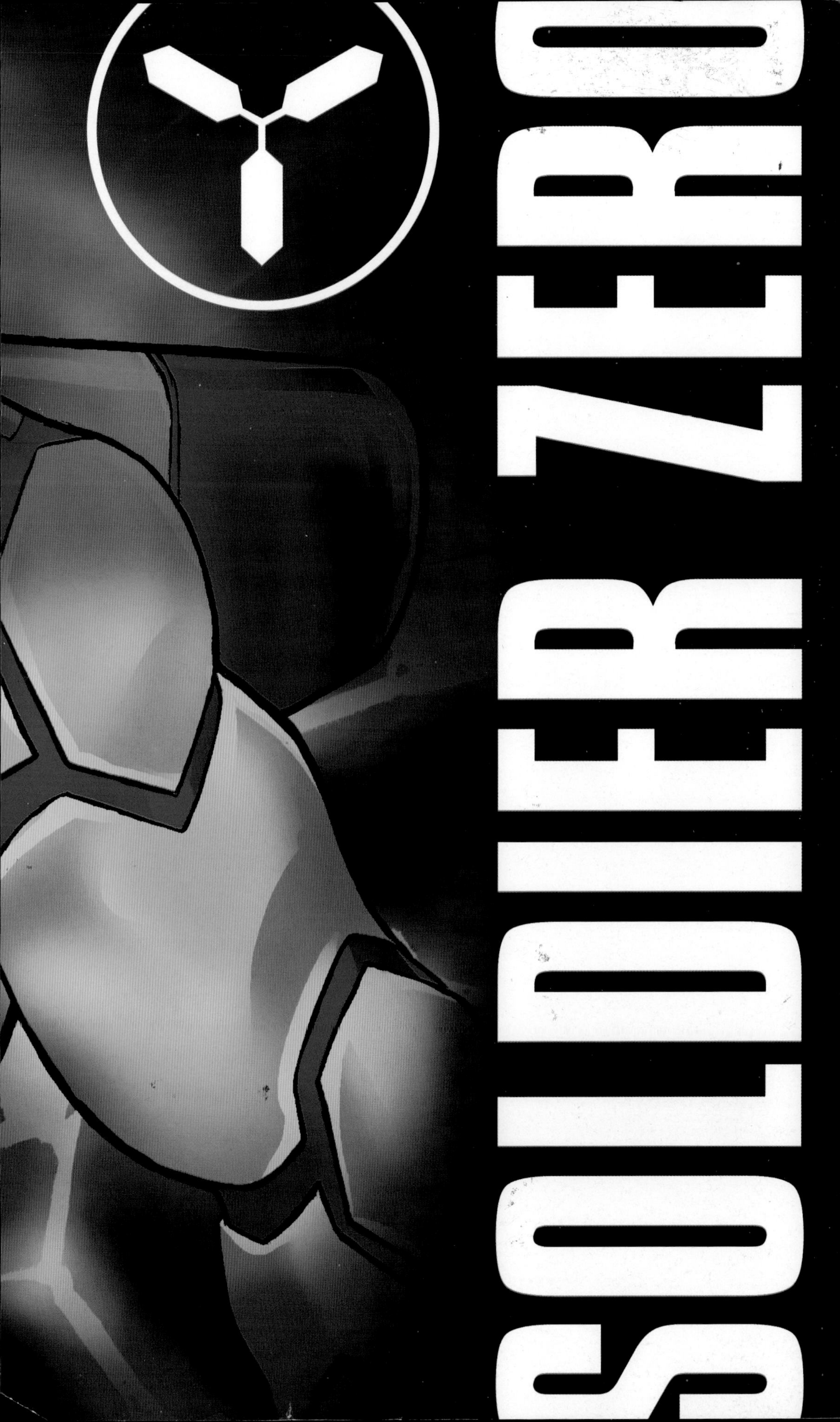
SOLDIER ZERO

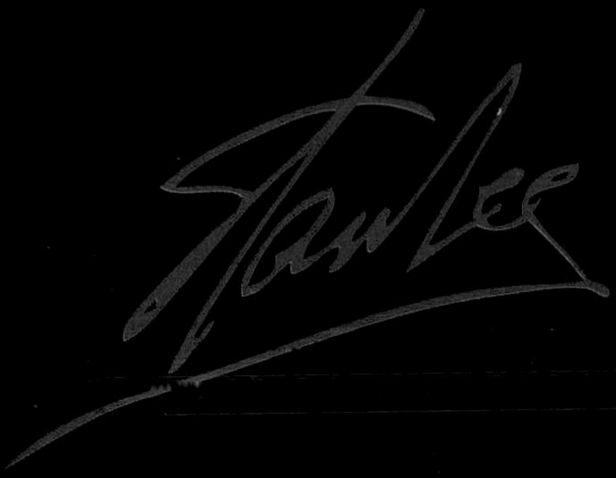